GLENCOE LANGUAGE ARTS

Grammar and Language Workbook

GRADE 11

D1306614

Glencoe
McGraw-Hill

New York, New York   Columbus, Ohio   Woodland Hills, California   Peoria, Illinois

Glencoe/McGraw-Hill

A Division of The McGraw·Hill Companies

Copyright © by The McGraw-Hill Companies, Inc. All rights reserved. Except as permitted under the United States Copyright Act of 1976, no part of this publication may be reproduced or distributed in any form or means, or stored in a database or retrieval system, without the prior written permission of the publisher.

Send all inquiries to:
Glencoe/McGraw-Hill
8787 Orion Place
Columbus, Ohio 43240-4027

ISBN 0-02-818303-7

Printed in the United States of America

27 28 29 30 HES 12 11 10

Contents

Copyright © by Glencoe/McGraw-Hill

Handbook of Definitions and Rules

PARTS OF SPEECH

Nouns

1. A **singular noun** is a word that names one person, place, thing, or idea: brother, classroom, piglet, and joy. A **plural noun** names more than one person, place, thing, or idea: brothers, classrooms, piglets, and joys.

2. To help you determine whether a word in a sentence is a noun, try adding it to the following sentences. Nouns will fit in at least one of these sentences:
   I know something about _____. I know something about a(n) _____.
   I know something about **brothers**. I know something about a **classroom**.

3. A **collective noun** names a group. When the collective noun refers to the group as a whole, it is singular. When it refers to the individual group members, the collective noun is plural.
   The class meets two days a week. (singular)
   The board of trustees come from all walks of life. (plural)

4. A **common noun** names a general class of people, places, things, or ideas: soldier, country, month, or theory. A **proper noun** specifies a particular person, place, thing, event, or idea. Proper nouns are always capitalized: **G**eneral **S**chwartzkopf, **A**merica, **J**uly, or **B**ig Bang.

5. A **concrete noun** names an object that occupies space or that can be recognized by any of the senses: tuba, music, potato, and aroma. An **abstract noun** names an idea, a quality, or a characteristic: courage, sanity, power, and memory.

6. A **possessive noun** shows possession, ownership, or the relationship between two nouns: Raul's house, the cat's fur, and the girls' soccer ball.

Pronouns

1. A **pronoun** takes the place of a noun, a group of words acting as a noun, or another pronoun.

2. A **personal pronoun** refers to a specific person or thing. **First person** personal pronouns refer to the speaker, **second person** pronouns refer to the one spoken to, and **third person** pronouns refer to the one spoken about.

	Nominative Case	Possessive Case	Objective Case
First Person, Singular	I	my, mine	me
First Person, Plural	we	our, ours	us
Second Person, Singular	you	your, yours	you
Second Person, Plural	you	your, yours	you
Third Person, Singular	he, she, it	his, her, hers, its	him, her, it
Third Person, Plural	they	their, theirs	them

3. A **reflexive pronoun** refers to the subject of the sentence. An **intensive pronoun** adds emphasis to a noun or another pronoun. A **demonstrative pronoun** points out specific persons, places, things, or ideas.
   Reflexive:　　　　**They** psyched **themselves** up for the football game.
   Intensive:　　　　**Freddie himself** asked Julie out.
   Demonstrative:　　**That** is a good idea!　**Those** are my friends.

4. An **interrogative pronoun** is used to form questions. A **relative pronoun** is used to introduce a subordinate clause. An **indefinite pronoun** refers to persons, places, or things in a more general way than a noun does.
   Interrogative:　　**Which** is your choice?　　　With **whom** were you playing video games?

Copyright © by Glencoe/McGraw-Hill

Relative: The cake **that** we baked was delicious.
Indefinite: **Everyone** has already voted.   **No one** should enter without knocking.

5. The **antecedent** of a pronoun is the word or group of words referred to by the pronoun.
Ben rode **his** bike to school. (*Ben* is the antecedent of *his*.)

Verbs

1. A **verb** is a word that expresses action or a state of being and is necessary to make a statement. Most verbs will fit one or more of these sentences:
We _____.   We _____ loyal.   We _____ it.   It _____.
We **sleep**.   We **remain** loyal.   We **love** it!   It **snowed**.

2. An **action verb** tells what someone or something does. The two types of action verbs are transitive and intransitive. A **transitive verb** is followed by a word or words that answer the question *what?* or *whom?* An **intransitive verb** is not followed by a word that answers *what?* or *whom?*
Transitive: Children **trust** their parents.   The puppy **carried** the bone away.
Intransitive: The team **played** poorly.   The light **burned** brightly.

3. A **linking verb** links, or joins, the subject of a sentence with an adjective, a noun, or a pronoun.
The concert **was** loud. (adjective)   I **am** a good card player. (noun)

4. A **verb phrase** consists of a main verb and all its **auxiliary**, or helping, verbs.
My stomach **has been growling** all morning.   I **am waiting** for a letter.

5. Verbs have four **principal parts** or forms: base, past, present participle, and past participle.
Base: I **eat**.   Present Participle: I am **eating**.
Past: I **ate**.   Past Participle: I have **eaten**.

6. The principal parts are used to form six verb tenses. The **tense** of a verb expresses time.
Simple Tenses
Present Tense: She **eats**. (present or habitual action)
Past Tense: She **ate**. (action completed in the past)
Future Tense: She **will eat**. (action to be done in the future)
Perfect Tenses
Present Perfect Tense: She **has eaten**. (action done at some indefinate time or still in effect)
Past Perfect Tense: She **had eaten**. (action completed before some other past action)
Future Perfect Tense: She **will have eaten**. (action to be completed before some future time)

7. **Irregular verbs** form their past and past participle without adding *-ed* to the base form.

PRINCIPAL PARTS OF IRREGULAR VERBS

Base	Past	Past Participle	Base	Past	Past Participle
be	was, were	been	catch	caught	caught
beat	beat	beaten	choose	chose	chosen
become	became	become	come	came	come
begin	began	begun	do	did	done
bite	bit	bitten *or* bit	draw	drew	drawn
blow	blew	blown	drink	drank	drunk
break	broke	broken	drive	drove	driven
bring	brought	brought	eat	ate	eaten

Copyright © by Glencoe/McGraw-Hill

Base Form	Past Form	Past Participle	Base Form	Past Form	Past Participle
fall	fell	fallen	run	ran	run
feel	felt	felt	say	said	said
find	found	found	see	saw	seen
fly	flew	flown	set	set	set
freeze	froze	frozen	shrink	shrank *or* shrunk	shrunk *or* shrunken
get	got	got *or* gotten			
give	gave	given	sing	sang	sung
go	went	gone	sit	sat	sat
grow	grew	grown	speak	spoke	spoken
hang	hung *or* hanged	hung *or* hanged	spring	sprang *or* sprung	sprung
have	had	had	steal	stole	stolen
know	knew	known	swim	swam	swum
lay	laid	laid	take	took	taken
lead	led	led	tear	tore	torn
lend	lent	lent	tell	told	told
lie	lay	lain	think	thought	thought
lose	lost	lost	throw	threw	thrown
put	put	put	wear	wore	worn
ride	rode	ridden	win	won	won
ring	rang	rung	write	wrote	written
rise	rose	risen			

8. **Progressive forms** of verbs, combined with a form of *be,* express a continuing action. **Emphatic forms**, combined with a form of *do,* add emphasis or form questions.
   Kari **is scratching** the cat.   Loni **has been washing** the walls.
   We **do support** our hometown heroes. (present)   He **did want** that dinner. (past)

9. The **voice** of a verb shows whether the subject performs the action or receives the action of the verb. The **active voice** occurs when the subject performs the action. The **passive voice** occurs when the action of the verb is performed on the subject.
   The owl **swooped** upon its prey. (active)   The ice cream **was scooped** by the cashier. (passive)

10. A verb can express one of three moods. The **indicative mood** makes a statement or asks a question. The **imperative mood** expresses a command or request. The **subjunctive mood** indirectly expresses a demand, recommendation, suggestion, statement of necessity, or a condition contrary to fact.
    I **am** overjoyed. (indicative)   **Stop** the car. (imperative)
    If I **were** angry, I would not have let you in. (subjunctive)

Adjectives

1. An **adjective** modifies a noun or pronoun by giving a descriptive or specific detail. Adjectives can usually show comparisons. (See Using Modifiers Correctly on pages 9 and 10.)
   cold winter   **colder** winter   **coldest** winter

2. Most adjectives will fit this sentence:
   The _____ one looks very _____.
   The **dusty** one looks very **old.**

3. Articles are the adjectives *a, an,* and *the.* Articles do not meet the above test for adjectives.

Copyright © by Glencoe/McGraw-Hill

4. A **proper adjective** is formed from a proper noun and begins with a capital letter.
Marijka wore a **Ukrainian** costume.   He was a **Danish** prince.

5. An adjective used as an **object complement** follows and describes a direct object.
My aunt considers me **funny.**

Adverbs

1. An **adverb** modifies a verb, an adjective, or another adverb. Most adverbs can show comparisons. (See Using Modifiers Correctly on pages 9 and 10.)

   a. Adverbs that tell how, where, when, or to what degree modify verbs or verbals.
   The band stepped **lively.** (how)   Maria writes **frequently.** (when)
   Put the piano **here.** (where)   We were **thoroughly** entertained. (to what degree)

   b. Adverbs of degree strengthen or weaken the adjectives or other adverbs that they modify.
   A **very** happy fan cheered. (modifies adjective)   She spoke **too** fast. (modifies adverb)

2. Many adverbs fit these sentences:
   She thinks _____.   She thinks _____ fast.   She _____ thinks fast.
   She thinks **quickly.**   She thinks **unusually** fast.   She **seldom** thinks fast.

Prepositions, Conjunctions, and Interjections

1. A **preposition** shows the relationship of a noun or a pronoun to some other word. A **compound preposition** is made up of more than one word.
The first group **of** students arrived.   They skated **in spite of** the cold weather.

2. Some common prepositions include these: *about, above, across, after, against, along, among, around, at, before, behind, below, beneath, beside, besides, between, beyond, but, by, concerning, down, during, except, for, from, into, like, near, of, off, on, out, outside, over, past, round, since, through, till, to, toward, under, underneath, until, up, upon, with, within, without.*

3. A **conjunction** is a word that joins single words or groups of words. A **coordinating conjunction** joins words or groups of words that have equal grammatical weight. **Correlative conjunctions** work in pairs to join words and groups of words of equal weight. A **subordinating conjunction** joins two clauses in such a way as to make one grammatically dependent on the other.
Coordinating conjunction: He **and** I talked for hours.
Correlative conjunctions: Russ wants **either** a cat **or** a dog.
Subordinating conjunction: We ate lunch **when** it was ready.

4. A **conjunctive adverb** clarifies a relationship.
He did not like cold weather; **nevertheless,** he shoveled the snow.

5. An **interjection** is an unrelated word or phrase that expresses emotion or exclamation.
Wow, that was cool!   **Aha!** You fell right into my trap!

PARTS OF THE SENTENCE
Subjects and Predicates

1. The **simple subject** is the key noun or pronoun that tells what the sentence is about. A **compound subject** is made up of two or more simple subjects that are joined by a conjunction and have the same verb.
My **father** snores.   My **mother** and **I** can't sleep.

Copyright © by Glencoe/McGraw-Hill

2. The **simple predicate** is the verb or verb phrase that expresses the essential thought about the subject of the sentence. A **compound predicate** is made up of two or more verbs or verb phrases that are joined by a conjunction and have the same subject.

The night **was** cold. The elves **sang** and **danced** in the flower garden.

3. The **complete subject** consists of the simple subject and all the words that modify it.

The bright lights of the city burned intensely. **The warm, soothing fire** kept us warm.

4. The **complete predicate** consists of the simple predicate and all the words that modify it or complete its meaning.

Dinosaurs **died out 65 million years ago.** The sun **provides heat for the earth.**

5. Usually the subject comes before the predicate in a sentence. In inverted sentences, all or part of the predicate precedes the subject.

There **are** two **muffins** on the plate Over the field **soared** the **glider.**

Complements

1. A **complement** is a word or a group of words that complete the meaning of the verb. There are four kinds of complements: direct objects, indirect objects, object complements, and subject complements.

2. A **direct object** answers *what?* or *whom?* after an action verb.

Sammi ate the **turkey.** (Sammi ate what?)

Carlos watched his **sister** in the school play. (Carlos watched whom?)

3. An **indirect object** receives what the direct object names.

Marie wrote **June** a letter. George Washington gave his **troops** orders.

4. A **subject complement** follows a subject and a linking verb and identifies or describes the subject. A **predicate nominative** is a noun or pronoun that follows a linking verb and further identifies the subject. A **predicate adjective** follows a linking verb and further describes the subject.

Predicate Nominative: The best football player is **Jacob.**

Predicate Adjective: The people have been very **patient.**

5. An **object complement** describes or renames a direct object.

Object Complement: Ami found the man **handsome.**

Object Complement: Carlos thought the woman a **genius.**

PHRASES

1. A **phrase** is a group of words that acts in a sentence as a single part of speech.

2. A **prepositional phrase** is a group of words that begins with a preposition and usually ends with a noun or pronoun called the **object of the preposition.** Aprepositional phrase can modify a noun or a pronoun, a verb, an adjective, or an adverb.

One of my favorite meals is pigs **in a blanket.** (modifies the noun *pigs*)

The supersonic jet soared **into the sky.** (modifies the verb *soared*)

The love of a household pet can be valuable **for a family.** (modifies the adjective *valuable*)

The child reads well **for a six-year-old.** (modifies the adverb *well*)

3. An **appositive** is a noun or a pronoun that is placed next to another noun or pronoun to identify it or give more information about it. An **appositive phrase** is an appositive plus its modifiers.

My grandfather **Géza** takes me fishing. C.S. Lewis, **my favorite author,** lived in England.

Copyright © by Glencoe/McGraw-Hill

4. A **verbal** is a verb form that functions in a sentence as a noun, an adjective, or an adverb. A **verbal phrase** is a verbal plus any complements and modifiers.

   a. A **participle** is a verbal that functions as an adjective: Gary comforted the **crying** baby.

   b. A **participial phrase** contains a participle plus any complements or modifiers: **Thanking everyone**, my uncle began to carve the turkey.

   c. A **gerund** is a verbal that ends with *-ing*. It is used in the same way a noun is used: **Skiing** is a popular sport.

   d. A **gerund phrase** is a gerund plus any complements or modifiers: **Singing the national anthem** is traditional at many sports events.

   e. An **infinitive** is a verbal that is usually preceded by the word *to*. It is used as a noun, an adjective, or an adverb: I never learned **to dance**. (noun) She has an errand **to run**. (adjective) I will be happy **to help**. (adverb)

   f. An **infinitive phrase** contains an infinitive plus any complements or modifiers: My father woke up **to watch the news on television**.

5. An **absolute phrase** consists of a noun or a pronoun that is modified by a participle or a participial phrase but has no grammatical relation to the sentence.
   His legs terribly tired, Honori sat down.

CLAUSES AND SENTENCE STRUCTURE

1. A **clause** is a group of words that has a subject and a predicate and is used as a sentence or part of a sentence. There are two types of clauses: main and subordinate. A **main clause** has a subject and a predicate and can stand alone as a sentence. A **subordinate clause** has a subject and a predicate, but it cannot stand alone as a sentence.

      main   sub.
   The book bored me until I read Chapter 5.

2. There are three types of subordinate clauses: adjective, adverb, and noun.

   a. An **adjective clause** is a subordinate clause that modifies a noun or a pronoun.
   The students **who stayed after school for help** did well on the test.

   b. An **adverb clause** is a subordinate clause that modifies a verb, an adjective, or an adverb. It tells *when, where, how, why, to what extent,* or *under what conditions.*
   When the sun set, everyone watched from the window. (modifies a verb)
   Today is warmer **than yesterday was.** (modifies an adjective)

   c. A **noun clause** is a subordinate clause used as a noun.
   Who will become president has been declared.   I now remember **what I need to buy.**

3. Main and subordinate clauses can form four types of sentences. A **simple sentence** has only one main clause and no subordinate clauses. A **compound sentence** has two or more main clauses. A **complex sentence** has one main clause and one or more subordinate clauses. A **compound-complex sentence** has more than one main clause and at least one subordinate clause.

                              main
   Simple: The stars fill the sky.

                          main   main
   Compound: The plane landed,   and the passengers left.

                          sub.   main
   Complex: Although the children found the letter,   they couldn't read it.

                          main   main   sub.
   Compound-Complex: The earth is bountiful;   we may destroy it   if we abuse it.

Copyright © by Glencoe/McGraw-Hill

4. A sentence that makes a statement is classified as a **declarative sentence**: The Cleveland Browns are my favorite team. An **imperative sentence** gives a command or makes a request: Please go to the dance with me. An **interrogative sentence** asks a question: Who would abandon a family pet? An **exclamatory sentence** expresses strong emotion: Look out!

SUBJECT-VERB AGREEMENT

1. A verb must agree with its subject in person and number.
   Doli **runs.** (singular)   Doli and Abay **run.** (plural)
   He **is** singing. (singular) They **are** singing. (plural)

2. In **inverted sentences** the subject follows the verb. The sentence may begin with a prepositional phrase, the words *there* or *here,* or the verb form of *do.*
   Out of the bushes **sprang** the *leopard.*   There **is** never enough *time.*
   Do those *pigs* **eat** leftover food?

3. Do not mistake a word in a prepositional phrase for the subject.
   The **boss** of the employees **works** very hard. (The verb *works* tells the action of the boss.)

4. Make the verb in a sentence agree with the subject, not with the predicate nominative.
   Her problem **was** the twins.   The twins **were** her problem.

5. A title is always singular, even if nouns in the title are plural.
   The War of the Worlds **was** a radio broadcast that caused widespread panic.

6. Subjects combined with *and* or *both* use plural verbs unless the parts are of a whole unit. When compound subjects are joined with *or* or *nor,* the verb agrees with the subject listed last.
   Chocolate, strawberry, and vanilla are common ice cream flavors.
   Peanut butter and jelly is a good snack.   Neither **books nor a briefcase is** needed.

7. Use a singular verb if the compound subject is preceded by the words *many a, every,* or *each.*
   Every **dog and cat** needs to be cared for.   Many a **young man** has stood here.

8. A subject remains singular or plural regardless of any intervening expressions.
   Gloria, as well as the rest of her family, **was** late.
   The **players,** accompanied by the coach, **enter** the field.

9. A verb must agree in number with an indefinite pronoun subject.
   Always singular: *each, either, neither, one, everyone, everybody, everything, no one, nobody, nothing, anyone, anybody, anything, someone, somebody,* and *something.*
   Always plural: *several, few, both,* and *many.*
   Either singular or plural: *some, all, any, most,* and *none.*
   Is any of the **lemonade** left?   **Are** any of the **biscuits** burnt?

10. When the subject of an adjective clause is a relative pronoun, the verb in the clause must agree with the antecedent of the relative pronoun.
    He is one of the singers who dance. (The antecedent of *who* is *singers,* plural: singers dance.)

USING PRONOUNS CORRECTLY

1. Use the **nominative case** when the pronoun is a subject or a predicate nominative.
   She eats cake.   Is **he** here?   That is **I.** (predicate nominative)

Copyright © by Glencoe/McGraw-Hill

2. Use the objective case when the pronoun is an object.
   Clarence invited **us.** (direct object)   Chapa gave **me** a gift. (indirect object)
   Spot! Don't run around **me!** (object of preposition)

3. Use the possessive case to replace possessive nouns and precede gerunds. Never use an apostrophe in a possessive pronoun.
   That new car is **hers.**   They were thrilled at **his** playing the violin.

4. Use the nominative case when the pronoun is a subject or a predicate nominative.
   We three—Marijian, his sister, and I—went to camp.

5. Use the objective case to rename an object.
   The teacher acknowledged **us,** Burny and **me.**

6. When a pronoun is followed by an appositive, choose the case of the pronoun that would be correct if the appositive were omitted.
   We the jury find the defendant guilty.   That building was erected by **us** workers.

7. In elliptical adverb clauses using *than* and *as,* choose the case of the pronoun that you would use if the missing words were fully expressed.
   Kareem is a better sprinter than **I.** (I am)   It helped you more than **me.** (it helped me)

8. Use a reflexive pronoun when it refers to the person who is the subject of the sentence. Avoid using *hisself* or *theirselves.*
   Jerry found **himself** in a mess.   The candidates questioned **themselves** about their tactics.

9. In questions, use *who* for subjects and *whom* for objects. Use *who* and *whoever* for subjects and predicate nominatives in subordinate clauses. Use the objective pronouns *whom* and *whomever* for objects of subordinate clauses.
   Who roasted these marshmallows?   **Whom** will you hire next?
   This medal is for **whoever** finishes first.
   The newspaper will interview **whomever** the editor chooses.

10. An antecedent is the word or group of words to which a pronoun refers or that a pronoun replaces. All pronouns must agree with their antecedents in number, gender, and person.
    Colleen's **friends** gave up **their** free time to help.   The **Senate** passed **its** first bill of the year.

11. Make sure that the antecedent of a pronoun is clearly stated.
    VAGUE: The people who lost their dogs stayed in their yards, hoping **they** would return.
    CLEAR: The people who lost their dogs stayed in their yards, hoping **the dogs** would return.

    INDEFINITE: If you park the car under the sign **it** will be towed away.
    CLEAR: If you park the car under the sign **the car** will be towed away.

USING MODIFIERS CORRECTLY

1. Most adjectives and adverbs have three degrees of form. The positive form of a modifier cannot be used to make a comparison. The comparative form of a modifier shows two things being compared. The superlative form of a modifier shows three or more things being compared.
   The year went by **fast.**   This year went by **faster** than last year.
   I expect next year to go by the **fastest** of all.

Copyright © by Glencoe/McGraw-Hill

2. One- and two-syllable adjectives add *-er* to form comparative and *-est* to form superlative.

POSITIVE:	bold	happy	strong
COMPARATIVE:	bolder	happier	stronger
SUPERLATIVE:	boldest	happiest	strongest

3. For adverbs ending in *-ly* and modifiers with three or more syllables, use *more* and *most* or *less* and *least* to form the comparative and superlative degrees.

He was the **least** exhausted of the group.   She spoke **more** caringly than some others.

4. Some modifiers have irregular forms.

POSITIVE:	good, well	badly, ill	far	many, much	little
COMPARATIVE:	better	worse	farther	more	less
SUPERLATIVE:	best	worst	farthest	most	least

5. Do not make a double comparison using both *-er* or *-est* and *more* or *most.*

INCORRECT: That musical was the **most funniest** I have ever seen.
CORRECT: That musical was the **funniest** I have ever seen.

6. Do not make an incomplete or unclear comparison by omitting *other* or *else* when you compare one member of a group with another.

UNCLEAR: Joey has missed more school than any kid in the ninth grade.
CLEAR: Joey has missed more school than any **other** kid in the ninth grade.

7. Avoid double negatives, which are two negative words in the same clause.

INCORRECT: I have **not** seen **no** stray cats.
CORRECT: I have **not** seen **any** stray cats.

8. For clarity, place modifiers as close as possible to the words they modify.

MISPLACED: The fire was snuffed out by the storm **that we accidentally started.**

CLEAR: The fire **that we accidentally started** was snuffed out by the storm.

DANGLING: **To avoid the long walk,** a friend drove us.

CLEAR: **To avoid the long walk,** we were driven by a friend.

9. Place the adverb *only* immediately before the word or group of words it modifies.
Only Afi wants choir rehearsal next week. (No one but Afi wants rehearsal.)
Afi wants **only** choir rehearsal next week. (She wants no other rehearsal.)
Afi wants choir rehearsal **only** next week. (She does not want rehearsal any other week.)

USAGE GLOSSARY

a, an Use the article *a* when the following word begins with a consonant sound. Use *an* when the following word begins with a vowel sound.
   a house   **an** understudy   **an** hour   **a** united front

a lot, alot Always write this expression, meaning "a large amount," as two words.
   With his help, we will learn **a lot** about photography.

a while, awhile *In* or *for* often precedes *a while,* forming a prepositional phrase. *Awhile* is used only as an adverb.
   Let us listen to the forest for **a while.**   The students listened **awhile.**

Copyright © by Glencoe/McGraw-Hill

accept, except *Accept,* a verb, means "to receive" or "to agree to." *Except* may be a preposition or a verb. As a preposition it means "but." As a verb it means "to leave out."
I will **accept** all of your terms **except** the last one.

adapt, adopt *Adapt* means "to adjust." *Adopt* means "to take something for one's own."
Species survive because they **adapt** to new situations. My church will **adopt** a needy family.

advice, advise *Advice,* a noun, means "helpful opinion." *Advise,* a verb, means "to give advice."
I must **advise** you to never take Jakel's **advice**.

affect, effect *Affect,* a verb, means "to cause a change in, to influence." *Effect* may be a noun or a verb. As a noun it means "result." As a verb it means "to bring about."
Is it true that the observer can **affect** the results? (verb)
I have no idea what **effect** that may have. (noun)
How can the president **effect** a good approval rating? (verb)

ain't *Ain't* is unacceptable in speaking and writing. Use only in exact quotations.

all ready, already *All ready* means "completely ready." *Already* means "before or by this time."
We had **already** purchased our plane tickets, and we were **all ready** to board.

all right, alright Always write this expression as two words. *Alright* is unacceptable.
Because she is your friend, she is **all right** with me.

all together, altogether The two words *all together* mean "in a group." The single word *altogether* is an adverb meaning "completely" or "on the whole."
The hikers gathered **all together** for lunch, and they were **altogether** exhausted.

allusion, illusion *Allusion* means "an indirect reference." *Illusion* refers to something false.
Mr. Lee made an **allusion** to *The Grapes of Wrath*.   The magician performed **illusions**.

anyways, anywheres, everywheres, somewheres Write these words and others like them without a final *-s: anyway, anywhere, everywhere, somewhere.*

bad, badly Use *bad* as an adjective and *badly* as an adverb.
We watched a **bad** movie.   He sang the national anthem quite **badly**.

being as, being that Use these only informally. In formal writing and speech, use *because* or *since*.

beside, besides *Beside* means "next to." *Besides* means "moreover" or "in addition to."
Who, **besides** Antonio, will offer to sit **beside** the window?

between, among Use *between* to refer to or to compare two separate nouns. Use *among* to show a relationship in a group.
I could not choose **between** Harvard and Princeton.   Who **among** the class knows me?

borrow, lend, loan *Borrow* is a verb meaning "to take something that must be returned." *Lend* is a verb meaning "to give something that must be returned." *Loan* is a noun.
People **borrow** money from banks.   Banks will **lend** money to approved customers.
People always must apply for a **loan**.

bring, take Use *bring* to show movement from a distant place to a closer one. Use *take* to show movement from a nearby place to a more distant one.
Bring in the paper, and **take** out the trash.

can, may *Can* indicates the ability to do something. *May* indicates permission to do something.
Anyone **can** use a credit card, but only the cardholder **may** authorize it.

can't hardly, can't scarcely These terms are considered double negatives. Do not use them. Use *can hardly* and *can scarcely*.

Copyright © by Glencoe/McGraw-Hill

continual, continuous *Continual* describes repetitive action with pauses between occurrences. *Continuous* describes an action that continues with no interruption in space or time.

We make **continual** trips to the grocery.   **Continuous** energy from our sun lights the sky.

could of, might of, must of, should of, would of Do not use *of* after *could, might, must, should,* or *would.* Instead, use the helping verb *have.*

That **must have been** the longest play ever!

different from, different than The expression *different from* is preferred to *different than.*

Baseball is **different from** the English sport of cricket.

doesn't, don't *Doesn't* is the contraction of *does not* and should be used with all singular nouns. *Don't* is the contraction of *do not* and should be used with *I, you,* and all plural nouns.

My dog **doesn't** like the mail carrier.   Bobsled riders **don't** take their job lightly.

emigrate, immigrate Use *emigrate* to mean "to move from one country to another." Use *immigrate* to mean "to enter a country to settle there." Use *from* with *emigrate* and *to* with *immigrate.*

Refugees **emigrate** from war-torn countries.   My great-grandfather **immigrated** to America.

farther, further *Farther* refers to physical distance. *Further* refers to time or degree.

Traveling **farther** from your home may **further** your understanding of different places.

fewer, less Use *fewer* to refer to nouns that can be counted. Use *less* to refer to nouns that cannot be counted. Also use *less* to refer to figures used as a single amount or quantity.

If **fewer** crimes were committed, there would be **less** misery in the world.
The box measured **less** than 100 cm².

good, well *Good* is an adjective, and *well* is an adverb.

That spot is a **good** place for a picnic.   We dined **well** that day.

had of Do not use *of* between *had* and a past participle.

I wish I **had eaten** my sundae when I had the chance.

hanged, hung Use *hanged* to mean "put to death by hanging." Use *hung* in all other cases.

In the Old West, many were convicted and **hanged.**   I **hung** my coat on the hook.

in, into, in to Use *in* to mean "inside" or "within" and *into* to indicate movement or direction from outside to a point within. *In to* is made up of an adverb *(in)* followed by a preposition *(to).*

The fish swim **in** the sea.   We moved **into** a new house last year.
The student walked **in to** see the principal for a meeting.

irregardless, regardless Always use *regardless. Irregardless* is a double negative.

Root beer tastes great **regardless** of the brand.

this kind, these kinds Because *kind* is singular, it is modified by the singular form *this* or *that.* Because *kinds* is plural, it is modified by the plural form *these* or *those.*

I love **these kinds** of desserts!   I do not feel comfortable with **this kind** of situation.

lay, lie *Lay* means "to put" or "to place," and it takes a direct object. *Lie* means "to recline" or "to be positioned," and it never takes an object.

I taught my dog to **lay** the paper at my feet and then **lie** on the ground.

learn, teach *Learn* means "to receive knowledge." *Teach* means "to impart knowledge."

I want to **learn** a new language and later **teach** it to others.

leave, let *Leave* means "to go away." *Let* means "to allow" or "to permit."

My guest had to **leave** because his parents do not **let** him stay up too late.

like, as *Like* is a preposition and introduces a prepositional phrase. *As* and *as if* are subordinating

Copyright © by Glencoe/McGraw-Hill

conjunctions and introduce subordinate clauses. Never use *like* before a clause.

I felt **like** a stuffed crab after the feast.   The pigeons flew away, **as** they always do when scared.

loose, lose Use *loose* to mean "not firmly attached" and *lose* to mean "to misplace," or "to fail to win."

You don't want to **lose** your nice pair of **loose** jeans.

passed, past *Passed* is the past tense and the past participle of the verb *to pass*. *Past* can be an adjective, a preposition, an adverb, or a noun.

He **passed** the exit ramp because he could not see the sign **past** the bushes.

precede, proceed *Precede* means "to go or come before." *Proceed* means "to continue."

We can **proceed** with the plans.   From a distance, lightning appears to **precede** thunder.

raise, rise *Raise* means "to cause to move upward," and it always takes an object. *Rise* means "to get up"; it is intransitive and never takes an object.

Raise the drawbridge!   For some, it is difficult to **rise** in the morning.

reason is because Use either *reason is that* or *because*.

The **reason** he left **is that** he was bored. He left **because** he was bored.

respectfully, respectively *Respectfully* means "with respect." *Respectively* means "in the order named."

We **respectfully** bowed to the audience.

Abla, Héctor, and Shelly, **respectively,** play first, second, and third base.

says, said *Says* is the third-person singular of *say*. *Said* is the past tense of *say*.

Listen carefully to what she **says**.   I love what the keynote speaker **said**.

sit, set *Sit* means "to place oneself in a sitting position." It rarely takes an object. *Set* means "to place" or "to put" and usually takes an object. *Set* can also refer to the sun's going down.

Sit anywhere you would like.   **Set** the nozzle back in its slot before paying for the gas.

Today the sun will **set** at seven o'clock.

than, then *Than* is a conjunction that is used to introduce the second element in a comparison; it also shows exception. *Then* is an adverb.

Julio hit more home runs **than** Jacob this year.   Call for help first, and **then** start CPR.

this here, that there Avoid using *here* and *there* after *this* and *that*.

This bunk is yours.

who, whom *Who* is a subject, and *whom* is an object.

Who first sang the song "Memories"?   To **whom** should I throw the ball now?

CAPITALIZATION

1. Capitalize the first word in a sentence, including direct quotes and sentences in parentheses unless they are contained within another sentence.

   Shakespeare asked, "**W**hat's in a name?" (**T**his is from *Romeo and Juliet*.)

2. Always capitalize the pronoun *I* no matter where it appears in a sentence.

   Because **I** woke up late, **I** had to race to school.

3. Capitalize the following proper nouns.

   a. Names of individuals, titles used in direct address or preceding a name, and titles describing a family relationship used with a name or in place of a name.

   President Nixon   **George Burns**   **Sir Anthony Hopkins**   **Uncle Jay**   **Sis**

Copyright © by Glencoe/McGraw-Hill

b. Names of ethnic groups, national groups, political parties and their members, and languages

African Americans   **Mexicans**   **Republican party**   **Hebrew**

c. Names of organizations, institutions, firms, monuments, bridges, buildings, and other structures

National Honor Society   **Vietnam War Memorial**   **Brooklyn Bridge**   **Parliament**

d. Trade names and names of documents, awards, and laws

Kleenex tissues   **Declaration of Independence**   **Academy Award**   **Bill of Rights**

e. Geographical terms and regions or localities

North Carolina   **Arctic Ocean**   **Nile River**   **West Street**   the **South**   **Central Park**

f. Names of planets and other heavenly bodies

Jupiter   **Horsehead Nebula**   the **Milky Way**

g. Names of ships, planes, trains, and spacecraft

Challenger   **USS** *George Washington*   *Spirit of St. Louis*

h. Names of most historical events, eras, calendar items, and religious terms

Fourth of July   **Jurassic**   **Gulf War**   **Friday**   **Yom Kippur**   **Protestant**

i. Titles of literary works, works of art, and musical compositions

"The Road Less Traveled" (poem)   *The Old Man and the Sea* (book)
Venus de Milo (statue)   **The Magic Flute** (opera)

4. Capitalize proper adjectives (adjectives formed from proper nouns).

Socratic method   **Jungian theory**   **Chinese food**   **Georgia clay**   **Colombian coffee**

PUNCTUATION, ABBREVIATIONS, AND NUMBERS

1. Use a period at the end of a declarative sentence and at the end of a polite command.

Robin Hood was a medieval hero.   Pass the papers to the front.

2. Use an exclamation point to show strong feeling or to give a forceful command.

What a surprise that is!   Watch out!   That's just what I need!

3. Use a question mark to indicate a direct question. Use a period to indicate an indirect question.

DIRECT: Who ruled France in 1821?
INDIRECT: Gamal wanted to know how much time was left before lunch.

4. Use a colon to introduce a list or to illustrate or restate previous material.

For my team, I choose the following people: Zina, Ming, and Sue.
In light of the data, the conclusion was not hard to obtain: Earth is not flat.

5. Use a colon for precise time measurements, biblical chapter and verse references, and business letter salutations.

10:02 A.M.   John 3:16   Dear Ms. Delgado:

6. Use a semicolon in the following situations:

a. To separate main clauses not joined by a coordinating conjunction

My computer isn't working; perhaps I need to call a technician.

b. To separate main clauses joined by a conjunctive adverb or by *for example* or *that is*

Cancer is a serious disease; however, heart disease kills more people.

c. To separate items in a series when those items contain commas

I have done oral reports on Maya Angelou, a poet; Billy Joel, a singer; and Mario van Peebles, a director and actor.

Copyright © by Glencoe/McGraw-Hill

Handbook

d. To separate two main clauses joined by a coordinating conjunction when such clauses already contain several commas
According to Bruce, he spent his vacation in Naples, Florida; but he said it was a business, not a pleasure, trip.

7. Use a comma in the following situations:

a. To separate the main clauses of compound sentences
She was a slow eater, but she always finished her meal first.

b. To separate three or more words, phrases, or clauses in a series
Apples, oranges, grapefruit, and cherries are delicious.

c. To separate coordinate modifiers
The prom was a happy, exciting occasion.

d. To set off parenthetical expressions
He will, of course, stay for dinner.   Mary, on the other hand, is very pleasant.

e. To set off nonessential clauses and phrases; to set off introductory adverbial clauses, participial phrases, and long prepositional phrases.
Adjective clause: The bride, who is a chemist, looked lovely.
Appositive phrase: The parade, the longest I've ever seen, featured twelve bands.
Adverbial clause: After we had eaten, I realized my wallet was still in the car.
Participial phrase: Laughing heartily, Milan quickly left the room.
Prepositional phrase: At the sound of the final buzzer, the ball slid through the hoop.

f. To separate parts of an address, a geographical term, or a date
1640 Chartwell Avenue, Edina, Minnesota   September 11, 1982

g. To set off parts of a reference
Read *Slaughterhouse-Five*, pages 15–20.   Perform a scene from *Hamlet*, Act II.

h. To set off words or phrases of direct address and tag questions
Sherri, please pass the butter.   How are you, my friend?   We try hard, don't we?

i. After the salutation and close of a friendly letter and after the close of a business letter
Dear Richard,   Sincerely,   Yours,   Dear Mother,

8. Use dashes to signal a change in thought or to emphasize parenthetical matter.
"Remember to turn off the alarm—oh, don't touch that!"

9. Use parentheses to set off supplemental material. Punctuate within the parentheses only if the punctuation is part of the parenthetical expression.
I saw Bill Cosby (he is my favorite comedian) last night.

10. Use brackets to enclose information inserted by someone besides the original writer.
The paper continues, "The company knows he [Watson] is impressed."

11. Ellipsis points, a series of three spaced points, indicate an omission of material.
The film critic said, "The show was great . . . a must see!"

12. Use quotation marks to enclose a direct quotation. When a quotation is interrupted, use two sets of quotation marks. Use single quotation marks for a quotation within a quotation.
"This day," the general said, "will live on in infamy."
"Yes," the commander replied. "The headlines today read, 'Allies Retreat.'"

13. Use quotation marks to indicate titles of short works, unusual expressions, and definitions.
"The Gift of the Magi" (short story)   "Ave Maria" (song)
Large speakers are called "woofers," and small speakers are called "tweeters."

Copyright © by Glencoe/McGraw-Hill

14. Always place commas and periods *inside* closing quotations mark. Place colons and semicolons *outside* closing quotation marks. Place question marks and exclamation points *inside* closing quotation marks only when those marks are part of the quotation.

"Rafi told me," John said, "that he could not go."

Let me tell you about "Piano Man": it is a narrative song.

He yelled, "Who are you?"

Did she say "Wait for me"?

15. Italicize (underline) titles of books, lengthy poems, plays, films, television series, paintings and sculptures, long musical compositions, court cases, names of newspapers and magazines, ships, trains, airplanes, and spacecraft.

The Last Supper (painting)   *Bang the Drum Slowly* (film)   *Roe v. Wade* (court case)
Titanic (ship)   *Time* (magazine)   *Boston Globe* (newspaper)

16. Italicize (underline) foreign words and expressions that are not used frequently in English and words, letters, and numerals used to represent themselves.

Please discuss the phrase *caveat emptor.*

Today, *Sesame Street* was sponsored by the letters *t* and *m* and the number *6.*

17. Add an apostrophe and *-s* to all singular indefinite pronouns, singular nouns, plural nouns not ending in *-s,* and compound nouns to make them possessive. Add only an apostrophe to plural nouns ending in *-s* to make them possessive.

anyone**'s** guess   the dog**'s** leash   the women**'s** club
students**'** teacher   singers**'** microphones   runners**'** shoes

18. If two or more people possess something jointly, use the possessive form for the last person's name. If they possess things individually, use the possessive form for both names.

mom and dad**'s** checkbook   Carmen**'s** and Sumil**'s** projects

19. Use a possessive form to express amounts of money or time that modify a noun.

a day**'s** pay   fifty dollars**'** worth   a block**'s** walk

20. Use an apostrophe in place of omitted letters or numerals. Use an apostrophe and *-s* to form the plural of letters, numerals, and symbols.

cannot is *can't*   *do not* is *don't*   1978 is **'**78
Mind your **p's** and **q's.**

21. Use a hyphen after any prefix joined to a proper noun or a proper adjective. Use a hyphen after the prefixes *all-, ex-,* and *self-* joined to a noun or adjective, the prefix *anti-* joined to a word beginning with *i-,* the prefix *vice-* (except in vice *president*), and the prefix *re-* to avoid confusion between words that are spelled the same but have different meanings.

all-inclusive   ex-wife   self-reliance
anti-immigrant   vice-principal   re-call instead of recall

22. Use a hyphen in a compound adjective that precedes a noun. Use a hyphen in compound numbers and in fractions used as adjectives.

a green-yellow jersey   a red-hot poker   jet-black hair
ninety-nine   one-fifth cup of sugar

23. Use a hyphen to divide words at the end of a line.

daz-zle   terri-tory   Mediter-ranean

24. Use one period at the end of an abbreviation. If punctuation other than a period ends the sentence, use both the period and the other punctuation.

Bring me the books, papers, pencils, etc.   Could you be ready at 2:00 P.M.?

Copyright © by Glencoe/McGraw-Hill

25. Capitalize the abbreviations of proper nouns and some personal titles.
    U.K.   C.E.O.   R. F. Kennedy   B.C.   A.D.   Ph.D.

26. Abbreviate numerical measurements in scientific writing, but not in ordinary prose.
    Measure 89 g into the crucible.   Jim ran ten yards when he heard that dog barking!

27. Spell out cardinal and ordinal numbers that can be written in one and two words and those that appear at the beginning of a sentence.
    Five hundred people attended.   I look forward to my **eighteenth** birthday.

28. Use numerals for dates; for decimals; for house, apartment, and room numbers; for street and avenue numbers greater than ten; for sums of money involving both dollars and cents; and to emphasize the exact time of day and with A.M. and P.M.
    April **1, 1996**   Room **251**   **$2.51**   **2:51** P.M.

29. Express all related numbers in a sentence as numerals if any one should be a numeral.
    The subscriptions gradually rose from **10** to **116**.

30. Spell out numbers that express decades, amounts of money that can be written in one or two words, streets and avenues less than ten, and the approximate time of day.
    the **seventies**   **fifty** cents   **Fifth** Avenue   half past **five**

VOCABULARY AND SPELLING

1. Clues to the meaning of an unfamiliar word can be found in its context. Context clues include definition, the meaning stated; example, the meaning explained through one familiar case; comparison, similarity to a familiar word; contrast, opposite of a familiar word; and cause and effect, a cause described by its effects.

2. Clues to the meaning of a word can be obtained from its base word, its prefix, or its suffix.
    telegram **gram** = writing   psychology **psych** = soul, mind
    antibacterial **anti** = against   biology **-logy** = study

3. The *i* comes before the *e*, except when both letters follow a *c* or when both letters are pronounced together as an *ā* sound. However, many exceptions exist to this rule.
    f**ie**ld (*i* before *e*)   dec**ei**ve (*ei* after *c*)   r**ei**gn (*ā* sound)   w**ei**rd (exception)

4. Most word endings pronounced *sēd* are spelled *-cede.* In one word, *supersede,* the ending is spelled *-sede.* In *proceed, exceed,* and *succeed,* the ending is spelled *-ceed.*
    pre**cede**   re**cede**   con**cede**

5. An unstressed vowel sound is not emphasized when a word is pronounced. Determine the spelling of this sound by comparing it to a known word.
    hesitant (Compare to *hesitate.*)   *fantasy* (Compare to *fantastic.*)

6. When adding a suffix that begins with a consonant to a word that ends in silent *e*, generally keep the *e*. If the suffix begins with a vowel or *y*, generally drop the *e*. If the suffix begins with *a* or *o* and the word ends in *ce* or *ge*, keep the *e*. If the suffix begins with a vowel and the word ends in *ee*, or *oe*, keep the *e*.
    encourag**ement**   scary   chang**eable**   fle**eing**

7. When adding a suffix to a word ending in a consonant +*y*, change the *y* to *i* unless the suffix begins with *i*. If the word ends in a vowel +*y*, keep the *y*.
    heart**iness**   read**iness**   sp**ying**   stra**ying**

Copyright © by Glencoe/McGraw-Hill

8. Double the final consonant before adding a suffix that begins with a vowel to a word that ends in a single consonant preceded by a single vowel if the accent is on the root's last syllable.

planned   finned   misfitted

9. When adding -ly to a word that ends in a single *l*, keep the *l*. If it ends in a double *l*, drop one *l*. If it ends in a consonant +*le*, drop the *le*.

real becomes really   dull becomes dully   inexplicable becomes inexplicably

10. When adding -ness to a word that ends in *n*, keep the *n*.

leanness   meanness   greenness

11. When joining a word or prefix that ends in a consonant to a suffix or word that begins with a consonant, keep both consonants.

quietness   greatly   redness

12. Most nouns form their plurals by adding -s. However, nouns that end in -ch, -s, -sh, -x, or -z form plurals by adding -es. If the noun ends in a consonant +y, change y to i and add -es. If the noun ends in -lf, change f to v and add -es. If the noun ends in -fe, change f to v and add -s.

cans   churches   faxes   spies   halves   loaves

13. To form the plural of proper names and one-word compound nouns, follow the general rules for plurals. To form the plural of hyphenated compound nouns or compound nouns of more than one word, make the most important word plural.

Shatners   Stockholders   brothers-in-law   Master Sergeants

14. Some nouns have the same singular and plural forms.

sheep   species

COMPOSITION

Writing Themes and Paragraphs

1. Use **prewriting** to find ideas to write about. One form of prewriting, **freewriting**, starts with a subject or topic and branches off into related ideas. Another way to find a topic is to ask and answer questions about your starting subject, helping you to gain a deeper understanding of your chosen topic. Also part of the prewriting stage is determining who your readers or **audience** will be and deciding your **purpose** for writing. Your purpose—as varied as writing to persuade, to explain, to describe something, or to narrate—is partially shaped by who your audience will be, and vice versa.

2. To complete your first **draft**, organize your prewriting into an introduction, body, and conclusion. Concentrate on unity and coherence of the overall piece. Experiment with different paragraph orders: **chronological order** places events in the order in which they happened; **spatial order** places objects in the order in which they appear; and **compare/contrast order** shows similarities and differences in objects or events.

3. **Revise** your composition if necessary. Read through your draft, looking for places to improve content and structure. Remember that varying your sentence patterns and lengths will make your writing easier and more enjoyable to read.

4. In the **editing** stage, check your grammar, spelling, and punctuation. Focus on expressing your ideas clearly and concisely.

5. Finally, prepare your writing for **presentation**. Sharing your composition, or ideas, with others may take many forms: printed, oral, or graphic.

Copyright © by Glencoe/McGraw-Hill

Outlining

1. The two common forms of outlines are sentence outlines and topic outlines. Choose one type of outline and keep it uniform throughout.

2. A period follows the number or letter of each division. Each point in a sentence outline ends with a period; the points in a topic outline do not.

3. Each point begins with a capital letter.

4. A point may have no fewer than two subpoints.

SENTENCE OUTLINE
I. This is the main point.
   A. This is a subpoint of *I*.
      1. This is a detail of *A*.
         a. This is a detail of *1*.
         b. This is a detail of *1*.
      2. This is a detail of *A*.
   B. This is a subpoint of *I*.
II. This is another main point.

TOPIC OUTLINE
I. Main point
   A. Subpoint of *I*
      1. Detail of *A*
         a. Detail of *1*
         b. Detail of *1*
      2. Detail of *A*
   B. Subpoint of *I*
II. Main point

Writing letters

1. Personal letters are usually handwritten in indented form (the first lines of paragraphs, each line of the heading, the complimentary close, and the signature are indented). Business letters are usually typewritten in block or semiblock form. Block form contains no indents; semiblock form indents the heading, the complimentary close, and the signature.

2. The five parts of a personal letter are the heading (the writer's address and the date), the salutation (greeting), the body (message), the complimentary close (such as "Yours truly"), and the signature (the writer's name). The business letter has the same parts and also includes an inside address (the recipient's address).

PERSONAL LETTER

Heading

Salutation

Body

Complimentary Close
Signature

BUSINESS LETTER

Heading

Inside Address

Salutation

Body

Complimentary Close
Signature

Copyright © by Glencoe/McGraw-Hill

3. Reveal your personality and imagination in colorful personal letters. Keep business letters brief, clear, and courteous.

4. **Personal letters** include letters to friends and family members. **Thank-you notes** and **invitations** are personal letters that may be either formal or informal in style.

5. Use a **letter of complaint** to convey a concern. Begin the letter by telling what happened. Then use supporting details as evidence. Complete the letter by explaining what you want done. Avoid insults and threats, and make reasonable requests. Use a **letter of request** to ask for information or to place an order of purchase. Be concise, yet give all the details necessary for your request to be fulfilled. Keep the tone of your letter courteous and be generous in allotting time for a response.

6. Use an **opinion letter** to take a firm stand on an issue. Make the letter clear, firm, rational, and purposeful. Be aware of your audience, their attitude, how informed they are, and their possible reactions to your opinion. Support your statements of opinion with facts.

7. Use a **résumé** to summarize your work experience, school experience, talents, and interests. Be clear, concise, and expressive. Use a consistent form. You do not need to write in complete sentences, but use as many action verbs as possible.

8. Use a **cover letter** as a brief introduction accompanying your résumé.

Copyright © by Glencoe/McGraw-Hill

*T*roubleshooter

●●●●●●●●●●●●●●●●●●●●●●●●

Sentence Fragments

PROBLEM 1

Fragment that lacks a subject

frag	Ali baked a chocolate cake. Took it to the party.
frag	Maria thought the comedian was funny. Laughed at his jokes.

SOLUTION

Ali baked a chocolate cake. He took it to the party.
Maria thought the comedian was funny. She laughed at his jokes.

Make a complete sentence by adding a subject to the fragment.

PROBLEM 2

Fragment that lacks a complete verb

frag	Helen is a photographer. She becoming well-known for her work.
frag	Alicia has a new computer. It very powerful.

SOLUTION A

Helen is a photographer. She is becoming well-known for her work.
Alicia has a new computer. It is very powerful.

Make a complete sentence by adding a complete verb or a helping verb.

SOLUTION B

Helen is a photographer and is becoming well-known for her work.
Alicia has a new computer, which is very powerful.

Combine the fragment with another sentence.

Copyright © by Glencoe/McGraw-Hill

PROBLEM 3

Fragment that is a subordinate clause

frag   Akira repaired the old boat. <u>Because it was beautiful.</u>

frag   Jennifer has two race car magazines. <u>Which she bought at the store.</u>

SOLUTION A

Akira repaired the old boat because it was beautiful.

Jennifer has two race car magazines, which she bought at the store.

Combine the fragment with another sentence.

SOLUTION B

Akira repaired the old boat. It was beautiful.

Jennifer has two race car magazines. She bought them at the store.

Make the fragment a complete sentence by removing the subordinating conjunction or the relative pronoun and adding a subject or other words necessary to make a complete thought.

PROBLEM 4

Fragment that lacks both subject and verb

frag   The soft rustle of the trees makes me sleepy. <u>In the afternoon.</u>

frag   <u>The next morning.</u> We talked about our adventure.

SOLUTION

The soft rustle of the trees makes me sleepy in the afternoon.

The next morning, we talked about our adventure.

Make the fragment part of a sentence.

Need More Help?

More help in avoiding sentence fragments is available in Lesson 30.

Copyright © by Glencoe/McGraw-Hill

Run-on Sentences

PROBLEM 1

Comma splice—two main clauses separated only by a comma

run-on (I don't know where the oil paints are, they were over by the easel.)

SOLUTION A

I don't know where the oil paints are. They were over by the easel.

Make two sentences by separating the first clause from the second with end punctuation, such as a period or a question mark, and start the second sentence with a capital letter.

SOLUTION B

I don't know where the oil paints are; they were over by the easel.

Place a semicolon between the main clauses of the sentence.

SOLUTION C

I don't know where the oil paints are, but they were over by the easel.

Add a coordinating conjunction after the comma.

PROBLEM 2

No punctuation between two main clauses

run-on (Deelra ran the hurdles in record time Shawna placed second.)

SOLUTION A

Deelra ran the hurdles in record time. Shawna placed second.

Make two sentences out of the run-on sentence.

Copyright © by Glencoe/McGraw-Hill

Copyright © by Glencoe/McGraw-Hill

SOLUTION B

Deelra ran the hurdles in record time; Shawna placed second.

Separate the main clauses with a semicolon.

SOLUTION C

Deelra ran the hurdles in record time, but Shawna placed second.

Add a comma and a coordinating conjunction between the main clauses.

PROBLEM 3

Two main clauses without a comma before the coordinating conjunction

run-on The robins usually arrive in the spring and they start building nests at once.

run-on Emily won the scholarship last year but she decided not to accept it.

SOLUTION

The robins usually arrive in the spring, and they start building nests at once.

Emily won the scholarship last year, but she decided not to accept it.

Separate the main clauses by adding a comma before the coordinating conjunction.

More help in avoiding run-on sentences is available in Lesson 31.

Troubleshooter

Lack of Subject-Verb Agreement

PROBLEM 1

A prepositional phrase between a subject and its verb

agr	The arrangement of those colorful pictures (make) a vivid, exciting combination.
agr	One of those big, gray seagulls (have perched) on the roof.

SOLUTION

The arrangement of those colorful pictures makes a vivid, exciting combination.

One of those big, gray seagulls has perched on the roof.

Make the verb agree with the subject, not with the object of the preposition.

PROBLEM 2

A predicate nominative differing in number from the subject

agr	Fast-paced adventure movies (was) always Jenny's choice.

SOLUTION

Fast-paced adventure movies were always Jenny's choice.

Make the verb agree with the subject, not with the predicate nominative.

PROBLEM 3

A subject following the verb

agr	On the sun deck there (was) several chairs and a table.
agr	Here (comes) the rain clouds and the heavy, slanting rain.

Copyright © by Glencoe/McGraw-Hill

SOLUTION

On the sun deck there were several chairs and a table.

Here come the rain clouds and the heavy, slanting rain.

Look for the subject after the verb in an inverted sentence. Make sure that the verb agrees with the subject.

PROBLEM 4

Collective nouns as subjects

agr   The crowd really (like) the music, doesn't it?

agr   Margaret's company (arrives) tomorrow by bus and by train.

SOLUTION A

The crowd really likes the music, doesn't it?

Use a singular verb if the collective noun refers to a group as a whole.

SOLUTION B

Margaret's company arrive tomorrow by bus and by train.

Use a plural verb if the collective noun refers to each member of a group individually.

PROBLEM 5

A noun of amount as the subject

agr   The past two days (seems) like a week.

agr   One thousand millimeters (equal) a meter.

SOLUTION

The past two days seem like a week.

One thousand millimeters equals a meter.

A noun of amount that refers to one unit is singular. A noun of amount that refers to a number of individual units is plural.

Copyright © by Glencoe/McGraw-Hill

Troubleshooter

PROBLEM 6

Compound subject joined by **and**

agr	A clear day and a light breeze (brightens) a summer afternoon.
agr	Pop and pizza (are) a common meal.

SOLUTION A

A clear day and a light breeze brighten a summer afternoon.

Use a plural verb if the parts of the compound subject do not belong to one unit or if they refer to different people or things.

SOLUTION B

Pop and pizza is a common meal.

Use a singular verb if the parts of the compound subject belong to one unit or if they refer to the same person or thing.

PROBLEM 7

Compound subject joined by **or** *or* **nor**

agr	Neither Yuri nor Sarah (like) the menu.

SOLUTION

Neither Yuri nor Sarah likes the menu.

Make your verb agree with the subject closer to it.

PROBLEM 8

Compound subject preceded by **many a, every,** *or* **each**

agr	Many a brush and tube of paint (were scattered) around the studio.

Copyright © by Glencoe/McGraw-Hill

SOLUTION

Many a brush and tube of paint was scattered across the studio.

The subject is considered singular when *many a, each,* or *every* precedes a compound subject.

PROBLEM 9

Subjects separated from the verb by an intervening expression

agr Jamal's new sculpture, in addition to his other recent works, (reflect) his abiding love of nature.

SOLUTION

Jamal's new sculpture, in addition to his other recent works, reflects his abiding love of nature.

Expressions that begin with *as well as, in addition to,* and *together with,* do not change the number of the subject. Make the verb agree with its subject, not with the intervening expression.

PROBLEM 10

Indefinite pronouns as subjects

agr Each of the trees along the old canal (have) different colors in the fall.

SOLUTION

Each of the trees along the old canal has different colors in the fall.

Some indefinite pronouns are singular, some are plural, and some can be either singular or plural depending on the noun they refer to. (A list of indefinite pronouns is on page 54.)

 More help with subject-verb agreement is available in Lessons 44–51.

Copyright © by Glencoe/McGraw-Hill

Lack of Agreement Between Pronoun and Antecedent

PROBLEM 1

A singular antecedent that can be either male or female

| ant | A great coach inspires (his) athletes to be their best on or off the field. |

Traditionally, masculine pronouns referred to antecedents that might have been either male or female.

> ### SOLUTION A
>
> **A great coach inspires his or her athletes to be their best on or off the field.**
>
> Use *he* or *she, him* or *her*, and so on, to reword the sentence.

> ### SOLUTION B
>
> **Great coaches inspire their athletes to be their best on or off the field.**
>
> Make both the antecedent and the pronoun plural.

> ### SOLUTION C
>
> **Great coaches inspire athletes to be their best on or off the field.**
>
> Eliminate the pronoun.

PROBLEM 2

A second-person pronoun that refers to a third-person antecedent

| ant | Mary and Jodi prefer the new bridle trail because (you) get long stretches for galloping. |

Copyright © by Glencoe/McGraw-Hill

Do not use the second-person pronoun *you* to refer to an antecedent in the third person.

> ## SOLUTION A
>
> **Mary and Jodi prefer the new bridle trail because they get long stretches for galloping.**
>
> Replace *you* with the appropriate third-person pronoun.

> ## SOLUTION B
>
> **Mary and Jodi prefer the new bridle trail because the horses have long stretches for galloping.**
>
> Replace *you* with an appropriate noun.

PROBLEM 3

Singular indefinite pronouns as antecedents

> ant   Each of the women in the boat received a rowing medal for their victory.

> ## SOLUTION
>
> **Each of the women in the boat received a rowing medal for her victory.**
>
> Determine whether the antecedent is singular or plural, and make the personal pronoun agree with it.

More help with pronoun-antecedent agreement is available in Lessons 57–59.

Copyright © by Glencoe/McGraw-Hill

Unclear Pronoun References

PROBLEM 1

Unclear antecedent

| ref | The wind was fair and the water calm, and (that) made sailing across the bay an absolute pleasure. |
| ref | The traffic was snarled, (which) was caused by an accident. |

SOLUTION A

The wind was fair and the water calm, and those conditions made sailing across the bay an absolute pleasure.

Substitute a noun for the pronoun.

SOLUTION B

The traffic was snarled in a massive tie-up, which was caused by an accident.

Rewrite the sentence, adding a clear antecedent for the pronoun.

PROBLEM 2

A pronoun that refers to more than one antecedent

| ref | The team captain told Karen to take (her) guard position. |
| ref | The buses came early for the students, but (they) were not ready. |

SOLUTION A

The team captain told Karen to take the captain's guard position.

Substitute a noun for the pronoun.

Copyright © by Glencoe/McGraw-Hill

Copyright © by Glencoe/McGraw-Hill

SOLUTION B

Because the buses came early, the students were not ready.

Rewrite the sentence, eliminating the pronoun.

PROBLEM 3

Indefinite uses of you *or* they

ref   In those hills (you) rarely see mountain lions.

ref   In some movies (they) have too much violence.

SOLUTION A

In those hills hikers rarely see mountain lions.

Substitute a noun for the pronoun.

SOLUTION B

Some movies have too much violence.

Eliminate the pronoun entirely.

Need More Help?

More help in making clear pronoun references is available in Lesson 60.

Shifts in Pronouns

PROBLEM 1

Incorrect shift in person between two pronouns

pro	They went to the stadium for the game, but you could not find a place to park.
pro	One needs to remember to always keep their study time free from other commitments.
pro	We were on the hill at dawn, and you could see the most wondrous sunrise.

Incorrect pronoun shifts occur when a writer or speaker uses a pronoun in one person and then illogically shifts to a pronoun in another person.

SOLUTION A

They went to the stadium for the game, but they could not find a place to park.

One needs to remember to always keep one's study time free from other commitments.

Replace the incorrect pronoun with a pronoun that agrees with its antecedent.

SOLUTION B

We were on the hill at dawn, and Mary and I could see the most wondrous sunrise.

Replace the incorrect pronoun with an appropriate noun.

 More help with shifts in pronouns is available in Lessons 57–60.

Copyright © by Glencoe/McGraw-Hill

Shift in Verb Tenses

PROBLEM 1

Unnecessary shifts in tense

> shift t   Akira waits for the bus and (worked) on the computer.
>
> shift t   Jenny hit the home run and (runs) around the bases.

       Two or more events occurring at the same time must have the same verb tense.

SOLUTION

Akira waits for the bus and works on the computer.
Jenny hit the home run and ran around the bases.

Use the same tense for both verbs.

PROBLEM 2

Tenses do not indicate that one event precedes or succeeds another

> shift t   By the time the movie finally started, we (waited) impatiently through ten minutes of commercials.

       If events being described occurred at different times, shift tenses to show that one event precedes or follows another.

SOLUTION

By the time the movie finally started, we had waited impatiently through ten minutes of commercials.

Use the past perfect tense for the earlier of two actions to indicate that one action began and ended before another action began.

More help with shifts in verb tenses is available in Lessons 37–39 and 41.

Copyright © by Glencoe/McGraw-Hill

Incorrect Verb Tenses or Forms

PROBLEM 1

Incorrect or missing verb endings

tense   Ricardo said it (snow) last night.

tense   Karen and her family (travel) to Costa Rica last year.

SOLUTION

Ricardo said it snowed last night.

Karen and her family traveled to Costa Rica last year.

Regular verbs form the past tense and the past participle by adding *-ed*.

PROBLEM 2

Improper formation of irregular verbs

tense   The sun (rised) out of scarlet clouds into a clear, blue sky.

SOLUTION

The sun rose out of scarlet clouds into a clear, blue sky.

An irregular verb forms its past tense and past participle in some way other than by adding *-ed*.

PROBLEM 3

Confusion between the past form of the verb and the past participle

tense   The horses (have ate) their feed already.

tense   The coach (has wore) the old team jacket to every graduation.

Copyright © by Glencoe/McGraw-Hill

SOLUTION

The horses have eaten their feed already.

The coach has worn the old team jacket to every graduation.

When you use the auxiliary verb *have,* use the past participle form of an irregular verb, not its simple past form.

PROBLEM 4

Improper use of the past participle

tense   Deemee (drawn) the winning ticket for the door prize at the dance.

tense   The old rowboat (sunk) just below the surface of the lake.

Past participles of irregular verbs cannot stand alone as verbs. They must be used in conjunction with a form of the auxiliary verb *have.*

SOLUTION A

Deemee had drawn the winning ticket for the door prize at the dance.

The old rowboat had sunk just below the surface of the lake.

Form a complete verb by adding a form of the auxiliary verb *have* to the past participle.

SOLUTION B

Deemee drew the winning ticket for the door prize at the dance.

The old rowboat sank just below the surface of the lake.

Use the simple past form of the verb instead of the past participle.

Need More Help?

More help with correct verb forms is available in Lessons 35, 36, and 40.

Copyright © by Glencoe/McGraw-Hill

Misplaced or Dangling Modifiers

PROBLEM 1

Misplaced modifier

|---|---|
| mod | Untended and overgrown since last summer, Marlene helped Keshia in her garden. |
| mod | Sarah won the jumping contest with her mother's horse, wearing western riding gear. |

A misplaced modifier appears to modify the wrong word or group of words.

> **SOLUTION**
>
> **Marlene helped Keshia in her garden, untended and overgrown since last summer.**
>
> **Wearing western riding gear, Sarah won the jumping contest with her mother's horse.**
>
> Place the modifying phrase as close as possible to the word or words it modifies.

PROBLEM 2

Misplacing the adverb only

mod	Akiko only runs hurdles in track.

> **SOLUTION**
>
> **Only Akiko runs hurdles in track.**
> **Akiko runs only hurdles in track.**
> **Akiko runs hurdles only in track.**
>
> Each time *only* is moved in the sentence, the meaning of the sentence changes. Place the adverb immediately before the word or group of words it is to modify.

Copyright © by Glencoe/McGraw-Hill

38   *Grammar and Language Workbook, Grade 11*

PROBLEM 3

Dangling modifiers

> mod   (Branches swaying in the breeze,) we rested in the shade.
>
> mod   (Trying out the new exercise equipment,) the new gym is a great improvement over the old one.

A dangling modifier does not modify any word in the sentence.

SOLUTION

Branches swaying in the breeze, the tree provided us with shade.

Trying out the new exercise equipment, Mary said the new gym is a great improvement over the old one.

Add a noun to which the dangling phrase clearly refers. You might have to add or change other words, as well.

More help with misplaced or dangling modifiers is available in Lesson 66.

Copyright © by Glencoe/McGraw-Hill

Troubleshooter

Misplaced or Missing Possessive Apostrophes

PROBLEM 1

Singular nouns

> poss   (Charles) car is the white one, but (Jamals) is the red convertible.

SOLUTION

Charles's car is the white one, but Jamal's is the red convertible.

To form the possessive of a singular noun, even one that ends in -*s*, use an apostrophe and an -*s* at the end of the word.

PROBLEM 2

Plural nouns that end in -s

> poss   The seven maple (trees) cool, delicious shade is the best in the park.

SOLUTION

The seven maple trees' cool, delicious shade is the best in the park.

To form the possessive of a plural noun that ends in -*s*, use an apostrophe by itself after the final -*s*.

PROBLEM 3

Plural nouns that do not end in -s

> poss   The (childrens) movies are on that rack next to the nature films.

SOLUTION

The children's movies are on that rack next to the nature films.

Form the possessive of a plural noun that does not end in -*s* by using an apostrophe and -*s* at the end of the word.

Copyright © by Glencoe/McGraw-Hill

Copyright © by Glencoe/McGraw-Hill

PROBLEM 4

Pronouns

> poss That painting cannot be just (anybodys) work.
>
> poss (Their's) is the trophy in the center of the display case.

SOLUTION A

That painting cannot be just anybody's work.

Form the possessive of a singular indefinite pronoun by adding an apostrophe and -*s* to it.

SOLUTION B

Theirs is the trophy in the center of the display case.

With any of the possessive personal pronouns, do not use an apostrophe.

PROBLEM 5

Confusing *its* with *it's*

> poss The computer is booting up; I see (it's) power light blinking.
>
> poss (Its) going to be a great victory party.

SOLUTION

**The computer is booting up; I see its power light blinking.
It's going to be a great victory party.**

It's is the contraction of *it is,* not the possessive of *it.*

 Need More Help?

More help with apostrophes and possessives is available in Lessons 3 and 92.

Missing Commas with Nonessential Elements

PROBLEM 1

Missing commas with nonessential participles, infinitives, and their phrases

com	Lois scowling fiercely turned her back on Clark.
com	The detective mystified by the fresh clue scratched his head in bewilderment.
com	Television to tell the truth just doesn't interest me.

SOLUTION

Lois, scowling fiercely, turned her back on Clark.

The detective, mystified by the fresh clue, scratched his head in bewilderment.

Television, to tell the truth, just doesn't interest me.

If the participle, infinitive, or phrase is not essential to the meaning of the sentence, set off the phrase with commas.

PROBLEM 2

Missing commas with nonessential adjective clauses

com	The sailboat which looked like a toy in the storm rounded the point into the breakwater.

SOLUTION

The sailboat, which looked like a toy in the storm, rounded the point into the breakwater.

If the clause is not essential to the meaning of the sentence, set it off with commas.

Copyright © by Glencoe/McGraw-Hill

Copyright © by Glencoe/McGraw-Hill

PROBLEM 3

Missing commas with nonessential appositives

com   The palomino a beautiful horse with almost golden hair is often seen in parades.

SOLUTION

The palomino, a beautiful horse with almost golden hair, is often seen in parades.

If the appositive is not essential to the meaning of the sentence, set it off with commas.

PROBLEM 4

Missing commas with interjections and parenthetical expressions

com   Wow did you see that falling star?

com   I would have told you by the way but you weren't home.

SOLUTION

Wow, did you see that falling star?

I would have told you, by the way, but you weren't home.

Set off the interjection or parenthetical expression with commas.

 More help with commas and nonessential elements is available in Lesson 80.

Troubleshooter

PROBLEM 1

Commas missing in a series of words, phrases, or clauses

s com   Mona said that Amy Tan James Baldwin and Charles Dickens were her favorite authors.

s com   Sailing on the Great Lakes can be as challenging adventurous and rewarding as sailing on the ocean.

s com   Our forensic team practiced hard did their research and used all their wit and intelligence to win the championship.

s com   The wind shifted the clouds parted and the sunlight streamed down.

SOLUTION

Mona said that Amy Tan, James Baldwin, and Charles Dickens were her favorite authors.

Sailing on the Great Lakes can be as challenging, adventurous, and rewarding as sailing on the ocean.

Our forensics team practiced hard, did their research, and used all their wit and intelligence to win the championship.

The wind shifted, the clouds parted, and the sunlight streamed down.

Use a comma between each item in a series except the last.

Copyright © by Glencoe/McGraw-Hill

More help with commas is available in Lessons 78–85.

Grammar

Unit 1: Parts of the Speech

Lesson 1
Nouns: Singular, Plural, Possessive, Concrete, and Abstract

A noun is a word that names a person, place, thing, or idea. A singular noun names one person, place, thing, or idea, and a plural noun names more than one.

	SINGULAR	PLURAL
Person:	visitor	visitors
Place:	valley	valleys
Thing:	hammer	hammers
Idea:	belief	beliefs

The possessive form of a noun shows possession, ownership, or the relationship between two nouns.

	SINGULAR POSSESSIVE	PLURAL POSSESSIVE
Possession:	teacher's desk	teachers' desks
Ownership:	student's term paper	students' term papers
Relationship:	country's beauty	countries' beauty

▶ **Exercise 1** Write *S* above each singular noun, *P* above each plural noun, and *poss.* above each possessive noun.

         S   P   poss.   S
The announcer told the fans the game's score.

1. Beautiful white snow covered the mountain's flanks.

2. The audience enjoyed the speaker's anecdotes about the hike.

3. Kentucky's pastures produce many fine thoroughbreds.

4. Alaina received three scholarships after her audition.

5. Did your puppy run under Mrs. Swenson's porch?

6. The parakeet squawks while the canary sings.

7. Our excursion to the park was shortened by warnings of an approaching tornado.

8. Driving hurriedly through the countryside, Jaleel seemed careless about avoiding potholes.

9. The committee's decision to suspend the rules gave Adam more freedom to present his proposal.

10. The figurine on the trophy cracked when the cheering teammates broke the shelf.

11. Su-Lin scrubbed the car's tires while Tom polished the chrome.

Copyright © by Glencoe/McGraw-Hill

12. Jamal's understanding of the technology involved in storing information on a disk seems correct.

13. Many persons in our hectic society have forgotten the beautiful art of sewing.

14. Geraldo insisted on playing devil's advocate whenever discussions arose.

15. Running around the house, the children could not find their father's hat.

16. Having scored twenty-three points in the game, Dowana received the lion's share of praise on the nightly broadcast.

17. Beethoven's fifth symphony is one of his most popular works.

18. Paul's personal library is becoming so large there is no place to add any more shelves.

A **concrete noun** names an object that occupies space or can be recognized by any of the senses. An **abstract noun** names an idea, a quality, or a characteristic.

music (concrete)   value (abstract)   scent (concrete)   loyalty (abstract)

▶ **Exercise 2** Write *con.* (concrete) or *abst.* (abstract) above each italicized noun.

        con.
John ardently studies *heraldry.*

1. Kwang showed his *affection* for his sister Annette by writing her three poems.

2. The *sound* of singing birds makes one's spirits rise.

3. Olaf had not yet reached the *peak* of his abilities.

4. *Hate* is a dangerous emotion.

5. Are you a member of the Republican or Democratic *party*?

6. One of Americans' most prized possessions is *freedom.*

7. Sherri's *urgency* caused Kim to make more mistakes than she normally would have.

8. His cold feet were soothed by the *warmth* from the evening campfire.

9. Kevin was mesmerized by the *aroma* of the bread baking in the kitchen.

10. Muriel's two cats and her dog brought her much *enjoyment.*

11. I was not impressed with his *singing* during the student choir concert.

12. There are several theories as to what caused the *rings* around Saturn.

13. Throughout the entire *kingdom,* none was as brave as Sir Lancelot, the famous knight.

14. Making the team and passing English were two of Ping's *goals* for this semester.

Copyright © by Glencoe/McGraw-Hill

Lesson 2
Nouns: Proper, Common, and Collective

A **proper noun** names a specific person, place or thing. Capitalize proper nouns. A common noun refers to people, places or things in general.

	PROPER NOUNS	COMMON NOUNS
Person:	Robert Walls	superintendent
Place:	Africa	continent
Thing:	Iguanodon	dinosaur
Idea:	Renaissance	thought

A **collective noun** names a group. A collective noun is singular when it refers to the group as a whole. A collective noun is plural when it refers to the individual members of a group.

The **committee** studies the issue. (singular)   The **committee** have gone to lunch. (plural)

▶ **Exercise 1** Label each italicized noun as *prop.* for proper, *com.* for common, or *col.* for collective. Assume the collective nouns are also common nouns.

                col.   com.
The Air Force *squadron* flew over the Olympic *field*.

1. The international sports *festival* known as the *Olympic Games* began in ancient *Greece*.

2. These *games*, which started in the eighth *century* B.C., were held every four *years* for *centuries*.

3. The ancient *Greeks* used the *games* to salute their *god Zeus* and to honor their *cities*.

4. They included *competition* in music, *oratory*, and theater as well as *sport*.

5. Abandoned for several centuries, the *games* were revived in 1894 by an international *committee*.

6. Today that *commission*, the International Olympic Committee, bases itself in *Lausanne, Switzerland*.

7. The original governing *board* consisted of fourteen *members*.

8. Each participating *country* must have a *National Olympics Committee* to sponsor the *team* and physically manage it.

9. *Participants* held the first modern games in the *year* 1896 in *Athens*, Greece.

10. The games were revived to salute the collective athletic *talents* of the *family* of *nations*.

11. Today's *Olympics* concentrate on *sport* only and have a much expanded *venue*.

12. They foster the *ideal* of a "sound *mind* in a sound *body*" and promote *friendship* among nations.

Copyright © by Glencoe/McGraw-Hill

Grammar

13. Participation is open to all, regardless of political *affiliation* or *creed*.

14. Thirteen *countries* competed in that first *revival*.

15. Nine *sports* made up the entire *agenda*.

16. These *events* generated sufficient *interest* to justify continuing the *games*.

17. The *United States* entered a *squad* of fourteen *men* who dominated the track and field events.

18. By the fourth modern *Olympiad* (1908), the *number* of *competitors* had grown from 311 to 2,082.

19. The Olympic governing *council* added the *Winter Games* in 1924.

20. *Chamonix,* France, hosted the first winter *extravaganza*.

21. By 1988, 167 *nations* had Olympic *chapters*.

22. The summer *festivities* that year in Seoul, Korea, drew *athletes* from a record 160 *countries*.

23. The largest *assembly* of *competitors* gathered in Munich, *Germany,* which showcased ten

    thousand *athletes* in 1972.

24. The international *committee* currently has more than seventy *members*.

25. By 1992, the *Winter Olympics* alone boasted 2,174 athletic *colleagues* from sixty-three *countries*.

26. The *Olympiads* have not always been successful in keeping *politics* and *prejudices* outside

    their *events*.

27. Hitler tried to use the 1936 games in *Berlin* to propagandize the Nazi racist *cause*.

28. African American *Jesse Owens* upset those *plans* by winning four gold *medals* in track
    and field.

29. Several *instances* of *boycotts* have shocked the global *audience* and lessened universal

    participation.

30. Even *terrorism* has plagued the games, as in the murder of a *group* of *Israelis* in 1972.

31. Almost all Olympians stress the *camaraderie* of the great *assembly*.

32. While there is much *pride* in competing for one's *country,* the feeling of international *unity* is

    even more important.

33. *Prizes* for the *events* are purposely kept to token *awards*.

34. *Medals* of *gold,* bronze, and *silver* reward the top three *finishers* in each event.

35. This is one *way* of keeping the *emphasis* on the sport rather than the *reward*.

36. In this way the modern *Olympiads* remain true to the *ideals* of their founders, the citizens of

    classical *Greece*.

Copyright © by Glencoe/McGraw-Hill

Lesson 3
Pronouns: Personal, Possessive, Reflexive, and Intensive

Copyright © by Glencoe/McGraw-Hill

A **pronoun** takes the place of a noun, a group of words acting as a noun, or another pronoun. We call the word or group of words that a pronoun refers to its **antecedent**.

A **personal pronoun** refers to a specific person or thing by indicating the person speaking (the first person), the person being addressed (the second person), or any other person or thing being discussed (the third person).

	SINGULAR	PLURAL
First Person:	I, me	we, us
Second Person:	you	you
Third Person:	he, him, she, her, it	they, them

A **possessive pronoun** shows possession or control. It takes the place of a possessive noun.

	SINGULAR	PLURAL
First person	my, mine	our, ours
Second person	your, yours	your, yours
Third person	his, her, hers, its	their, theirs

▶ **Exercise 1** Draw one line under each personal pronoun and two lines under each possessive pronoun.

She makes her own clothes.

1. Does she have the stamina to climb to the top of the cathedral tower?

2. You are the best friend anyone could ask for.

3. Ms. Kowalski signed her autograph on this theater program.

4. Franklin, does that incident have anything to do with your shyness?

5. If Stella asks, just say that I quit for today but will be back tomorrow to finish the job.

6. Did you say this blue and gold notebook was hers?

7. The dog shook its wet fur and splattered water over the entire room.

8. Manny and John have their own version of what happened yesterday at the game.

9. Our substitute teacher, Mr. Pennyworth, told us about his archaeological experiences.

10. Will you give him a helping hand if he asks you for your help?

11. Dad, how long will it take us to reach the first rest area?

12. Mr. Ramirez showed us how to fix a flat tire on a motorcycle.

13. None of the trash scattered all over their yard is ours.

14. My time is very limited today; could I see you tomorrow?

15. How much did the handyman charge them to fix the cracked cement on their porch?

16. Maria said that her mother would help us with the arrangements tomorrow.

17. We try always to be dependable when she asks us to assist her.

18. No matter how many times they try, the Livingston twins just don't show much progress in painting their house.

19. Did you see how many pancakes he ate this morning for breakfast?

20. Debbie and I practiced our instruments for an hour; how long did Russ and Dejuana practice theirs?

A **reflexive pronoun** refers to a noun or another pronoun and indicates that the same person or thing is involved. An **intensive pronoun** adds emphasis to a noun or another pronoun. Reflexive and intensive pronouns look alike. Their usage reveals the difference.

Pedro presented **himself** the award. (reflexive)
Pedro **himself** presented the award. (intensive)

	SINGULAR	PLURAL
First person	myself	ourselves
Second person	yourself	yourselves
Third person	himself, herself, itself	themselves

▶ **Exercise 2** Write *ref.* above each reflexive pronoun and *int.* above each intensive pronoun.

            ref.
Roberto bought himself a new jacket.

1. The chimpanzee itself opened the lock on the laboratory door.

2. Did you ever find yourselves wondering why we keep doing this?

3. Marvin, why don't you attend the meeting and see for yourself?

4. Kellie and Mika arranged a meeting between Garth Brooks and themselves.

5. I continually surprise myself at my own genius.

6. Akira and Bob, did you do this whole project yourselves?

7. I rented myself a three-wheeler for the weekend.

8. Arthur gave her the book himself.

Copyright © by Glencoe/McGraw-Hill

Lesson 4

Pronouns: Demonstrative, Interrogative, Relative, and Indefinite

Use an **interrogative pronoun** to form questions. Interrogative pronouns are *who, whom, whose, what,* and *which.* The intensive forms of the interrogative pronouns are *whoever, whomever, whatever,* and *whichever.*

Whoever heard of such a silly request?

Use a **relative pronoun** to begin a special subject-verb word group called a subordinate clause (see Lesson 23).

The lady **who** came late was my sister. (*Who* begins the subordinate clause *who came late.*)

RELATIVE PRONOUNS

who	whom	what	which	that
whoever	whomever	whatever	whichever	whose

▶ **Exercise 1** Draw one line under each interrogative pronoun and two lines under each relative pronoun.

<u>Who</u> is coming to my party?

1. Is Pat the person who parked in the principal's reserved space?

2. I never thought that you would say such a thing.

3. Bill is a friend on whom you can always depend.

4. Whom did the sheriff want to see?

5. For her birthday Jenny got a calculator that prints out its results.

6. Aunt Carey, who is my mother's sister, will visit us next week.

7. What do you mean?

8. May I take whichever I choose?

9. A long nap is what I need right now.

10. The accident that had happened three years ago left her with a severe limp.

11. Whoever heard of such an outrageously funny thing?

12. It was Kalina's vote that broke the tie in the student election yesterday.

13. Tara or Rico, whoever arrives first, will adjust the thermostat.

14. After that long study session, which sounds better, ice cream or pizza?

Copyright © by Glencoe/McGraw-Hill

Grammar

15. Our neighbors, whose tree blew over, borrowed our chain saw.

16. I gave it to Fred and Ping, who are my best friends.

A **demonstrative pronoun** points out specific persons, places, things, or ideas.

These are the days that try men's souls.

DEMONSTRATIVE PRONOUNS

Singular:	this	that
Plural:	these	those

An **indefinite pronoun** refers to persons, places, or things in a more general way than does a personal pronoun.

Do you really believe that **everyone** is going?

INDEFINITE PRONOUNS

all	both	everything	none	some
another	each	few	nothing	somebody
any	either	many	one	someone
anybody	enough	most	other	something
anyone	everybody	neither	others	
anything	everyone	nobody	several	

▶ **Exercise 2** Write *ind.* above each indefinite pronoun and *dem.* above each demonstrative pronoun.

dem.   ind.
These are the times that everyone enjoys so much.

1. Waking suddenly, I heard something in the hallway.

2. How expensive are those?

3. Please save some for Mandy.

4. As far as problems are concerned, we have few with your son because he is so well behaved, Mrs. Windsor.

5. Place that on the end table, please.

6. I know how disappointed he felt, but I liked neither of the movies he rented.

7. When the meeting adjourned, everybody headed for the soda shop across the street.

8. These are the types of problems that make me want to scream.

9. Some days it seems that everything goes wrong.

10. Take several of these so that you won't run short on your trip tomorrow.

Copyright © by Glencoe/McGraw-Hill

Lesson 5
Verbs: Action

A **verb** expresses action or a state of being and is necessary to make a statement. An **action verb** tells what someone or something does. Action verbs can express either physical or mental action. A **transitive verb** is an action verb that is followed by a word or words that answer the question *what?* or *whom?* An **intransitive verb** is an action verb that is not followed by a word that answers the question *what?* or *whom?*

Ellie **ate** the cake. (transitive)
Myron **jumped** over the fence. (intransitive)

Some verbs can be either transitive or intransitive, depending on their usage.

He **fought** for recognition. (intransitive)　　He **fought** the bad guys. (transitive)

▶ **Exercise 1** Draw two lines under each action verb. Write *trans.* in the blank if the verb is transitive and *int.* if it is intransitive.

___*int.*___ John Wesley Powell explored far and wide.

_____ 1. John Wesley Powell came from Mount Morris, New York.

_____ 2. His family soon moved to frontier Illinois, where the beauties of nature impressed the young boy.

_____ 3. Spending much time by himself on rivers in canoes, young John taught himself many things about nature.

_____ 4. He landed a job as a teacher, a post at which he prospered.

_____ 5. He accepted the post of superintendent of the county schools at age twenty-seven.

_____ 6. While he served in that position, the American Civil War erupted.

_____ 7. An early volunteer, John rushed to his country's service.

_____ 8. At the Battle of Shiloh, he lost his right arm to an enemy rifle ball.

_____ 9. After the war, John returned to Illinois.

_____ 10. The many empty spaces on American maps of the time intrigued Powell.

_____ 11. With the help of old army friends (including U.S. Grant), he succeeded in getting government approval and finance for an expedition to the Green and Colorado River canyons.

_____ 12. Major Powell and eight assorted adventurers began the mapping expedition on May 24, 1869.

Copyright © by Glencoe/McGraw-Hill

_____ **13.** Powell intended to map the entire country.

_____ **14.** In his explorations, Powell grew wise to the ways of the arid regions of the West.

_____ **15.** Powell also desired the development of the beautiful western lands of America.

_____ **16.** He developed irrigation techniques and argued for rights of the individual landowner.

_____ **17.** Water rights caused great problems in the growth of the West because local monopolies manipulated water use.

_____ **18.** Powell also conceived a love for the Native Americans.

_____ **19.** By 1879, the government appointed him director of both the United States Geological Survey and the United States Bureau of Ethnology.

_____ **20.** Under his leadership, topographical maps became the standard by which the rest of the world made maps.

_____ **21.** He angered a few senators when he funneled some of the Survey's federal monies into investigating the chemical possibilities of petroleum.

_____ **22.** Most people at that time saw no possible use for crude oil except as lighting fuel or as a lubricant.

_____ **23.** Congress slashed the Survey's funds, and Powell resigned.

_____ **24.** In the administration of the Bureau of Ethnology, however, Powell's enthusiasm soared.

_____ **25.** As part of his work in the bureau, Powell classified Native American languages.

_____ **26.** His *Introduction to the Study of Indian Languages* established Powell as an important anthropologist.

_____ **27.** The former superintendent of county schools achieved lasting fame and respect for his work with Native Americans.

_____ **28.** Under his tutelage, the bureau brought the new field of anthropology into adulthood.

_____ **29.** Powell wrote other works as well; his books concern his explorations and his work in anthropology.

_____ **30.** Meanwhile, his ideas on irrigation improved crop production in the West.

Copyright © by Glencoe/McGraw-Hill

Lesson 6
Verbs: Linking

A **linking verb** links, or joins, the subject of a sentence with a word or expression that
identifies or describes the subject. The most common linking verbs are the forms of *be*.
Some examples are *am, is, are, was, were, will be, has been,* and *was being.*

Gerald **is** handsome.   Marta **was** the president.

OTHER LINKING VERBS

appear	feel	look	seem	smell
become	grow	remain	sound	taste

▶ **Exercise 1** **Draw a line under the verb, and write *LV* in the blank if the verb is a linking verb
and *AV* if the verb is an action verb.**

__LV__   Frieda is a lucky person.

_____ **1.** Connie walks to the grocery store with Miki.

_____ **2.** Helen and Gary revealed the secret of their amazing discovery.

_____ **3.** After the morning session, many of the delegates went to a mall.

_____ **4.** My neighbors appear regularly on local television.

_____ **5.** Matching the pattern of that material will be difficult.

_____ **6.** Your speech sounds great.

_____ **7.** Tuani's dog obviously met a skunk last night.

_____ **8.** All of the evidence seems clear.

_____ **9.** Regardless of the weather, I am usually the first at practice.

_____ **10.** Inside twenty minutes, the forest rangers readied the campsite for the children.

_____ **11.** A jury member fell asleep after many hours in the courtroom.

_____ **12.** Karl evaded the tackler on the last play for the touchdown.

_____ **13.** How long has Akira been the team captain?

_____ **14.** Many of the members feel bad about the election.

_____ **15.** My playful collie requires a lot of my energy and time.

_____ **16.** Albert missed the best game of the year because of a flat tire.

_____ **17.** Ms. Toshio retains three attorneys for her corporation.

_____ **18.** I regretted my decision about the science fair.

Copyright © by Glencoe/McGraw-Hill

Grammar

_____ 19. The four girls remained in the cellar until the all-clear signal.

_____ 20. A 70 percent majority elected Heather president of the chess club.

_____ 21. My dislike of liver has grown stronger over the years.

_____ 22. Yana trains for the wrestling tournament next month in the state capital.

_____ 23. Kosey really liked his new school.

_____ 24. The Franklins hope for good weather for their trip this weekend.

_____ 25. The veterinarian gave my cat a shot last week.

_____ 26. The hamburger tasted absolutely delicious.

_____ 27. The neighbors loud music kept me awake until two in the morning.

_____ 28. Ernesto saw nothing funny about the practical joke.

_____ 29. Hundreds of visitors tour our local museum each month.

_____ 30. These footprints look fresh.

_____ 31. The computer at the library saves me a lot of research time.

_____ 32. The weather turned colder after those few sunny, warm days.

_____ 33. This turkey tastes good with the tart cranberry sauce.

_____ 34. Akira and Ramon are two of the nicest people in the world.

_____ 35. Ricardo and Minal became closer after the tragedy.

_____ 36. Mark plays cards often.

_____ 37. The wonderful old oak tree grew on the wide hillside to the north of the farm.

_____ 38. Two term papers and three book reports try the best of us.

_____ 39. Marilyn and Anna take trigonometry in summer school.

_____ 40. With no further business, the meeting adjourned fifteen minutes early.

▶ **Writing Link** **Write a paragraph comparing the personalities of two television characters. Use linking verbs whenever possible.**

_____

_____

_____

_____

_____

_____

Copyright © by Glencoe/McGraw-Hill

Lesson 7
Verb Phrases

The verb in a sentence may consist of more than one word. We call the words that accompany the main verb **auxiliary**, or helping, verbs. A **verb phrase** consists of a main verb and all its auxiliary verbs.

Jill **will have finished** by then. (*Will* and *have* help the main verb *finished*.)

AUXILIARY VERBS

Forms of *be*: am, is, are, was, were, being, been
Forms of *have*: has, have, had, having
Others: can, could, do, does, did, may, might, must, shall, should, will, would

▶ **Exercise 1 Draw one line under each verb phrase and two lines under each auxiliary verb.**

The rain has been falling steady all night.

1. Mr. Ho has been keeping bees on the hill behind his house for more than forty years.

2. The limbs of the elm tree were being shaken by the wind.

3. The babies are crying from hunger.

4. Melanie never did say the answer to the word puzzle correctly.

5. A mistake of that magnitude could wreck all of our financial hopes.

6. Many of us should be ready for a change of pace after that fast dance.

7. The young lieutenant can muster his troops in only fifteen minutes.

8. Have you ever been in Hawaii?

9. Jenny might have mentioned the party to Roger.

10. Grandad will be seventy-two next month on the thirteenth.

11. Marsha is not getting a new sweater today.

12. How can this confusion about the experiment be explained to Mr. Hawkfeather's satisfaction?

13. Michi might have been finished before Nui.

14. Our family will be having guests this Monday evening for dinner.

15. After school, will you be going straight home?

16. The innkeepers are concerned about the new tax laws for motels.

17. The rooster was crowing that fateful morning.

18. Before the last session with your new tutor, your fears of math may well disappear.

Copyright © by Glencoe/McGraw-Hill

19. Irene could only hope for her friends' understanding.

20. The occasion might have ended in disaster for the Sprank twins.

21. The accident might have done more damage to the car.

22. We shall never regret our decision.

23. Because of the snowstorm, the dance has been postponed until next week.

24. We must have lost the game.

25. The younger children will be frightened by certain scenes in the movie, Mom.

26. We could probably switch the gathering to Friday.

27. Will had eaten seven hot dogs by the end of the show.

28. Kajala has always been stronger than Osvaldo in cross-country skiing.

29. Miriam and Terra have seldom studied together before last night.

30. Without the wire top on the cage, the rabbit could jump out of it and into the reach of our dog.

31. Ollie may have deposited the money earlier than usual.

32. Because of the fog, Margaret's plane will be arriving two hours late tomorrow night.

33. The rust has certainly damaged the rocker panels on your brother's old car.

34. Billy Ray cannot remember his last visit to the doctor.

35. Red and green have been the traditional Christmas colors for many years.

36. In eight competitions this year, our school jazz band has received seven awards.

37. Hadi really does know the answers to the trick questions.

38. With a tight score, that game must have thrilled everyone there.

39. By combining all the clues, we can name a suspect in the baron's murder.

40. With her memory, she should seldom forget anything as important as my birthday.

▶ **Writing Link** **Write a short description of a typical day for one of your parents. Demonstrate the use of main verbs with auxiliary verbs.**

_____

_____

_____

_____

_____

Copyright © by Glencoe/McGraw-Hill

Lesson 8
Adjectives

An **adjective** modifies a noun or a pronoun by limiting its meaning. Adjectives include the articles *a, an,* and *the. A* and *an* are **indefinite** articles; *the* is a **definite** article. Because they modify nouns, possessive nouns and pronouns are considered adjectives as well.

Bill has **large** feet.   Give me **the** ball.   She takes **swimming** lessons.

A **proper adjective** is formed from a proper noun and begins with a capital letter. Proper adjectives are often created by using the following suffixes: *-an, -ian, -n, -ese,* and *-ish.*

We ate **Chinese** food and listened to **African** music at the international festival.

Many adjectives have different forms to indicate their degree of comparison.

POSITIVE	COMPARATIVE	SUPERLATIVE	
large	larger	largest	(regular formation of degree)
good	better	best	(irregular formation of degree)

▶ **Exercise 1** **Underline each adjective in the following sentences.**

<u>Some</u> villages developed into <u>huge</u> <u>urban</u> areas.

1. Cities did not become possible until ancient societies produced more food than they consumed and had found ways of storing the surplus.

2. Storing and preserving food was necessary to sustain large numbers of non-farming people.

3. Civil officials and religious priests inhabited the earliest cities.

4. Around them lived the lower classes of craft persons, artisans, and common laborers.

5. The labor of outside farmers supported the permanent inhabitants of the city.

6. The city officials collected the surplus food and distributed it among the workers.

7. Another reason for the development of the city was that it provided the best defense against outside aggressors.

8. Since it depended on the outlying areas for supplies, each city had to dominate and defend its entire region against enemies.

9. The city rulers sent out professional soldiers to keep order in the hinterland and to defend it from roving marauders and from attacks by other cities.

10. Large municipalities sprang up wherever commerce flourished, such as the intersections of trade routes, at sea harbors, and at the mouths of rivers.

Copyright © by Glencoe/McGraw-Hill

Grammar

11. The trading function has been an important source of employment and sustenance for cities throughout history.

12. All the major urban areas of the United States, including the cities of the Great Lakes and the Gulf of Mexico, began as small trade centers.

▶ **Exercise 2** **Write in the blank the degree of comparison (*pos.* for positive, *comp.* for comparative, or *sup.* for superlative) for the italicized adjective.**

_____sup._____ Ancient Athens might have been the *most beautiful* city ever built.

_____ 1. As cities grow *larger,* they develop many problems, some of which seem difficult to solve.

_____ 2. Depending on the state of the economy, *good* jobs become scarce or non-existent.

_____ 3. One of the *most frustrating* problems remains adequate housing.

_____ 4. Urban leaders consider providing proper utility and sanitation services an even *more difficult* task.

_____ 5. Many *clear* thinkers have dedicated themselves to solving and preventing such problems through urban planning.

_____ 6. The first step is to clearly define the needs, addressing the *worst* problems directly.

_____ 7. Planners organize these needs into specific goals that will give the *most complete* solutions.

_____ 8. The next step, the *hardest* one, focuses on producing the means with which to achieve the goals.

_____ 9. One of the *more difficult* obstacles is financing development projects.

_____ 10. Taxes provide *most* of the money.

_____ 11. The *most influential* pioneer in city planning was Ebenezer Howard.

_____ 12. Howard's ideas for social and ecomonic balance provided a basis for the *most significant* advancement in cities in centuries.

Copyright © by Glencoe/McGraw-Hill

Grammar

Lesson 9
Adverbs

Grammar

An **adverb** modifies a verb, an adjective, or another adverb by making its meaning more specific. Adverbs answer the questions *how? when? where?* and *to what degree?* When modifying a verb, an adverb may appear in various positions in a sentence. If modifying an adjective or another adverb, an adverb appears directly before the modified word.

The boy had run **quickly** home. (*Quickly* modifies the verb *had run*.)
Kate is **very** nervous about her performance. (*Very* modifies the adjective *nervous*.)
Dr. Delacorte removed the bandages **quite carefully**. (*Quite* modifies the adverb *carefully; carefully* modifies the verb *removed*.)

The negatives *no* and *not* and the contraction *-n't* are adverbs. Other negative words, such as *nowhere, hardly,* and *never,* can function as adverbs of time, place, and degree.

I could**n't** remember where I left it.   The rain **never** begins until softball practice starts.

▶ **Exercise 1 Draw an arrow from each adverb to the word it modifies.**

The dejected boy moved slowly.

1. Uncle Kwan laughed heartily.

2. The teacher had an unusually quiet classroom.

3. The driver turned the steering wheel very sharply.

4. The children eagerly awaited the clowns' entrance.

5. Myra suddenly saw the spider.

6. All single-spaced manuscripts will be summarily rejected.

7. Juana crept very slowly to the railing on the high balcony of the duke's palace.

8. Tillie's face turned really red because of her spoonerism.

9. This is an extremely slow copier.

10. My sister was sleeping comfortably on the couch.

11. Alexis couldn't believe Cheryl's words.

12. Rosa's aunt had become quite captivated with the tale.

Copyright © by Glencoe/McGraw-Hill

13. The rest of the play proceeded smoothly.

14. Mitch handles his tape player carelessly.

15. Esther rounded the building and nearly collided with an elderly man.

16. The instructions were given clearly and concisely.

17. The little girl carefully drew a picture of a very skinny dog.

18. The seriously injured player was carried to an ambulance.

19. "I wish I had kept my mouth shut," Ted said remorsefully.

20. The debate team had a rather mediocre record.

▶ **Exercise 2** **Underline each adverb. Write in the blank the type of word it modifies: *V* (verb),** *adj.* **(adjective), or** *adv.* **(adverb). Some sentences may have more than one adverb.**

_____*V*_____ Kim gazed lovingly at her little sister.

_____ **1.** The coach shouted hoarsely at the defensive back.

_____ **2.** The melody floated gracefully throughout the building.

_____ **3.** "I want tuba music at my wedding," said Rico jokingly.

_____ **4.** That extremely clean car belongs to Ms. Salvatore.

_____ **5.** Masu spoke rather shyly.

_____ **6.** After his reprieve, Soto skipped merrily down the hallway.

_____ **7.** Mr. Atkinson attributes his very green lawn to proper fertilizing and watering.

_____ **8.** Will you ever succeed in learning this procedure?

_____ **9.** Does such a hastily prepared assignment deserve a top grade?

_____ **10.** Betsy has never readily accepted responsibility for the accident.

_____ **11.** A rather large dog met the salesman at the front door.

_____ **12.** Winona is really intelligent.

_____ **13.** The suspiciously nervous boys were quite anxious.

_____ **14.** Every morning Mr. Chin greets his class cheerily.

_____ **15.** Lady Louisa's heavily powdered face significantly detracted from her beautiful gown.

_____ **16.** I think that Melody purposely lost her assignment.

Copyright © by Glencoe/McGraw-Hill

Lesson 10
Prepositions

A **preposition** shows the relationship of a noun or a pronoun to some other word in the sentence.

The bus stopped **by** the school.

COMMON PREPOSITIONS

aboard	as	but	in	out	toward
about	at	by	inside	outside	under
above	before	concerning	into	over	underneath
across	behind	despite	like	past	until
after	below	down	near	pending	unto
against	beneath	during	of	regarding	up
along	beside	except	off	since	upon
amid	besides	excepting	on	through	with
among	between	for	onto	throughout	within
around	beyond	from	opposite	to	without

A **compound preposition** is a preposition that is made up of more than one word.

Use something red **in front of** that black background.

COMMON COMPOUND PREPOSITIONS

according to	apart from	because of	in front of	next to	out of
ahead of	aside from	by means of	in spite of	on account of	owing to
along with	as to	in addition to	instead of	on top of	

Phrases that begin with a preposition usually end with a noun or pronoun called the **object of the preposition**.

Elaine left without her **sweater.** (*Sweater* is the object of the preposition *without*.)

▶ **Exercise 1** **Draw one line under each prepositional phrase and circle its object.**

Early in the (morning,) Sam acts grumpy.

1. The crowd leaped to their feet when Montana dropped back for a pass.

2. Without hesitation, Abdul volunteered to run for secretary.

3. Judy parked her car in front of Margie's house.

4. The boats were tied downstream below the dam.

5. Eluding the police, the burglar made his escape by means of the transom.

6. Terrence hugged Marlene amid the throng of cheering fans.

Copyright © by Glencoe/McGraw-Hill

Grammar

Grammar

7. According to Ellie, there will be no meeting this afternoon in the cafeteria.

8. "He isn't there," Bill said, pointing toward the closet door.

9. I can't wait until spring.

10. Jerilynn was thrilled beyond her wildest dreams at the beautiful sound.

11. On top of the hill, you will find a grassy plot with a wonderful apple tree.

12. They spend a lot of time out west at a dude ranch.

13. All members have paid their dues except Jeremy.

14. We served the Jeffersons mashed potatoes and succotash along with the barbecued ribs.

15. The dry weather ruined the crop despite our desperate irrigation attempts.

16. The doctors had a consultation concerning Ms. Devereaux's illness.

17. Aboard the train, the family settled down for the long ride from Paris to Marseilles.

18. Planting marigolds around the garden will keep the rabbits away from the vegetables.

19. Inside the card we found a twenty-dollar bill beneath a photo of Aunt Helen and Uncle Joe.

20. Three pieces of candy fell onto the floor and rolled along the wall.

21. We found the missing socks underneath the bed and on top of a comic book.

22. May I have the macaroni and cheese instead of the pilaf?

23. Ms. Sarmiento will be our advisor during Mr. Voss's sabbatical.

24. Taki waited near the telephone for an hour, but Kurt didn't call despite his promise.

25. Dean came to the Halloween party as an aardvark and Ed came as a green Martian.

26. His reputation among the athletes spread throughout the city after his winning touchdown.

27. We completed the project three weeks ahead of schedule.

28. Gasoline prices rose on account of the dramatic increase in demand.

29. We have a renewed enthusiasm since the retreat.

30. Upon his arrival, the contest began.

31. Because of Cal's shrewdness, we managed to get terrific bargains.

32. Will I see you at the concert?

33. Upon receipt of the letter, Daisy disappeared into her room.

34. The smoke rose lazily up the chimney by means of the draft through the flue.

35. Is Hector the man leaning against the wall?

36. The sporting goods store moved around the corner.

Copyright © by Glencoe/McGraw-Hill

Lesson 11
Conjunctions: Coordinating, Correlative, and Subordinating

A **conjunction** joins single words or groups of words. A **coordinating conjunction** joins words or groups of words that have equal grammatical importance. Coordinating conjunctions include *and, but, or, nor, for,* and *yet.*

Bob **and** Beth are waiting.   The lightning flashes, **yet** I hear no thunder.

Correlative conjunctions work in pairs to join words and groups of words of equal importance. Correlative conjunctions include *both...and, just as...so, not only...but also, either...or, neither...nor,* and *whether...or.*

Whether you send a printout **or** bring the disk in person, the data must be here by noon.

A **subordinating conjunction** joins a dependent idea or clause to a main clause.

Carlos called **before** you arrived.

COMMON SUBORDINATING CONJUNCTIONS

after	as though	provided (that)	until
although	because	since	when
as	before	so long as	whenever
as far as	considering (that)	so that	where
as if	if	than	whereas
as long as	inasmuch as	though	wherever
as soon as	in order that	unless	while

▶ **Exercise 1** Circle each conjunction. Write *coord.* in the blank if the conjunction is coordinating, *corr.* if the conjunction is correlative, or *sub.* if the conjunction is subordinating.

_____coord._____ Do you write letters to your friends, (or) do you use only the phone?

_____ 1. In the ancient world the establishment of large governments and the development of trade necessitated formal message-carrying systems.

_____ 2. At first, governments reserved these systems for their own use; commercial interests and the private sector were later included.

_____ 3. Around 550 B.C., the Persians began a postal service that not only proved dependable but also still serves as a model for communications.

_____ 4. The Romans established a large system that remained very reliable so long as the empire maintained its central world authority.

Copyright © by Glencoe/McGraw-Hill

Grammar

_____ 5. Based on the Persian model, Roman relay stations were both large and numerous.

_____ 6. Roman government posts carried only official letters, whereas commercial companies served businesses and private citizens.

_____ 7. After Rome's authority weakened, reliable posts either disappeared or became undependable.

_____ 8. The Renaissance in western Europe sparked a boom in official, commercial, ecclesiastical, and private correspondence.

_____ 9. This increase made it necessary for regional monarchies not only to rehabilitate the postal systems but also to extend them greatly.

_____ 10. France established a nationwide postal service in 1497 as England had done earlier in 1481.

_____ 11. In America, early colonial mail was neither regular nor organized.

_____ 12. To correspond with relatives abroad, colonists posted letters with sea captains unless they could find a friend to carry the letters for them.

_____ 13. Cities supervised early attempts at organized mail so that the demand for communications could be met.

_____ 14. Since the Colonial American authorities realized the necessity of centralized control, they appointed Benjamin Franklin deputy postmaster general for America in 1737.

_____ 15. Franklin made fundamental improvements in the domestic mail system while he established regular foreign deliveries.

_____ 16. The Continental Congress in 1775 appointed Franklin postmaster general because his innovations had been so successful.

_____ 17. After the constitution of 1789 mandated the establishment of a post office and post roads, Congress made the Post Office Department an organ of the federal government.

_____ 18. The government appointed Samuel Osgood as the first postmaster general of the fledgling yet burgeoning department.

Copyright © by Glencoe/McGraw-Hill

Lesson 12
Conjunctive Adverbs and Interjections

A **conjunctive adverb** is used to clarify the relationship between clauses of equal weight in a sentence.

COMMON CONJUNCTIVE ADVERBS

again	further	indeed	nevertheless	still
also	furthermore	instead	nonetheless	then
besides	hence	likewise	otherwise	therefore
consequently	however	moreover	similarly	thus

Becky managed the concession stand; **moreover,** she did a terrific job.

An **interjection** is a word or phrase that expresses emotion or exclamation. An interjection has no grammatical connection to other words. Commas follow mild ones; exclamation points follow stronger ones. Common interjections include: *oh; oh, my; good grief; my heavens; darn; drat;* and *gee whiz.*

Oh, my, how you've grown.   **Oh, no!** The gate is open again.

▶ **Exercise 1 Draw a line under each conjunctive adverb and circle each interjection.**

Alan sold his horse; thus, his equestrian days ended.

1. Marci forgot her umbrella; however, Felicia brought hers.

2. We'll weed the garden; meanwhile, you cut the grass away from the antique rosebush.

3. Yipes! Rover is loose again in the neighbor's yard.

4. Shhh! I am trying to study for the big test.

5. Oscar never opened the book; hence, he failed to read that beautiful story.

6. Oh, drat, I'll never get the hang of this new computer that I bought.

7. The rain poured down; still, no one left the ticket line.

8. Oh, no! The concert is sold out, and we haven't gotten in yet.

9. Jason moaned and groaned; nevertheless, no one would do his work for him.

10. Kara read three books on colonial dress; consequently, her costume looked the most authentic of all.

11. Everyone was restless; nevertheless, Hal continued his speech.

12. I've lost my notes from yesterday's class; however, there wasn't much new material in them anyway.

Copyright © by Glencoe/McGraw-Hill

13. Mr. Min talked about beekeeping; besides, he brought samples of foods made with honey.

14. Jeff submitted a terrific essay; indeed, he won first place in the writing contest.

15. Mercy! My feet are killing me.

16. You may have the ice cream if you have finished the chores; otherwise, you can do without it.

17. The trio had a difficult time at the audition; moreover, their second selection did not work out very well.

18. Doreen tore her jeans climbing the fence; similarly, Monty scratched his forearm.

19. You've spent all your money already? Good grief!

20. For heaven's sake, you should know better than to fall asleep in the sun.

21. Dad spends a lot of time working in the yard; consequently, our lawn is the nicest in the neighborhood.

22. Oh, pshaw, I dropped another stitch in my knitting.

23. Every member of the theatrical company did his or her job; therefore, the play was a huge success.

24. Twist off the cap; then, carefully squeeze till a drop of glue appears.

25. "My godness," uttered Grandma, "he looks just like his uncle Morty did forty years ago."

26. Erika isn't going skating with us; besides, she has a bad cold and should stay inside.

27. We all donated a dollar for the gift; also, Carol supplied the card.

28. The girl got the guy, the horse was saved from the dog food factory, and the underdog was elected president; thus, the cliché-ridden tale came to an end.

29. Alas, the ending of this miserable story was no better than the beginning.

30. Andi and Sue gave in to Cindy's demands; likewise, I finally capitulated, too.

31. Achim didn't have his part memorized; furthermore, he didn't even try.

32. "Great Caesar's ghost!" cried the foreman. "Why aren't these boxes loaded?"

▶ **Writing Link** **Compose a humorous paragraph about an imaginary camping trip. Include conjunctive adverbs and interjections.**

_____

_____

_____

_____

Copyright © by Glencoe/McGraw-Hill

☑ Unit 1 **Review**

▶ **Exercise 1 Write the part of speech above each italicized word:** *N* (noun), *pro.* (pronoun), *V* (verb), *adj.* (adjective), *adv.* (adverb), *prep.* (preposition), or *conj.* (conjunction). **Some may be compound words.**

                N   V   adv. prep.   adj.
The *cowboy rode slowly into* the *small* town.

1. *Because of* the approaching storm, all of the picnickers *gathered* their *belongings* and ran to the shelter houses.

2. Did you see that Nina and Sally *built* an *extremely large* decoration for the pep rally *on* Friday?

3. *After* eating every snack in the place, he *had* the nerve to ask if there would be more food *later*.

4. Placing his feet on the desk, Mr. Zahn read *slowly through* our request for an *extra* dance this semester.

5. *In spite of* the *noise*, An-Li *managed* to finish her homework during lunch.

6. If we plan that trip to *New Mexico, we* will have to travel on *inexpensive* transportation.

7. *Someone wedged* this invitation to the banquet into the storm door.

8. *I* want you to meet the *person* to whom I owe *everything* for teaching me the correct way to shoot free throws.

9. *Dennis* acted *as though* the teacher had asked us to read the *entire* encyclopedia in one evening.

10. Molly *and* Yani *are* excited about *their* interviews for a job with the newspaper.

11. *Both* my sister and I *gave* the *vanity* that was Grandma's to cousin Corinne.

12. Even for a thousand dollars, I will *never* say anything about a friend that *would* hurt him or her.

13. Kerry belonged *to* the French club and the science club *in addition to* several sports *teams*.

14. The circus offered *five* performances at the coliseum, *but* the Ke family wasn't able to attend any of them *because all* of the children had chicken pox.

15. Al *placed* himself on a *very* rigorous training schedule for wrestling, and it must have paid off for him since he is *undefeated* this year.

Copyright © by Glencoe/McGraw-Hill

Cumulative Review: Unit 1

► Exercise 1 **Write the part of speech above each italicized word:** *N* (noun), *pro.* (pronoun), *V* (verb), *adj.* (adjective), *adv.* (adverb), *prep.* (preposition), *conj.* (conjunction), or *int.* (interjection). **Some may be compounds.**

              adv.
The car sped *recklessly* around the corner.

1. Takeo *drank* in the *magnificence* of the mansion as he enjoyed the *warm* hospitality of its owner.

2. The sun set slowly in the western sky, the trees rustled lightly *in* the *gentle* breeze, and Wilma slept *more* soundly than she had slept in years.

3. Because he was *blinded* by the *intensely* bright car lights, *Elmer* never saw the sign.

4. The tables and chairs *were* in place *for* the meeting; *however,* no one remembered to prepare the *dais.*

5. *Who* would *have* the nerve to call at this *ridiculous* hour?

6. *These* are examples of my *grandmother's finest* needlework.

7. *Whew!* I hope we *never* come that close to another *moving* vehicle again.

8. Maurey carried his bag *himself because* he didn't *trust* the airline not to lose it.

9. We have resolved to do *whatever* is necessary to ensure that the job is *finished* on *time.*

10. The life of a writer may seem *very* unstructured, but *few* know the discipline it *takes* to achieve success in the profession.

11. We sat *next to* the celebrities, *who* were *warm* and friendly.

12. Squeaks *and* honks *told* me that the *beginners'* band practice had begun.

13. *Yucch! If* I have to eat boiled carrots one more time, I think I'll run *from* the table.

14. Harry *seems* content *with* his role, *but* don't let his facade fool you.

15. *When* one goes to *Lilly's* house for dinner, she always has *plenty* to eat.

16. The airport skycap *luckily* spied the *lost* wallet *underneath* the edge of a baggage cart.

17. He told me *in* the *locker room* he would win the long jump and, *by gum,* he did!

18. The farmer waded *clumsily* across the *rain-filled* ditch to rescue the bawling *calf.*

19. Did you *ever* see such a *uniformly matched* team of horses?

20. Ivan jumped *nearly* a foot, *but* he still denies being *scared.*

Copyright © by Glencoe/McGraw-Hill

Unit 2: Parts of the Sentence

Lesson 13
Subjects and Predicates

Every sentence has a subject and a predicate. A **simple subject** is the main noun or pronoun that tells what the sentence is about. A **simple predicate** is the verb or verb phrase that tells something about the subject.

Wolves howl.   The wolves howl loudly at night.
(In both sentences, *wolves* is the simple subject; *howl* is the simple predicate.)

▶ **Exercise 1** Draw one line under each simple subject and two lines under each simple predicate.

Martin's luggage stood next to the hall closet.

1. The building collapsed in a cloud of dust.

2. The captain is peering through the periscope.

3. The Cheshire cat stared at the impudent mouse.

4. The green grass shimmered in the morning sun.

5. Boris will paint the old porch.

6. Sheena searched for her airline tickets.

7. The dictator ordered the king into exile.

8. The water glitters in the brook.

9. A red hen pecked along the ground.

10. An old streetcar was clattering down the tracks.

11. A bright sun rose above the city.

12. Mighty bolts of lightning frightened us.

13. The Greeks fought the Persians.

14. Clark wrote a new story.

15. The scientist has solved the problem.

16. Children play in the city park.

17. The rocket shot high into the air.

18. A hawk is floating on the cool breezes.

Copyright © by Glencoe/McGraw-Hill

19. Deelra stopped at the library.

20. Frederick will sing in the varsity choir.

A **complete subject** includes the simple subject and any words that modify it.

The pack of wolves howled.

A **complete predicate** includes the simple predicate and any words that modify it.

The pack of wolves **howled at the moon.**

▶ **Exercise 2 Draw a vertical line between the complete subject and the complete predicate.**

The miniature leaves|covered the bonsai tree.

1. The robin hopped across the yard.

2. The huge elephant trumpeted loudly.

3. The heavy rain fell in gray, silvery sheets.

4. The legendary Greek King Oedipus answered the riddle of the Sphinx.

5. About 300 million people speak Spanish.

6. The chestnut horse runs swiftly over the field.

7. A rainbow shone beautifully against the dark clouds.

8. A flying fish leapt out of the splashing water.

9. The city buses stop down the street.

10. The famous general and dictator Napoleon conquered much of Europe.

11. Sandy's uncle will teach her about airplanes.

12. My homing pigeon will return soon.

13. I see the wheat field by the forest.

14. The Inca Empire stretched up and down the western coast of Peru.

15. The menacing iceberg loomed out of the dark.

16. The ore freighter *Edmund Fitzgerald* sank in Lake Superior.

17. My new friend Raji told me a lot about India.

18. Snow-mantled Aconcagua stands higher than any other mountain in the Americas.

19. The Greek poet Pindar composed victory poems for athletes.

20. Salina has a big collection of postage stamps.

Copyright © by Glencoe/McGraw-Hill

Grammar

Lesson 14
Compound Subjects and Predicates

A **compound subject** consists of two or more simple subjects joined by a conjunction. The subjects share the same verb. A **compound predicate** consists of two or more verbs or verb phrases joined by a conjunction. The verbs share the same subject.

Lloyd and Millie drove from Boston to Tallahassee. (compound subject)
Brad **washed and waxed** his old jalopy. (compound predicate)

▶ **Exercise 1** **Draw a vertical line between the subject and predicate. Write *S* above each simple subject and *P* above each simple predicate.**

   S   S   P   P
Lois and Clark|sat outside and looked up at the stars.

1. Our school library and cafeteria are under renovation.

2. The groundhog tunneled beneath the fence and poked its head into our yard.

3. Jules and his sister took pictures with their new camera.

4. Robins either find worms in the grass or dig for them underground.

5. The turbulent waves swirled and crashed to shore.

6. My friends and I borrow and wear each other's clothes.

7. A police car and an ambulance just whizzed by our house.

8. Erica sewed on the button and mended the tear.

9. Graham crackers, marshmallows, and chocolate taste delicious together.

10. The boy and the collie ran away but soon came back.

11. Salvador Dali, a surrealist artist, not only painted paintings but also made sculptures and designed jewelry.

12. Neither Yuri nor Bruno received mail today.

13. The mountain climbers hooked up their ropes and secured their backpacks.

14. Rea and Marissa auditioned for the lead roles in the school musical but got only chorus parts.

15. The alley cat yawned and stretched.

Copyright © by Glencoe/McGraw-Hill

Grammar

16. Darren and Brian washed and waxed their dad's car.

17. Wind and hail damaged our porch.

18. The tennis match and the track meet attracted many spectators.

19. Both the Senate and the House discuss and vote on legislation.

20. Jamaal and Keisha saw the movie and liked it.

▶ **Exercise 2** Draw a vertical line between the subject and predicate. Write *CS* in the blank if the subject is compound, *CP* if the predicate is compound, or *B* if both are compound.

_**CS**_   Purple hyacinths and yellow daffodils│bloom along the back fence.

_____ 1. Feng Ying wrote and edited the article for the school newspaper.

_____ 2. The Browns and the Sterns cooked outdoors and slept in a tent.

_____ 3. Luis popped the popcorn but did not put butter on it.

_____ 4. The novels of John Steinbeck and the poetry of Maya Angelou inspire me to write.

_____ 5. I will either borrow or buy a leotard for dance class.

_____ 6. Final exams and the SATs are the same week.

_____ 7. Both the bakery and the grocery bake and decorate birthday cakes.

_____ 8. My name, address, and social security number appear on the job application.

_____ 9. Community service projects keep me busy and give me self-esteem.

_____ 10. Claudio and Austin go to the gym and work out nearly every day after school.

_____ 11. The track star ran and jumped the hurdles in record time.

_____ 12. Quilts and baskets made up the special exhibit at the museum.

_____ 13. The Big Dipper and Orion were visible in the clear night sky.

_____ 14. My brother and one of his friends reviewed all the math questions and studied hard for the test.

_____ 15. Albert Schweitzer won the Nobel Peace Prize and established a leper colony with the money.

_____ 16. Chemistry and government are my favorite subjects.

Copyright © by Glencoe/McGraw-Hill

Lesson 15
Order of Subject and Predicate

In most sentences the subject comes before the predicate. In a sentence written in **inverted order**, the predicate comes before the subject. Some sentences are written in inverted order for variety or special emphasis. A prepositional phrase often begins this type of sentence. The verb must agree with the subject, not with the object of the preposition.

PREDICATE	SUBJECT
Across the field **run**	the gray **cats**.

The subject also follows the predicate in a sentence that begins with *there* or *here*.

PREDICATE	SUBJECT
There **is**	a **noise** in the basement.

When the subject *you* is understood, as in a request or command, the predicate appears without a subject.

(You) **Ask** your teacher to help you with these math problems.

▶ **Exercise 1** Draw one line under each simple subject and two lines under each simple predicate.

Behind us was an army ambulance.

1. There goes the best teacher in our school.

2. Here is the brownie recipe from my new cookbook.

3. Lead the way to the museum.

4. Beside our house runs a little creek.

5. Next to the library stand two big oak trees.

6. Under the pile of papers lies the missing letter.

7. Here are my car keys!

8. Around the park go the horse and buggies.

9. Don't exercise too soon after dinner.

10. Please help me in the garden.

11. On the desk in the den sits our new computer.

12. There is a recycling center at the west end of town.

13. Here on our patio gather the relatives.

14. Near one of the stores stands a mailbox.

15. On the beach scrambled the seagulls for the bread crumbs.

Copyright © by Glencoe/McGraw-Hill

Grammar

16. There in the water swims a lone dolphin.

17. Here comes Nina with her two children.

18. Always stretch your muscles before a race.

19. In my mom's hands is a list of my chores.

20. On the sidelines wait many players eager for victory.

▶ **Exercise 2** Write *C* beside each sentence that is a command (imperative). Write *I* beside each sentence that is in inverted order. If the sentence is in inverted order, draw one line under the simple subject and two lines under the simple predicate.

_____I_____   By the tree sits Isaac with a book in his lap.

_____   **1.** Please drive our new car very carefully.

_____   **2.** There is no excuse for rudeness.

_____   **3.** At the foot of the cliff galloped a black stallion.

_____   **4.** Write your grandfather a thank-you note for the CD.

_____   **5.** There will not be time for another game.

_____   **6.** Down the road hops a cute little bunny rabbit.

_____   **7.** There is a psychology course second period next term.

_____   **8.** Please be quiet during study hall.

_____   **9.** Here come the trombone players.

_____   **10.** In the desert walk three camels.

_____   **11.** Please wait for the bus with me.

_____   **12.** Tell Josh about the red sports car around the corner.

_____   **13.** There are no more baseball cards in the drawer.

_____   **14.** Donate your old clothes to the homeless.

_____   **15.** Take Rosa's dog for a walk around the neighborhood.

_____   **16.** There was I, all alone in the dark.

_____   **17.** In the barn mooed the cows.

_____   **18.** Across the street appeared a "For Sale" sign.

_____   **19.** Come to the pep rally after school tomorrow.

_____   **20.** In the kitchen boil the eggs.

Copyright © by Glencoe/McGraw-Hill

Lesson 16
Direct and Indirect Objects

A **complement** is a word or phrase that completes the meaning of a verb. A **direct object** is one type of complement. It answers the question *what?* or *whom?* after an action verb.

Martha cooked **chicken** for dinner. (*Chicken* answers the question *what?*)

An **indirect object** is also a complement. It answers the question *to whom? for whom? to what?* or *for what?* after an action verb.

I sent **June** an invitation to the masquerade party. (*June* answers the question *to whom?*)

▶ **Exercise 1 Draw two lines under each verb. Circle each direct object.**

The clay maker formed a lovely round (vase).

1. Barb will call us at home.

2. Li explained the phrase.

3. Amy asked Lisa and Todd to come.

4. Randolph designed the go-cart.

5. Bill tossed the volleyball over the net.

6. Shawna sang six songs at the concert.

7. Tess will paint the ceramic bird.

8. After school, Brad cleaned the garage.

9. Lucy carefully tilled the sprouting flowers.

10. The dashing colonel rallied his troops.

11. The moderator is concluding the discussion.

12. Jennifer closed the barn door behind her.

13. I adjusted my binoculars for the far horizon.

14. Jamal claimed the abandoned kite.

15. Yolanda rode her horse at the barrel riding contest.

Copyright © by Glencoe/McGraw-Hill

Grammar

16. Sean did not drop the card.

17. Carla really overdid that cheerleading performance.

18. The high pinnacles of the cumulus clouds formed fantastic battlements, bastions, and towers.

19. For centuries, the long tentacles of the giant squid have frightened mariners.

20. Sunee is saving her diaries for posterity.

▶ **Exercise 2** **Circle each direct object. Draw one line under each indirect object.**

Our math teacher gave us a quiz on variables today.

1. Little Cindy lent me a toy teacup.

2. Samantha will give Zack a valentine.

3. The white-bearded man offered Tricia the book of poems.

4. Liam bought Eileen the roses.

5. The duke sent Miss Emily the silver box.

6. Asford brought us the keys to the castle.

7. Deebra promised Edmund the video.

8. Walter, would you make me a translation of these hieroglyphs?

9. My little brother built me a model airplane.

10. Louise told the Smiths the tale of the broken window and the errant baseball.

11. But Sam guaranteed us better results!

12. Vanessa wrote the prince a long, sad letter about her change of heart.

13. General Pershing awarded my grandfather this medal.

14. Kenji, throw her the ball!

15. The mysterious lady on the foggy pier handed Monty a letter.

16. Well, I must teach him batting technique.

17. Camilla will show Henry her diary.

18. Oh, come on, Susan; sing us your song.

19. Tommy will paint Kara a portrait of herself on horseback.

20. I would have given them the truth had they asked for it.

Copyright © by Glencoe/McGraw-Hill

Lesson 17
Object and Subject Complements

An **object complement** is a noun, pronoun, or adjective that completes the meaning of a direct object by identifying or describing it.

Paul elected himself **president.** (noun)
Paul calls the car **his.** (pronoun)
Paul found the computer **useful.** (adjective)

▶ **Exercise 1** **Above each object complement, write *N* for noun, *P* for pronoun, or *A* for adjective.**

                                           A
The director considers Neal perfect for the lead role.

1. Mi-Ling made herself chairperson of the activities committee.

2. Carl Sagan finds the study of astronomy very fascinating.

3. My sister considers my clothes hers.

4. Claudio finds television a waste of time.

5. Grace hopes her classmates will elect her treasurer.

6. Roger plans to make history his major.

7. I find rollercoasters scary but fun.

8. Scientists call a cloud of interstellar gas and dust a *nebula.*

9. Our school makes Yom Kippur a holiday.

10. My dad considers the restaurant's prices exorbitant.

11. Isaiah's silly faces rendered his sister incoherent with laughter.

12. Sandy calls her cats "Taffy" and "Taboo."

13. The rock star appointed the wrestler her bodyguard.

14. Our neighbors call our fence theirs.

15. I consider chocolate mousse my favorite dessert.

16. Our class considers pollution an urgent problem.

Copyright © by Glencoe/McGraw-Hill

17. The detective found the circumstances extremely suspicious.

18. The magician found his assistant very helpful.

19. The referee called the basket ours.

20. Did I tell you that peanuts make me sick?

A **subject complement** follows a subject and a linking verb and identifies or describes the subject. One type of subject complement is a **predicate nominative**. It is a noun or pronoun that follows a linking verb and gives more information about the subject.

Montana is a northern **state.**

Another type of subject complement is a **predicate adjective**. It is an adjective that follows a linking verb and gives more information about the subject.

The whole issue seems **irrelevant.**

▶ **Exercise 1** Write *PN* above each predicate nominative and *PA* above each predicate adjective.

             PN   PA

Juan became class president, and his parents were proud.

1. The seats in our new sports car are tan leather.

2. Debussy's music sounds very dreamy.

3. Jenny was ecstatic that she got into the musical theater program.

4. Mrs. Lopez seemed upset that Jason forgot to mow her lawn.

5. Michael Jordan is a hero to many young people.

6. The sizzling bacon smelled delicious.

7. Tennis is a sport I like to watch.

8. Freud's ideas remain an important part of the study of psychology.

9. Diane's cat appeared weak and listless, so she took it to the vet.

10. Monet is my favorite impressionist painter.

11. The minestrone soup tasted too salty and spicy.

12. Karsten is a martial arts expert and a karate teacher.

Copyright © by Glencoe/McGraw-Hill

✓ Unit 2 **Review**

▶ **Exercise 1** **Draw a vertical line between the subject and the predicate. Draw one line under the simple subject and two lines under the simple predicate.**

A history <u>teacher</u> at our high school | <u><u>won</u></u> a prestigious award.

1. We researched, brain-stormed, and wrote an outline in one night.

2. The Amazon River contains one-fifth of the world's fresh river water.

3. There go Jake, Sara, Franco, and Diaz to the pool hall.

4. My mom, the best cook in the world, makes hot and steamy chicken noodle soup.

5. I wrote two letters and mailed them at the post office.

6. The race car, with the driver still in it, veered out of control during the last lap.

7. Across the street and through the park scrambled the gray squirrel.

8. Knights in the Middle Ages needed impenetrable armor for obvious reasons.

9. Our science class performed an experiment with polluted water.

10. In the gym at the club are exercise bikes, treadmills, weights, and chin-up bars.

▶ **Exercise 2** **Circle each direct object and underline each indirect object. Above each subject complement write *PN* (predicate nominative) or *PA* (predicate adjective). Above each object complement write *N* (noun), *P* (pronoun), or *A* (adjective).**

Ahmik brought <u>me</u> (roses) on our first date.

1. Mrs. Cathcart became the principal of our school.

2. The secret agent gave General Kiddoo and his assistant the government files.

3. The subway was quite noisy but clean.

4. I found the pizza too soggy and greasy.

5. Examples of endangered species are the American eagle, the red wolf, and the

   loggerhead turtle.

6. The student body elected Ramón president.

7. Rolf considers everything in his room his.

8. I grew cold and weary during the long football game.

Copyright © by Glencoe/McGraw-Hill

Cumulative Review: Units 1–2

▶ **Exercise 1** Draw a line between the complete subject and the complete predicate. In the blank write the part of speech of the italicized word.

_____noun_____ The *cleanliness* of Mia's room|shocked her mother.

_____ **1.** They saw the *white* tiger at the zoo.

_____ **2.** I *thought* long and hard about her advice.

_____ **3.** Soccer *remains* Scott's major source of exercise.

_____ **4.** Dr. Dawson is the one *who* signed my medical forms.

_____ **5.** *Nobody* can watch our dog while we're gone.

_____ **6.** *Both* trucks *and* cars had to stop at the roadblock.

_____ **7.** You climbed the hill *too* fast for me!

_____ **8.** Please empty the milk *into* the measuring cup.

_____ **9.** The book over there is *yours*.

_____ **10.** My dad, mom, sister, and I rode the *streetcar* in San Francisco.

_____ **11.** The reporter interviewed me for the school paper; *moreover,* the photographer took my picture.

_____ **12.** Please take *that* tray back to the cafeteria.

_____ **13.** *This* is the worst movie I've ever seen.

_____ **14.** My father is a professor of *philosophy*.

_____ **15.** We will meet for practice on the field tomorrow *unless* it rains.

_____ **16.** Mona *herself* braved the winter weather to shovel the snow.

_____ **17.** *Jonathan Swift* was an English author and satirist.

_____ **18.** The chef at Luigi's specializes in *Italian* cuisine.

_____ **19.** The pirate *is hiding* the treasure in the ship.

_____ **20.** Omar works in the bakery *but* doesn't eat sweets.

_____ **21.** The sun is *remarkably* bright today!

_____ **22.** *Oh, no!* I forgot to put on sunscreen!

Copyright © by Glencoe/McGraw-Hill

Unit 3: Phrases

Lesson 18
Prepositional Phrases

A **prepositional phrase** is a group of words that begins with a preposition and usually ends with a noun or a pronoun, called the **object of the preposition**.

I will meet you **at the movie.** (*Movie* is the object of the preposition *at.*)

Prepositional phrases may occur in a series and may have more than one object.

My skis sped **down the hill over the cliff into the river.** (three prepositional phrases)
We sent invitations **to Jack, Kumar,** and **Renee.** (three objects of the preposition *to*)

COMMON PREPOSITIONS

about	beneath	inside	since
above	beside	into	than
across	between	like	through
after	beyond	near	to
against	but (except)	of	toward
along	by	off	under
among	concerning	on	until
around	down	onto	up
as	during	out	upon
at	except	outside	with
before	for	over	within
behind	from	past	without
below	in		

A prepositional phrase functions as an adjective when it modifies a noun or a pronoun. It functions as an adverb when it modifies a verb, an adjective, or an adverb.

Can you identify that bird **in the garden?** (adjective phrase modifying the noun *bird*)
Please take this paint brush **to your father.** (adverb phrase modifying the verb *take*)

▶ **Exercise 1** Underline each prepositional phrase.

The biosphere is the total <u>of all biological communities</u> <u>on Earth</u>.

1. The biosphere extends for many miles; it begins at seven miles above sea level and continues

   for an equal distance into the ocean's depths.

2. Scientists divide the biosphere into ecosystems and study how organisms interact with each other.

3. Ecosystems are affected by environmental factors.

Copyright © by Glencoe/McGraw-Hill

4. Climate, the range of weather conditions over a period of time, affects ecosystems.

5. These conditions consist of rainfall, sunlight, temperature, wind, and humidity.

6. Climate itself is affected by latitude, a location's distance north or south of the equator.

7. Places near the Equator receive more of the sun's light than those near the poles.

8. Landforms in an ecosystem also affect the characteristics of its climate.

9. Large bodies of water moderate the temperatures of land along their shores.

10. Elevation, the distance of a place above sea level or below sea level, also has an effect on climate.

11. On land, higher elevations are colder than the areas beneath them.

12. In the deepest areas of the sea, many areas feel greater pressure from the waters above them.

13. This affects the kinds of organisms that can thrive under such conditions.

14. The soil within an area also affects ecosystems.

15. Soil contains various amounts of organic material, minerals, and rocks.

16. Soils also have air and water in varying amounts.

▶ **Exercise 2** Write *adj.* in the blank if the italicized phrase functions as an adjective and *adv.* if it functions as an adverb.

_____adv._____ Water is essential *to the biosphere.*

_____ 1. Carbon, oxygen, and nitrogen also cycle *through the biosphere.*

_____ 2. *In the water cycle,* water vapor condenses and falls *to Earth as precipitation.*

_____ 3. Some *of the precipitation* is absorbed *into the soil.*

_____ 4. Another part is used *by plants and animals.*

_____ 5. Most *of the remaining precipitation* makes its way *into rivers, lakes, and oceans.*

_____ 6. The process *of evaporation* takes this standing water back *into the atmosphere.*

_____ 7. *During this process,* liquid water changes *into a gas.*

_____ 8. This gas, or water vapor, is also put *into the atmosphere by breathing humans, animals, and plants.*

_____ 9. Nitrogen is another element essential *for life.*

_____ 10. Although much *of Earth's atmosphere* is nitrogen, most organisms cannot take nitrogen straight *from the air.*

Copyright © by Glencoe/McGraw-Hill

Lesson 19
Participles, Participial Phrases, and Absolute Phrases

Grammar

A **participle** is a verb form that can function as an adjective. Present participles always have an *-ing* ending. Past participles often end in *-ed*, but some take other forms. Many common adjectives are participles.

I tried to wash my **stained** shirt. (*Stained* is a participle that modifies the noun *shirt*.)

A **participial phrase** contains a participle plus its modifiers. Since it functions as an adjective, it can appear in various places in a sentence. When it appears at the beginning of a sentence or is nonessential, a participial phrase is set off by commas.

Stumbling over the junk, I decided to clean up the garage.
The farm, **devastated by the storm,** lay in ruins.

A past participle is sometimes used with the present participle of the helping verbs *have* and *be.*

Having studied for hours, I went for a walk. We watched the cliff **being dashed by the waves.**

▶ **Exercise 1** Underline each participle and participial phrase.

Packing carefully, we prepared for our camping trip.

1. Yelling with all our might, we sat in the cheering section.

2. Did anyone ever tell you that you have a winning smile?

3. Feeling like a fool, I appeared from behind the curtain in a checkered costume.

4. Blushing, Estrella accepted the praise of her cycling buddies.

5. What should we do with this picked fruit?

6. The leaning buildings were knocked down by the wrecking ball.

7. Breathing hard, the runners crossed the finish line.

8. The dog, caught between the two fierce cats, fled the yard.

9. Badly injured, the accident victims were helicoptered to the trauma center.

10. Holding our breaths, we watched the hero being stalked by the villain.

11. The crumpled shipment of dishes contained many cracked items.

12. Tires screaming, the racing car rounded the track.

13. The photographer shooting the wedding focused several pictures on the smiling parents.

14. The speaker at the museum was a respected environmentalist.

Copyright © by Glencoe/McGraw-Hill

15. My typing rate changed drastically due to my broken wrist.

16. Hoping for the best, we opened the basement door after the raging flood.

17. The team has finally broken its losing streak!

18. Don't forget your backpack lying behind the sofa.

19. Clutching her mother's hand, the child skated slowly over the frozen rink.

20. Slashing the vegetation ahead, the explorers ploughed through the overgrown jungle.

An **absolute phrase** consists of a noun or a pronoun that is modified by a participle or a participial phrase. It stands "absolutely" by itself, having no grammatical relation to the complete subject or the complete predicate of a sentence.

Its leaves burned off by the fire, the dead tree fell.

In some absolute phrases the participle *being* is understood rather than stated.

We hurried to the game, **our anticipation (being) high.**

▶ **Exercise 2** Underline each absolute phrase. Do not underline any participial phrase that is grammatically related to the rest of a sentence.

We hoped for a clear weekend, Friday being dreary.

1. Her suspicions confirmed, the police officer made the arrest.

2. Backing out of the driveway, I hit the mailbox.

3. They will take the daytime train, the landscape inviting.

4. My doubts relieved, I gained confidence as the game progressed.

5. Peering through a microscope, the scientist identified several microbes.

6. His dogs panting with exertion, Hagos took a break from his run.

7. Its shutters hanging limply in the wind, the house looked abandoned and forlorn.

8. The car rusted and worthless, I left it at the junkyard.

9. Wearing a red plaid outfit, Lydia looked like a character in a novel.

10. Everything planned in advance, the party went like clockwork.

11. We scrambled from the car, racing to the amusement park gates.

12. Moving quickly, the lion cut off the fleeing zebra.

13. My garden is dying, pesticides having been applied by mistake.

14. As the parole board met to decide the fates of several people, the prisoner was hoping for parole.

Copyright © by Glencoe/McGraw-Hill

Lesson 20

Gerunds and Gerund Phrases; Appositives and Appositive Phrases

Grammar

A **gerund** is a verb form that ends in *-ing* and functions as a noun.

Skating is my favorite sport. (gerund as subject)
My friends all love **skating**. (gerund as direct object)
We give **skating** much consideration. (gerund as indirect object)
I will teach a class in **skating**. (gerund as object of a preposition)
My father's favorites are **skiing** and **swimming**. (gerunds as predicate nominatives)
Two sports, **skiing** and **sledding**, are popular. (gerunds as appositives)

A **gerund phrase** is a gerund with its modifiers.

Running in marathons is my mother's constant passion.
Her success is due to **quality training**.

Though they both end in *-ing*, do not confuse a gerund, used as a noun, with a present participle, used as an adjective.

Standing in the rain, we wished we had brought umbrellas. (participial phrase)
Standing in the rain got us soaked to the skin. (gerund phrase)

▶ **Exercise 1** **Underline each gerund or gerund phrase.**

<u>Traveling under cover of night</u> helped slaves escape to the North.

1. I love walking in the moonlight and looking for nocturnal animals.

2. Rushing for the bus caused me to fall and scrape my knee.

3. Our class is committed to recycling, as well as to reducing the amount of package waste.

4. My sister's whining is her least appealing trait.

5. Shoving people aside, the thief leapt over the counter and fled the scene.

6. Chad's best track events are broad jumping and sprinting.

7. We all hate cleaning our rooms, but no one seems to be giving us any choice.

8. Do we get any credit for guessing?

9. Eating the dog's food is our cat's favorite activity.

10. Almost totaling the car last week really frightened my brother.

11. Returning to the campsite, the campers saw bear tracks.

12. I love waking up to the singing of the birds and the rising of the sun.

Copyright © by Glencoe/McGraw-Hill

13. Bringing in the hay and storing it in the barn was exhausting work.

14. Hovering over the mouse, the hawk plunged to Earth.

15. Painting the garage every summer is Gary's way to relieve stress.

16. We debated driving, but because of the distance decided on flying.

An **appositive** is a noun or pronoun that is placed next to another noun or pronoun to identify or give more information about it. An **appositive phrase** is an appositive plus its modifiers.

His cousin **Fred** is an astronomy whiz. (The appositive *Fred* identifies the noun *cousin*.) He writes for *Sky and Telescope,* **the astronomy magazine**. (The appositive phrase *the astronomy magazine* identifies *Sky and Telescope.*)

▶ **Exercise 2** Underline each appositive or appositive phrase.

The twins, Mark and Mabel, are both tall.

1. My aunt Helene bought a farm outside Toledo.

2. The comics, Seth and Josh, kept us in stitches for hours.

3. She moved to Albany, the capital of New York.

4. During first and second periods I have science and math, my best courses.

5. Kimane, the soccer captain, got an award.

6. I watched a documentary about Hank Aaron, the baseball great who broke Babe Ruth's home run record.

7. *Walden* is my favorite book by the naturalist Henry David Thoreau.

8. My fingers, cold sticks of ice, were frostbitten from being out in the cold too long.

9. I write for our student newspaper *Hall Pass*.

10. Was that your famous relative, the mountain climber?

11. My oldest brother, Tim, is on leave from the air force.

12. My cat Huckleberry lived for almost twenty years.

13. Let's see the theater's new production, *Arsenic and Old Lace.*

14. Rami, my best friend, is moving out of town.

15. The dancers, members of Ms. Contreras's class, leaped and twirled through the audience.

Copyright © by Glencoe/McGraw-Hill

Grammar

Lesson 21
Infinitives and Infinitive Phrases

An **infinitive** is a verb form that is usually preceded by the word *to* and is used as a noun, an adjective, or an adverb. The word *to* used before the base form of a verb is part of the infinitive form of the verb, not a preposition.

To lie is dishonorable. (infinitive as subject)
Everyone needs **to study**. (infinitive as direct object)
Their orders were **to retreat**. (infinitive as predicate nominative)
That would be a fun cave **to explore**. (infinitive as adjective)
The audience was waiting **to applaud**. (infinitive as adverb)

An **infinitive phrase** is an infinitive with its modifiers.

We hope **to climb the mountain by nightfall.**
Do you have **to play your music so loudly?**
To study after the test is a little backwards.

▶ **Exercise 1 Underline each infinitive.**

The space shuttle is designed <u>to launch</u> like a rocket and <u>to land</u> like an airplane.

1. It is large enough to carry as many as eight astronauts and over fifty thousand pounds of cargo.

2. The shuttle was designed to allow humans and equipment access to space on a regular basis.

3. Within the first ten years of its flight history, the shuttle managed to fly over forty missions.

4. The shuttle has many uses; it is often used to deploy satellites.

5. In a few cases the shuttle has been used to capture wandering spacecraft.

6. In a recovery mission in December of 1993, the shuttle *Endeavour* and its crew were sent to repair the Hubble Space Telescope.

7. Instruments aboard the shuttle are able to collect data on a variety of phenomena.

8. Mission to Planet Earth is a program geared to observe the effects that humans have on this planet.

9. A laboratory program called ATLAS has been created to study Earth's upper atmosphere and to collect data on the sun's environment and energy output.

10. The UARS satellite, carried by shuttle to Earth's orbit, was set up to examine the levels of life-sustaining gases above Earth.

11. Some scientists believe that data from this satellite reveal that the ozone layer is continuing to get thinner.

Copyright © by Glencoe/McGraw-Hill

12. A variety of telescopic instruments use the shuttle as a platform from which to observe the universe beyond Earth.

13. The *Galileo* probe, heading to Jupiter to observe the giant planet, was launched from the shuttle *Atlantis* in 1989.

14. *Ulysses,* launched from *Discovery* in 1990 and heading toward the sun, is programmed to collect information on the sun's poles starting in 1995.

15. Scientists think we will learn things about Earth and our environment that we cannot begin to imagine today.

▶ **Exercise 2** **Underline each *to* functioning as an infinitive and circle each *to* functioning as a preposition.**

Tamara Jernigan belongs (to) the United States Volleyball Association.

1. She is the only member of that organization to fly the space shuttle to Earth's orbit.

2. Jernigan has served as mission specialist on two shuttle flights, where she was able to test physical conditioning in space.

3. She notes that while all athletes have a duty to keep in shape, there are different things to deal with in space.

4. For example, few athletes ever have to adjust to microgravity.

5. The human experiment in space has taught astronauts that they have to counteract anti-gravity effects on the body by exercising while they are actually flying.

6. Jernigan uses the Russian space station *Mir* to point out the necessity of conditioning, both before and during flights.

7. She says the Russians exercise regularly on *Mir* because they do not want to get de-conditioned to Earth's gravitational forces.

8. Jernigan herself runs and tries to work out with a high school volleyball team, all in addition to her work with the USVA.

9. She describes the exercise equipment that the astronauts are able to take into space.

10. The ogometer is a bicycle-like device, and she discovered it was a fine way to exercise.

11. Unfortunately, she points out, exercising causes the shuttle to shake, which messes up the fine-tuned experiments that other astronauts are trying to carry out.

12. Obviously, someone needs to develop a way of exercising so as not to disturb the shuttle balance.

Copyright © by Glencoe/McGraw-Hill

Lesson 22
Distinguishing Participial, Gerund, and Infinitive Phrases

Grammar

The three types of verbal phrases—participial, gerund, and infinitive—are closely related to verbs. However, they are not used as verbs, but as nouns, adjectives, and adverbs. You can distinguish the kinds of phrases by identifying the way they are used in a sentence.

A participial phrase is used as an adjective and can be in the present or past tense.

A gerund phrase is used as a noun and ends in *-ing*.

An infinitive phrase can be used as a noun, an adjective, or an adverb, and is usually preceded by the word *to*.

▶ **Exercise 1** Write *P* in the blank if the italicized phrase is a participial phrase, *G* for gerund phrase, or *I* for infinitive phrase.

___I___ She hopes *to become a field biologist*.

_____ **1.** Matty bought me an elephant *carved from wood*.

_____ **2.** *Memorizing poetry* is a good way *to maintain brain power*.

_____ **3.** Do you want *to copy my notes*?

_____ **4.** The teacher handed back my theme, *edited by her assistant*.

_____ **5.** Jack's dream, *rafting the wild river*, was soon *to be realized*.

_____ **6.** The lifeguard, *swimming as quickly as possible*, approached the swimmer *calling for help*.

_____ **7.** *Weaving dangerously*, the truck managed *to stay on the slippery road*.

_____ **8.** Our fund raiser will help *to support the new environmental center*.

_____ **9.** My friend agreed *to keep my secret*.

_____ **10.** *Singing in the shower* is my greatest talent.

_____ **11.** Can you help me *to paint these lawn chairs*?

_____ **12.** The balloons *hanging from the ceiling* added the final touch to our decorations.

_____ **13.** I hope you don't plan *to meet my parents dressed as a pirate*!

_____ **14.** She is in training *to swim across the lake*.

_____ **15.** Do you expect me *to make excuses for you*?

_____ **16.** *Leaping into the air*, the kitten caught the butterfly.

_____ **17.** Everyone in class was confused and kept *missing the point*.

Copyright © by Glencoe/McGraw-Hill

_____ **18.** We traveled to Florida *to watch the launch of the space shuttle.*

_____ **19.** *Eating pizza* is one of my passions.

_____ **20.** I hate *to hear those mosquitoes droning around my bed.*

▶ **Exercise 2** **Draw a line under each verbal phrase below. Write *P* in the blank if it is a participial phrase, *G* if it is a gerund phrase, or *I* if it is an infinitive phrase.**

__P__   Climbing the tree, the kitten got trapped at the top.

_____ **1.** The residents heard the sound of shattering glass.

_____ **2.** Playing the trumpet is Jacky's best skill.

_____ **3.** Edging closer to the generals, the spy listened to their war plans.

_____ **4.** Where did you learn to make pottery?

_____ **5.** Working overtime is contributing to my savings.

_____ **6.** Searching for treasure attracts many people.

_____ **7.** Seeing its chance, the squirrel darted across the highway.

_____ **8.** In the spring, the hillsides covered with wildflowers attract many visitors.

_____ **9.** To abandon a pet is a crime.

_____ **10.** Taggart hates being shy.

_____ **11.** Hani plans to visit the Keck Telescope in Hawaii.

_____ **12.** Shivering with cold and fatigue, the stranded travelers huddled together under a blanket.

_____ **13.** Waving sadly, our aunt watched us drive out of the driveway.

_____ **14.** I don't want to argue with you any more!

_____ **15.** Broken in the fall, my leg took forever to heal soundly.

_____ **16.** Mowing the lawn is not my favorite task.

_____ **17.** My hobby, practicing magic tricks, takes up my spare time.

_____ **18.** The team, disappointed by their loss, could not be comforted.

_____ **19.** Judging by your mood, I don't think you want to hear the bad news.

_____ **20.** I thought I saw you hiding in the bushes.

Copyright © by Glencoe/McGraw-Hill

✓ Unit 3 **Review**

► **Exercise 1** **Draw one line under each participial phrase, two lines under each gerund phrase, and a circle around each infinitive phrase.**

Sighing in boredom, Rod waited for Jo to leave the house.

1. Excited over their victory, the players hurried to board the bus.

2. Be sure to watch out for deer crossing the highway.

3. Giving yourself credit for an accomplishment is often a hard thing to do with comfort.

4. A loon's cry sounded, breaking the evening silence.

5. I have to travel to the west side, but I don't know how to transfer on the bus.

6. Speaking in whispers, the adults tried not to awaken the children.

7. Bursting with pride, Keven showed us his trophy.

8. Stunned into silence, the spectators could not believe the final score.

9. Looking through binoculars is the best way to see many songbirds.

10. Renee, adjusting her backpack, started out to cross the canyon trail.

11. After thinking about it, I'd like to invite your sister to our party.

12. Where should we go to buy some snacks to feed our guests?

13. I plan to study sculpting in wood next summer.

14. Ms. Plunkett offered to teach us chess.

15. Rehearsing a play is hard work.

16. Pulling out all the drawers, the thieves ransacked the house.

17. Is it time to plant the tomatoes?

18. Seating herself on the lawn, Sarah began to eat her huge sandwich.

19. Watching the sky for meteors is a fine summer evening pastime.

20. Our dog limped home covered with mud and burrs.

21. I want to learn geometry, but I do not want to take any tests!

22. Smelling of skunk, the garage needed airing out.

Copyright © by Glencoe/McGraw-Hill

Cumulative Review: Units 1–3

▶ **Exercise 1** Draw a vertical line (|) between the complete subject and the complete predicate in each sentence.

The moaning wind|increased in intensity.

1. Millions of monarch butterflies migrate every year to trees in Mexico.

2. Some students actually complete their homework in study hall.

3. Mother takes classes in botany and geology at the local community college.

4. The sounds of coughing and sneezing came from the room full of cold-ridden students.

5. *The Terminator* movies are much too violent.

6. The spring rains, together with the heavy snow melt, turned the mountain trails into soggy, dripping bogs.

7. The rainforests, which produce so much oxygen, are often called the earth's lungs.

8. The Gingham Dog and the Calico Cat are characters in a nursery rhyme.

9. *Huckleberry Finn* is one of the finest novels ever written by an American.

10. My family, followed by my friends and neighbors, yelled "Surprise!"

11. Tami took her bird guide and her binoculars into the woods.

12. The animals ran, crawled, flew, or otherwise fled the forest fire.

13. Grandpa has to decide between chess and checkers.

14. Owls, which have no sense of smell, are able to prey on skunks.

15. To figure out the path through the ruins took some concentration.

16. A newly released pollution study warned about the dangers of chlorine.

17. To abandon a friend in need is a dishonorable act.

18. The runners, followed by several laughing children, crossed the finish line.

19. Our fund raiser collected enough money for two weeks' supplies for the food pantry.

20. Carrie can identify most plants in the wild.

21. The clock hands always pointed to 3:37, day and night.

22. Nelson controlled the marionette's strings.

23. The steam from the cocoa curled up through the frigid air.

24. Cutting the grass would be Cole's last chore for the day.

25. Stop here to fill your tank.

Copyright © by Glencoe/McGraw-Hill

Name _____ Class _____ Date _____

Unit 4: Clauses and Sentence Structure

Lesson 23
Main and Subordinate Clauses

A **main clause** is a group of words that contains a complete subject and a complete predicate. Also known as an **independent clause**, a main clause can stand alone as a complete sentence.

Tyler read the morning paper. (main clause)

A **subordinate clause** also contains a subject and a predicate, but it cannot stand alone. Because it depends on a main clause to make sense, it is also known as a **dependent clause**. A subordinate clause usually begins with a **subordinating conjunction**.

While he ate his toast [subordinate clause], Tyler read the morning paper.

SUBORDINATING CONJUNCTIONS

Time:	after, as, as soon as, before, since, until, when, whenever, while
Place:	where, wherever
Manner:	as, as if, as though
Cause:	a, because, inasmuch as, since, so that
Concession:	although, even though, though
Condition:	if, unless

A subordinate clause may also begin with a relative pronoun (such as *who, whose, whom, which, that,* or *what*). In some subordinate clauses, the connecting word also serves as the subject of the clause.

▶ **Exercise 1** Check (✔) the blank before each sentence that contains a subordinate clause.

✔_____ Louis Braille (1809–1852) lost his sight in an accident when he was three years old.

_____ **1.** When he was fourteen, he invented today's most common system of writing for the blind.

_____ **2.** As an adult, he became a teacher of the blind.

_____ **3.** In the Braille system, letters, numbers, and punctuation marks—even musical notes— are written in units called Braille "cells."

_____ **4.** Each cell contains between one and six raised dots.

_____ **5.** Visually impaired people who have been taught Braille can read these raised dots with their fingertips.

_____ **6.** Because sixty-three unique combinations of dots are possible, Braille is quite flexible.

_____ **7.** Louis Braille determined that these raised dots can be interpreted much faster than raised lettering.

Copyright © by Glencoe/McGraw-Hill

_____ 8. Even though it is more practical than raised lettering, the Braille system was not used widely until more than a century after its invention.

_____ 9. The six positions in a cell are arranged in two vertical columns of three positions each.

_____ 10. Each position in a cell is identified by a number.

_____ 11. For example, the number one position is the upper left-hand corner of the cell.

_____ 12. Immediately beneath it is the number two position.

_____ 13. When a single raised dot appears in the number one position, the cell represents the letter *a*.

_____ 14. When both the number one and number two positions contain dots, the cell represents the letter *b*.

_____ 15. Special signs are used to precede numbers and capital letters.

_____ 16. The number sign is a cell with dots in positions 3, 4, 5, and 6.

_____ 17. The first ten letters of the alphabet represent numerals if they are preceded by the number sign.

_____ 18. For example, a cell that would otherwise represent the letter *a* represents the Arabic numeral *1* if it is preceded by a number sign.

_____ 19. Similarly, whenever a cell with a single dot in position 6 appears, the reader knows that the next letter is a capital.

_____ 20. Braille can be written by manual or mechanical means.

_____ 21. A Braille writing machine is similar to a typewriter except that it has only six keys, one corresponding to each dot in the Braille cell.

_____ 22. An ordinary personal computer can convert printed material to Braille by using a special device that embosses dots on paper.

_____ 23. Another method of writing Braille involves using a slate and stylus to form raised dots on paper.

_____ 24. Although Braille provides visually impaired individuals with access to important information found in books, its usefulness doesn't stop there.

_____ 25. Because writing is such an intrinsic part of everyday life, Braille's most important role may be furnishing visually impaired people with a medium for letters, grocery lists, and phone messages.

▶ **Writing Link** **Write a brief paragraph about the reading and writing you do in the course of an ordinary day. Use at least two subordinate clauses.**

_____

_____

_____

Copyright © by Glencoe/McGraw-Hill

Lesson 24
Simple and Compound Sentences

A <u>simple sentence</u> has one complete subject and one complete predicate. The subject, the predicate, or both may be compound.

SUBJECT	PREDICATE
Most dogs	are pets
They	provide pleasure and companionship. (compound predicate)
Seeing Eye® dogs and other assistance dogs (compound subject)	give the gift of independence.

Two or more simple sentences, each considered a main clause, may be combined to form a <u>compound sentence</u>. Main clauses can be joined to build a compound sentence by using a comma followed by a conjunction, such as *or, and,* or *but.* However, a conjunction is not necessary to form a compound sentence. A semicolon may be used to join two main clauses without a conjunction. A semicolon is also used before a conjunctive adverb, such as *however.*

Laura can't hear the alarm clock, **and** her dog wakes her.
Laura can't hear the alarm clock; her dog wakes her.
Laura can't hear the alarm clock; **however,** her dog wakes her.

▶ **Exercise 1** **Write in the blank whether the sentence is *simple* or *compound.***

__compound__   Assistance dogs offer disabled people companionship, but they also play a more important role.

_____ **1.** A trained dog's help could make independent living possible for a disabled person.

_____ **2.** Someone in a wheelchair can't reach a light switch, and a deaf person can't hear a smoke alarm.

_____ **3.** Dogs can help in many everyday situations.

_____ **4.** Labrador retrievers open refrigerators, and Border collies nudge people awake.

_____ **5.** Assistance dogs push elevator buttons and pick up telephones.

_____ **6.** An assistance dog performs many duties, and these duties could change from one day to the next.

_____ **7.** Some dogs go to work or school, and others help with child care or housework.

_____ **8.** One dog might signal the whistle of a teakettle or the beep of a microwave oven.

_____ **9.** Assistance dogs serve as eyes, ears, legs, or arms; they empower those they help.

Copyright © by Glencoe/McGraw-Hill

_____ **10.** Many breeds become assistance dogs, but a few seem particularly well suited to the role.

_____ **11.** Labrador retrievers, golden retrievers, Welsh corgis, and Border collies generally respond well to training.

_____ **12.** These dogs are eager to please; praise and affection are their primary rewards.

_____ **13.** Assistance dogs face unfamiliar situations daily; thus, the single most important job qualification is a calm disposition.

_____ **14.** A dog might have to navigate a crowded bus or a noisy restaurant.

_____ **15.** Assistance dogs regularly encounter strangers; therefore, they should not be apprehensive.

_____ **16.** Nervous and excitable dogs might become frightened, and their unexpected moves could prove dangerous.

_____ **17.** Assistance dogs play another important role, and that is the part of social ice-breaker.

_____ **18.** Disabled people sometimes feel "invisible," but dogs make them very hard to ignore.

_____ **19.** Children especially are attracted to dogs; thus, assistance dogs are often included in disability awareness programs.

_____ **20.** The position of teacher can be added to the assistance dogs' long list of jobs.

▶ **Exercise 2** **Underline each main clause. If there is more than one main clause in a sentence, add a comma or a semicolon as needed.**

<u>Time was flying by</u>, and <u>the day of the wedding was fast approaching</u>.

1. Both of the sofas arrived but neither fit through the doorway.

2. Green is Angie's favorite color but her new coat is blue.

3. This is a great car and it gets good gas mileage.

4. The first game will be this Thursday at five.

5. I like skiing and Maria likes skating.

6. We don't order dessert when we eat out.

7. Martin expected bad weather therefore, he brought an umbrella.

8. This quilt might look old but my grandmother made it last year.

9. I'll call you when I get home from work.

10. We will sell tickets tomorrow or you may buy them at the door.

Copyright © by Glencoe/McGraw-Hill

Lesson 25
Complex and Compound-Complex Sentences

Grammar

A **complex sentence** contains a main clause and one or more subordinate clauses.

MAIN CLAUSE	SUBORDINATE CLAUSE
We ate popcorn	while we watched the movie.

Do not be confused by the phrase *we watched the movie,* which is a complete sentence. The complete subordinate clause is *while we watched the movie,* which cannot stand alone as a sentence.

A **compound-complex sentence** has more than one main clause and one or more subordinate clauses.

MAIN CLAUSE	SUBORDINATE CLAUSE	MAIN CLAUSE
I was in the back yard	when Tony called,	and I didn't hear the phone ring.

▶ **Exercise 1 Draw one line under the main clause and two lines under the subordinate clause. Write *C* in the blank if the sentence is complex and *CC* if it is compound-complex.**

___C___   Whenever I work at this computer, I get a stiff neck.

_____ **1.** After I had searched everywhere, I found my ring, and I put it in my jewelry box.

_____ **2.** Julia cooked the lasagna yesterday, because she wouldn't have time today.

_____ **3.** As long as you're driving that way, could you stop at the post office for me?

_____ **4.** While thinking of an answer, Jason stared at his feet.

_____ **5.** Tillie paused for a moment when she reached the landing, and then she continued up the stairs.

_____ **6.** Terese apologized because she had lost her temper.

_____ **7.** I gave him a pen so that he could write down the phone number.

_____ **8.** I wrote a letter to the owner because the restaurant was filthy, and I'm waiting for a reply.

_____ **9.** She did not have the shoes that I wanted to buy; however, she is ordering them for me.

_____ **10.** The kite didn't fly because there wasn't enough wind.

_____ **11.** I met Dr. Wolfe while I was attending college, and now I work in her office.

_____ **12.** Mary never called because she got home too late.

_____ **13.** When the weather is hot, gardening can be drudgery.

_____ **14.** He didn't raise his voice, but we knew that he meant business, and we got back to work.

_____ **15.** As long as you're calling, ask her for the salsa recipe.

Copyright © by Glencoe/McGraw-Hill

_____ **16.** Lee is worried, and I agree that we should take the cat to the vet.

_____ **17.** Because it was directed at toddlers, the program had to be brief.

_____ **18.** As he described his trip to sunny Puerto Rico, the rain continued to fall.

_____ **19.** Even though I was scheduled to leave early, I'll stay until closing, and then I'll make the bank deposit.

_____ **20.** When small children need sleep, they become short-tempered.

_____ **21.** My sister is moving because she got a new job.

_____ **22.** Although I promised I'd be there, I couldn't make it because my car wouldn't start.

_____ **23.** Even if you mail the card today, it won't arrive until after her birthday, and you will have to call anyway.

_____ **24.** If this snow continues, school will be canceled, and we'll have to stay home.

_____ **25.** The snack bar, which is open all year, is behind the boathouse.

_____ **26.** Angela called while you were out, but she didn't leave a message.

_____ **27.** Even though Carey is gone for the weekend, the cat sleeps on her bed, and the dog sleeps in her doorway.

_____ **28.** Unless it rains, she will take her binoculars and go birdwatching.

_____ **29.** Will the person who lost a pearl necklace please come to the front desk?

_____ **30.** If you simply paint over them, the cracks will return, and you'll have to paint again.

▶ **Writing Link** **Write a brief paragraph about a book you have read. Use at least two complex sentences and one compound-complex sentence.**

_____

_____

_____

_____

_____

_____

_____

_____

_____

_____

Copyright © by Glencoe/McGraw-Hill

Lesson 26
Adjective Clauses

When a subordinate clause modifies a noun or a pronoun, it is called an **adjective clause**. Often, adjective clauses begin with a relative pronoun. An adjective clause can also begin with *where* or *when*.

The banner **that I made for your parents' anniversary** was ruined by the rain. (modifies the noun *banner*)

RELATIVE PRONOUNS

that	whom	whomever
which	whose	what
who	whoever	whatever

▶ **Exercise 1** Draw one line under each adjective clause and two lines under each word that introduces an adjective clause.

The pictures that I saw in the yearbook brought back many memories.

1. The dog that Peter owns is a well-trained golden retriever.

2. Tell everyone whose time is up to please move on to the next booth.

3. I don't like standing in lines where there is no room to breathe.

4. The car, which was parked in the sun, became extremely hot.

5. I finally got to see the holography exhibit that you recommended.

6. Perry saw many desserts on the menu that sounded delicious.

7. There is no family whose reunions are more fun than ours.

8. For his research project, Kareem examined every sample that he could find.

9. Corky often visits the park where she saw the red fox.

10. The new movie, which was quite violent, contained some scenes that upset me.

11. Dave chose the T-shirts that had the college insignia on them.

12. The spot where we set up camp was twelve miles from the trailhead.

13. His vacation begins on the tenth, which is a Friday.

14. The car that my sister wants to buy has many extras.

15. The boy whom we met at the zoo is from Germany.

16. Will the person whose car is blocking the driveway please move it?

17. This is the intersection where the accident happened.

Copyright © by Glencoe/McGraw-Hill

Grammar

18. Francisco often visits the store that his grandfather owns.

19. Sam's car, which is the same year as mine, is in better condition.

20. My sister sold lemonade to the people who came to the garage sale.

Adjective clauses may be either essential or nonessential. **Essential clauses** are necessary to make the meaning of a sentence clear. A clause beginning with *that* is essential.

Projects that are completed before the science fair will earn extra credit. (essential clause)

Nonessential clauses add interesting information but are not necessary for the meaning of a sentence. Use commas to set off nonessential clauses from the rest of the sentence. A clause beginning with *which* is usually nonessential.

Massie's project, which demonstrated the effects of sound on plants, earned extra credit. (nonessential clause)

▶ **Exercise 2** Underline each adjective clause in the sentences below. Write *E* (essential) or *non.* (nonessential) in the space provided to identify the type of clause.

__non.__ My brother, <u>who goes to Yale</u>, will be home for the weekend.

_____ 1. Cars that have malfunctioning exhaust systems should be repaired or taken off the road.

_____ 2. I will point out the Thai restaurant that serves my favorite food.

_____ 3. Uncle Charles, whose cabin we stayed in last summer, has invited us back this year.

_____ 4. Use the plastic measuring spoons, which are in the top drawer.

_____ 5. The woman who owns the florist shop is visiting mom.

_____ 6. The popcorn that they sell at the fair is the best I've ever tasted.

_____ 7. Julio showed us the spot where he had last seen his camera.

_____ 8. Ridge Road, which is quite steep, leads to the ski area.

_____ 9. P.J. is the student who designed the poster for the play.

_____ 10. Joanna gave a performance that I will never forget.

_____ 11. This artist, whom I once met, used only watercolors.

_____ 12. Nick told us to take the road that runs straight through town.

_____ 13. Clarence, who is visiting Barbados, sent me this hat.

_____ 14. Volunteers who can follow directions make the job easier.

_____ 15. Ted showed us the tracks that were left by the grizzly bear.

_____ 16. The man who donated the refreshments owns a grocery store.

Copyright © by Glencoe/McGraw-Hill

Lesson 27
Adverb Clauses

An **adverb clause** is a subordinate clause that modifies a verb, an adjective, or an adverb. It is used to tell *when, where, why, to what extent,* or *under what conditions.* An adverb clause is usually introduced by a subordinating conjunction.

I'll take a turn **after Liana takes hers.**

▶ **Exercise 1** **Underline the adverb clause in each sentence.**

Wild potatoes grew in South America for thousands of years <u>before European explorers</u> <u>arrived.</u>

1. Spanish explorers brought potatoes with them when they returned from the Americas in the 1500s.

2. Potatoes were initially shunned by Europeans because some closely related plants are poisonous.

3. Even though some people were skeptical at first, the potato became an important food crop worldwide.

4. Potatoes are very practical because yield per acre is high.

5. Provided that the growing season is long enough, two plantings per year are usually possible.

6. Potatoes grow in difficult locations where other food will not grow.

7. Potatoes can't survive where the humidity is too high.

8. Because they are so hardy, potatoes have saved many lives.

9. Soldiers throughout history have been spared starvation when potatoes were available.

10. Few other crops can withstand the ravages of war as potatoes can.

11. Because they grow underground, potatoes can survive even fires.

12. The potato became the mainstay of the Irish diet until a blight destroyed the crop in 1845.

13. A million people died, and millions more fled Ireland so that they could live.

14. Potatoes were not an important crop in North America until great numbers of Irish immigrants began arriving in the mid-1800s.

15. As meat consumption increased, however, potatoes played a less important role in North American diets.

Copyright © by Glencoe/McGraw-Hill

16. Because people mistakenly believed that potatoes were fattening, this nutritious food was once again avoided.

17. Potatoes are not fattening unless they are combined with high-fat ingredients.

18. When people hear the word *potatoes,* one of the first things that comes to mind is probably French fries.

19. Even though they are made of potatoes, French fries are not very nourishing.

20. Provided they are prepared the right way, potatoes can be a major component of a well-rounded diet.

21. So that potatoes' nutritional virtues can be retained, low-fat cooking techniques should be employed.

22. If you use a little imagination, most potato dishes can be "lightened up."

23. Although butter is the most popular dressing for baked potatoes, it is probably the most fattening.

24. Even if you forego butter, other toppings such as sour cream or bacon are also high in empty fat calories.

25. Before you eat any potato dish, you might want to stop and consider its fat content.

26. Substituting low-fat ingredients is simple, once you know a few tricks.

27. Whenever sour cream is called for, you might try nonfat yogurt.

28. Before you add cheese to potatoes, ask yourself whether a little pepper might add more flavor.

29. Whenever you buy processed potatoes such as French fries or potatoes au gratin, don't forget about that hidden fat.

30. If you buy fresh potatoes, they are low in fat, high in carbohydrates, and packed with nutrients.

▶ **Writing Link** **Write a brief paragraph about a food you enjoy. Use at least three adverb clauses.**

_____

_____

_____

_____

_____

_____

Copyright © by Glencoe/McGraw-Hill

Lesson 28
Noun Clauses

A **noun clause** is a subordinate clause that acts as a noun.

Our **profits** depend on our pricing formula. (noun)
Whether we make a profit depends on our pricing formula. (noun clause)

The clause in the second sentence above replaces the noun in the first sentence. Noun clauses can be used in the same way as nouns—as subject, direct object, object of a preposition, and predicate noun.

Whoever takes the last ice cube should refill the tray. (subject)
Do you know **how Russians say "yes"**? (direct object)
We were anxious about **what would come next**. (object of preposition *about*)

The following words are used to introduce noun clauses:

how	what	where	who	whomever
however	whatever	which	whom	whose
that	when	whichever	whoever	why

▶ **Exercise 1** Underline each noun clause. In the blank, indicate its function in the sentence: *S* (subject), *DO* (direct object), *OP* (object of a preposition), or *PN* (predicate noun).

__DO__   The article described <u>how carpenters build chairs</u>.

_____ **1.** The assumption is that we will reach the coast before Friday.

_____ **2.** Whatever you want is fine with me.

_____ **3.** Will someone please tell me why the basement light is on?

_____ **4.** We were worried about what would happen to the senior center .

_____ **5.** That the team will make it to the state finals is the hope of all the players.

_____ **6.** Luanne wondered aloud why the car was so muddy.

_____ **7.** This open window must be where the burglar entered.

_____ **8.** What we wished for came true after all.

_____ **9.** Why she had chosen that college was never even discussed.

_____ **10.** Marnie asked the author why he wrote the story in the present tense.

_____ **11.** This covered bridge is where my mother proposed to my father.

_____ **12.** Whichever route you want to take is fine with me.

_____ **13.** We talked about what she would do with her free time.

_____ **14.** Please save those stones for when we build the path from the cabin to the creek.

Copyright © by Glencoe/McGraw-Hill

Grammar

_____ **15.** Birthdays are when I really appreciate my big family.

_____ **16.** I can't remember why I chose that morbid poem.

_____ **17.** Aunt Carol told me all about where she grew up.

_____ **18.** That they will hear a world-class orchestra is the expectation of the audience.

_____ **19.** No one can tell me what I should do about this problem.

_____ **20.** Holidays are when I miss my grandfather the most.

_____ **21.** The winner will be whoever sells the most subscriptions.

_____ **22.** Whoever wrote this perfume ad needs a good editor.

_____ **23.** I had a dream about when we were in Canada.

_____ **24.** Does anyone here know how tadpoles become frogs?

_____ **25.** Theo's advice was for whoever would listen.

_____ **26.** When we leave the party is up to you.

_____ **27.** Which flight we should take was a real dilemma.

_____ **28.** She'll give me whatever is left of the cake.

_____ **29.** College is whatever you make of it.

_____ **30.** Save this sample for whoever is in charge of printing the brochures.

_____ **31.** March drew whatever we asked her to.

_____ **32.** This deserted exit is where we ran out of gas.

_____ **33.** That Daniel missed his sister was apparent.

_____ **34.** The police officer talked about how his dog had saved his life.

_____ **35.** Jimmy could hit whatever I pitched him.

▶ **Writing Link Write a brief paragraph about a family get-together. Use each of the four types of noun clauses (subject, direct object, object of a preposition, and predicate noun) at least once.**

_____

_____

_____

_____

_____

_____

Copyright © by Glencoe/McGraw-Hill

Lesson 29
Kinds of Sentences

A **declarative sentence** makes a statement. It usually ends with a period.

We went to the state fair last summer.

An **imperative sentence** gives a command or makes a request. The subject "you" is understood. An imperative sentence ends with a period or exclamation point.

Please turn the lights off.

An **interrogative sentence** asks a question. It ends with a question mark.

Did you notice whether she was carrying an umbrella?

An **exclamatory sentence** expresses strong emotion. It ends with an exclamation point.

What a hectic day this has been!

▶ **Exercise 1** Label each sentence *dec.* (declarative), *imp.* (imperative), *int.* (interrogative), or *exc.* (exclamatory). Insert the correct punctuation—a period, a question mark, or an exclamation point.

___int.___ How much do you really know about bats?

_____ 1. Bats might be the world's most misunderstood animals

_____ 2. Do you think of bats as villainous, vampire-like creatures

_____ 3. This is not true

_____ 4. Out of more than nine hundred bat species, only three in South America drink animal blood

_____ 5. Did you know that bats are the only mammals capable of true flight

_____ 6. They navigate in the dark by echolocation

_____ 7. Few people realize bats' ecological importance

_____ 8. What do you suppose makes bats so beneficial

_____ 9. They consume huge quantities of insects, including mosquitoes

_____ 10. Some bats eat the equivalent of their body weight in insects in one night

_____ 11. Did you know there is a bat colony in Texas that consumes up to 250,000 pounds of insects in a single night

_____ 12. That's quite a few bugs

_____ 13. Every summer, a cave in Texas is home to the world's largest concentration of mammals

Copyright © by Glencoe/McGraw-Hill

_____ **14.** With the birth of new pups each summer, the population in Bracken Cave swells to 40 million

_____ **15.** Have you ever seen a bat

_____ **16.** Don't think bats live exclusively in caves

_____ **17.** They live in all parts of the world except the polar regions

_____ **18.** You might be able to spot bats in your neighborhood

_____ **19.** Pay close attention

_____ **20.** Many bats live in cities

_____ **21.** Did you know that the world's largest urban bat population is in the United States

_____ **22.** In Austin, Texas, nearly a million bats roost under a downtown bridge

_____ **23.** In Texas, bats are actually a tourist attraction

_____ **24.** Would you like to attract bats for insect-control purposes

_____ **25.** Consider building a bat nesting house

_____ **26.** Many books and articles about bats contain plans for bat houses

_____ **27.** Does it sound as if the public's perception of bats is changing

_____ **28.** Governments are even passing bat-protection laws

_____ **29.** If you're interested in bats, visit your library

_____ **30.** While you're there, look into bat conservation societies

▶ **Writing Link Write a paragraph about an animal. Use all four types of sentences—declarative, interrogative, imperative, and exclamatory.**

_____

_____

_____

_____

_____

_____

_____

_____

Copyright © by Glencoe/McGraw-Hill

Lesson 30
Sentence Fragments

A **sentence fragment** is an incomplete sentence. It may lack a subject, a verb, or both. It might also be a subordinate clause that cannot stand alone. Correct sentence fragments by adding the missing words or phrases.

Knocked for five minutes but got no answer (lacks subject)
The restaurant with three hundred items on the menu (lacks verb)
On my birthday (lacks subject and verb)
Because the dog was barking (subordinate clause only)

▶ **Exercise 1** Write *frag.* next to each sentence fragment. Write *S* next to each complete sentence.

<u>frag.</u>   Yesterday, the rain falling lightly.

_____ **1.** An oil tanker leaking gallons of crude.

_____ **2.** Many adults return to college after years in the working world.

_____ **3.** Even though we invited her again.

_____ **4.** The painting, which includes all three primary colors.

_____ **5.** The marathon starting line early on Saturday morning.

_____ **6.** California and Oregon, both experiencing a drought this year.

_____ **7.** When starting the elementary Spanish class, knew only three words.

_____ **8.** Small birds are nesting on the porch.

_____ **9.** His first professional acting role in nearly twenty years.

_____ **10.** That is precisely what I mean.

_____ **11.** Where you go to college is your decision.

_____ **12.** Her mother, the famous author of best-selling mystery novels.

_____ **13.** Ready to jump in the pool the children threw down their towels.

_____ **14.** I wore the blue hat and she the green.

_____ **15.** No one but Marella in the car when the accident occurred.

_____ **16.** Panicking, I called everyone again at the last minute.

_____ **17.** To announce the sidewalk sale and promote our new spring merchandise.

_____ **18.** Because my mother will be in Japan this summer.

_____ **19.** When Garrison gets hungry, he gets out the cookbooks.

Copyright © by Glencoe/McGraw-Hill

Grammar

Grammar

_____ 20. Describing the many benefits of a new cancer drug.

_____ 21. Before long, bluebirds had found the nesting boxes we'd built.

_____ 22. Whenever I need to return clothing received as a gift.

_____ 23. Walking at low tide yields the most interesting seashell finds.

_____ 24. *Charlotte's Web*, which I fondly remember reading in fourth grade.

_____ 25. Three boys riding mountain bikes and wearing brightly colored helmets.

▶ **Exercise 2** **Tell whether you should add a subject *S*, verb *V*, or a main clause *M* to form a complete sentence.**

___M___ Even tough Caleb's mother had sold him her old car at a reasonable price.

_____ 1. If you wait until Gilberto gets home from work.

_____ 2. More rain and flooding in California.

_____ 3. Taxpayers who wait until the last minute to file their returns.

_____ 4. Barked continually from midnight until 4:00 A.M.

_____ 5. My older sister Becky, who had twins at the beginning of January.

_____ 6. Walked along Sixth Street, looked up, and saw a hot-air balloon.

_____ 7. Without any instructions to guide me in assembling the new bookcase.

_____ 8. Right in the middle of the courtyard where all the neighbors could see.

_____ 9. Didn't really have very nice weather for the festival.

_____ 10. Not wanting to hurt the feelings of those who had contributed long hours to the project.

_____ 11. The painted bowl that my sister brought back from her semester in Mexico last year.

_____ 12. Later than he usually got home.

_____ 13. The washing machine, which was just repaired last week.

_____ 14. When you decided whether to take the job painting houses for the summer.

_____ 15. Carried on as if it were the end of the world.

_____ 16. Yesterday, crowds of people lining up to buy tickets for the opening day game.

_____ 17. Waited in line all afternoon to get a former astronaut's autograph.

_____ 18. If Peter and Tamara get home from school before I get home from work.

_____ 19. Disco music, which was quite popular for a short period in the 1970s.

_____ 20. Waiting in the open-air pavilion for the orchestra to begin playing Vivaldi's *Four Seasons*.

Copyright © by Glencoe/McGraw-Hill

Lesson 31
Run-On Sentences

A **run-on sentence** is two or more complete sentences written as though they were one. There are three basic kinds of run-on sentences.

A comma splice, perhaps the most common kind of run-on sentence, occurs when two main clauses are separated by a comma rather than a semicolon or period.

E. B. White was an essayist, he was also a children's author.

Correct a comma splice by adding a coordinating conjunction such as *and,* by replacing the comma with a semicolon, or by making each main clause a separate sentence.

E. B. White was an essayist, and he was also a children's author.
E. B. White was an essayist; he was also a children's author.
E. B. White was an essayist. He was also a children's author.

Another kind of run-on sentence is formed when there is no punctuation between two main clauses.

Walt Whitman was a poet he wrote *Leaves of Grass.*

Correct by adding a comma and a coordinating conjunction, by adding a semicolon, or by making each main clause a separate sentence.

Walt Whitman was a poet, and he wrote *Leaves of Grass.*
Walt Whitman was a poet; he wrote *Leaves of Grass.*
Walt Whitman was a poet. He wrote *Leaves of Grass.*

A third kind of run-on sentence is formed when there is no comma before the coordinating conjunction that joins two main clauses.

Stephen King is a popular author and his books are often turned into movies.

Correct by adding a comma before the conjunction.

Stephen King is a popular author, and his books are often turned into movies.

▶ **Exercise 1** Write *R* in the blank in front of each run-on sentence.

__R__   Two kinds of fish native to this area are endangered, many more are threatened.

_____ **1.** There are seventeen species of penguins, emperor penguins are the largest.

_____ **2.** The snow was gray, and so was the sky.

_____ **3.** Choose reusable products, use cloth napkins instead of paper.

_____ **4.** We heard noises in the chimney, a raccoon had moved in.

_____ **5.** Some are grizzlies, some are black bears.

Copyright © by Glencoe/McGraw-Hill

_____ 6. The squirrel zigzagged across the lawn, then it dashed up a tree.

_____ 7. A manatee is a mammal, so is a whale.

_____ 8. Komodo dragons are the largest lizards, some grow to more than ten feet long.

_____ 9. It is smaller than the crane, it has a longer neck.

_____ 10. Visit the zoo in cool weather, and the animals will be more active.

_____ 11. The bird I saw had a black throat, this one has a white throat.

_____ 12. Most cockroaches are brown, some are green or blue.

_____ 13. The cougar has many names, including mountain lion, puma, and panther.

_____ 14. Dolphins and porpoises are not the same, they are closely related.

_____ 15. Spotted salamanders migrate here, they cross this road.

_____ 16. Loons walk awkwardly, they're graceful swimmers.

_____ 17. My jeans were hanging on the clothesline, and a wren tried to build a nest in them.

_____ 18. Sea turtles get caught in nets, and so do dolphins.

_____ 19. Roadrunners are real birds, they live in the southwest.

_____ 20. The robin's egg is blue, so is the bluebird's.

_____ 21. Lightning sometimes strikes the ocean, sometimes sea animals get shocked.

_____ 22. Fish sleep, they don't close their eyes.

_____ 23. We visited the rainforest exhibit, but we didn't have time to see the butterflies.

_____ 24. Songbird populations are decreasing, there is still time to reverse the trend.

_____ 25. Tasmanian devils are real animals, and they have pouches like kangaroos.

_____ 26. Those are purple martins, they are the biggest swallows.

_____ 27. Elephants use their ears to cool off, they flap them like fans.

_____ 28. An orange half is an inexpensive birdfeeder, and it's easy to make.

_____ 29. Squirrels are rodents, so are porcupines.

_____ 30. Terrapins live in salt marshes, they crawl ashore to lay eggs.

_____ 31. It had been raining steadily when the sun peeked out from behind the clouds.

_____ 32. This isn't my umbrella nor, for that matter, is this my raincoat.

_____ 33. The pictures Kayla took will appear in today's paper.

_____ 34. Mr. Bils ruled the office but Mrs. Bils presided over their home.

_____ 35. Nora typed in the last word and hit "enter."

Copyright © by Glencoe/McGraw-Hill

☑ Unit 4 **Review**

▶ **Exercise 1** **Underline each main clause, and add commas as needed.**

<u>March was almost over</u>, and <u>I still hadn't finished the project.</u>

1. Three buses arrived but Carlos wasn't on any of them.

2. I always get nervous when my sister drives.

3. This coat is ancient but it's my favorite.

4. Mom cooks her special chicken with the honey-mustard sauce on the grill.

5. Carol expected me at seven; therefore she arrived at six forty-five.

6. You may order these cards through the mail or you may call in your order.

7. We don't go on packaged tours when we travel.

8. The baby stays with his grandmother while his mother is at work.

9. Call Terese when the movie is over and she will give you a ride home.

10. If you don't tell my secret I won't tell yours.

11. Whenever Johnnie shows up the dog goes crazy.

12. Greg likes tennis and his sister likes golf.

13. We didn't order green peppers and we didn't order mushrooms either.

14. My sister doesn't call very often because a call would be expensive.

15. We usually take the bus downtown so that we can avoid parking problems.

16. We put the feeder out for the birds but the squirrels eat most of the food.

17. Jackie won the piano competition and Carlisle won the guitar.

18. Regina took these pictures of Mono Lake when she lived in California.

19. My Aunt Debra owns three dogs and she wants to get another one.

20. Because I was tired from the long drive I rested on the sofa for an hour.

21. Pizza is our favorite; we have it every Friday.

22. Danielle wanted to watch a basketball game; Tim wanted to watch a movie.

23. If you call the accounting office on Monday, I'm sure they could help you.

24. I've waited long enough; I'll wait no longer.

25. Exactly where she misplaced her new sunglasses, I haven't a clue.

Copyright © by Glencoe/McGraw-Hill

Cumulative Review: Units 1–4

▶ **Exercise 1** Label each italicized word with its part of speech: *N* (noun), *V* (verb), *adj.* (adjective), *adv.* (adverb), *pro.* (pronoun), *prep.* (preposition), *conj.* (conjunction), or *int.* (interjection).

　　　　　　　　　　　　　　　　　　　　　　N
Hey! Did you see that runner steal second *base*?

1. Alta *scored* higher on the PSAT than I did.

2. The runner was exhausted, *and* she drank the proffered water in one gulp.

3. My new *checks* have pictures of movie stars on them.

4. *Someone* left a beautifully wrapped present on the back porch!

5. Why didn't you *warn* me about the wet paint on that chair?

6. I'll call Manny *after* the playoffs are over.

7. The downtown bus is always running *late.*

8. Otto forgot to watch for low branches, and before long—*whump!*—he was sitting on the ground watching his horse gallop away without him.

9. I haven't decided whether to take advanced math *or* trigonometry next year.

10. We made *Hungarian* goulash in Home Economics today.

11. The pink blossoms stood out vividly against *their* green stems.

12. Her appearance was *too* sudden, and it sent a quick chill up my spine.

13. I had come to a crossroads and *did* not *know* which way to go.

14. Why weren't *these* deadlines changed?

15. The boat's captain ordered the *sailor* to swab the deck.

16. The *lazy* sales clerk missed a lot of opportunities.

17. The raft was strong and *spacious;* we were not afraid to attempt the crossing.

18. If I've told that cat once, I've told it a thousand times, "Get *off* the couch!"

19. Of all the going-away presents I received, I liked best the framed photo of my *friends.*

20. "*Lands' sakes,*" my grandmother was always saying, "how did you ever grow to be such a handsome fella?"

Copyright © by Glencoe/McGraw-Hill

▶ **Exercise 2** Write *F* in the blank for each sentence fragment, *R* for each run-on sentence, and *C* for each sentence that is correct.

___R___   The bus was early, I missed it again.

_____   **1.** The book, which includes a chapter on the history of the town.

_____   **2.** From my balcony, I can see the lake.

_____   **3.** We saw John in the one-show, he got us free tickets.

_____   **4.** We walked to the wedding then we drove to the reception.

_____   **5.** Andy walked.

_____   **6.** At the grand opening of the supermarket in the new shopping center.

_____   **7.** That color is acceptable, the other is a better choice.

_____   **8.** What you choose to eat is your business.

_____   **9.** Elizabeth wore her linen suit and tan shoes to her interview.

_____ **10.** Michael and Lisa both having a hard time finding summer jobs.

_____ **11.** Her headache, which started during the final exam in trigonometry.

_____ **12.** Jenny's station was neat, Hannah's was immaculate.

_____ **13.** Time to get into the car and head home.

_____ **14.** In just two days they built the entire deck.

_____ **15.** Without any help Mia cooked Thanksgiving dinner for twelve.

▶ **Exercise 3** Write *S* in the blank if the sentence is a simple sentence, *C* if it is a compound sentence, *CX* if it is a complex sentence, and *CC* if it is a compound-complex sentence.

___S___   Behind them stood a great, pacing tiger.

_____   **1.** We hunted high and low, but there was no sign of the other cufflink.

_____   **2.** My little sister enjoys *Green Eggs and Ham,* and I enjoy reading it to her.

_____   **3.** The constant droning of loud music is giving me a headache.

_____   **4.** When Mom took the pies out of the oven, Rover sat up and begged for a slice.

_____   **5.** The sun was hot, our labor was intense, and we dreamed of lakes and canals and oceans.

_____   **6.** I simply can't keep up with Elizabeth.

_____   **7.** I do the kind of work that I enjoy; I don't believe that money is everything.

_____   **8.** Clark's the only person I know who wears a tam-o'-shanter.

Copyright © by Glencoe/McGraw-Hill

Grammar

_____ 9. Don't use the designs that Joonie suggested; your own are much better than hers.

_____ 10. The long, leafy branches swayed gracefully with the breeze.

_____ 11. Peg learned too late that Jack had stuffed all his exercise equipment into the hall closet.

_____ 12. It is true that time is priceless, and so, whatever you do, don't waste it.

▶ **Exercise 4** Write *prep.* before each sentence that contains a prepositional phrase and *inf.* before each sentence that contains an infinitive phrase. Some sentences may contain both.

_____prep._____ I was headed out to sea in the flimsiest of vessels.

_____ 1. Don wants to make chili tonight.

_____ 2. Let's go to a movie after we clean the living room.

_____ 3. Sylvia invited her friends to afternoon tea.

_____ 4. For the first time in my life, I was able to finish the marathon.

_____ 5. Rubbing sticks together is a hard way to start a fire!

_____ 6. To go to Harvard is Alissa's goal.

_____ 7. I ran to the school nurse.

_____ 8. Did you say that Mr. Clancy is going to teach that class?

_____ 9. To "grin and bear it" sometimes takes more effort than I realized.

_____ 10. Someday, I hope to write and to publish a novel.

▶ **Exercise 5** Write *ger.* before each sentence that contains a gerund or a gerund phrase and *part.* before each sentence that contains a participle or a participial phrase.

__ger.__ Stating your objectives clearly will help you reach your goals.

_____ 1. The horse, whinnying and snorting all the way, clearly did not want to be ridden.

_____ 2. Lar's racing pulse pounded against his eardrums.

_____ 3. On snowy days I enjoy curling up on the couch and reading a good book.

_____ 4. Knocking on the door, Carson hollered, "Is anybody home?"

_____ 5. I was surprised to see a delapidated outhouse behind the elegant home.

_____ 6. Is staring your way of showing disrespect?

_____ 7. Laughing and cooing, the baby delighted the guests.

_____ 8. Listening to the stranger's dialect, Adam deduced he was from Aragon.

_____ 9. Determining our next move proved to be a puzzle.

_____ 10. Charlotte, pausing for only a second, plunged into the cold water.

Copyright © by Glencoe/McGraw-Hill

Unit 5: Diagraming Sentences

Lesson 32
Diagraming Simple Sentences

Grammar

Diagraming is a method of showing the relationship of various words and parts of a sentence to the sentence as a whole. Use the following models as a guide in diagraming simple sentences with adjectives and adverbs, direct objects and indirect objects, object complements, and subject complements.

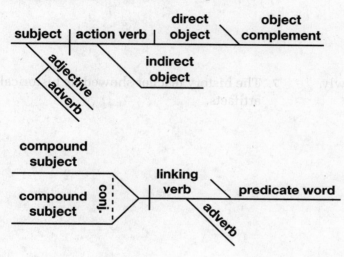

▶ **Exercise 1 Diagram each sentence.**

1. Brave pioneers settled the American West.

2. The men and women considered the journey dangerous.

Copyright © by Glencoe/McGraw-Hill

3. The desert was the most dangerous section.

6. The Santa Fe Trail was an important trail.

4. The weary pioneers advanced quite slowly.

7. The history teacher showed us historical artifacts.

5. The settlers' journey was frightening and exciting.

8. Our class thought the pioneers' stories inspiring.

Copyright © by Glencoe/McGraw-Hill

Lesson 33
Diagraming Simple Sentences with Phrases

Use the following models as a guide in diagraming simple sentences with prepositional phrases, appositives and appositive phrases, participles and participial phrases, gerunds and gerund phrases, infinitives and infinitive phrases, and absolute phrases.

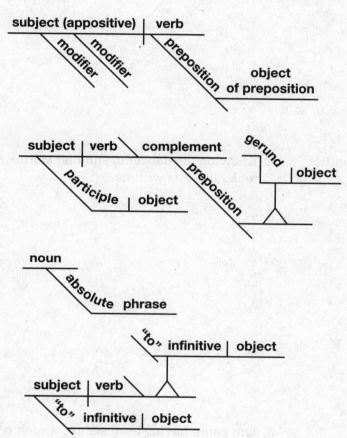

▶ **Exercise 1 Diagram each sentence.**

1. Seeking an enjoyable holiday, millions of tourists come to the Smoky Mountains.

2. Camping is a popular way of experiencing the mountains.

Copyright © by Glencoe/McGraw-Hill

3. To hike in the Smokies would be a wonderful way to spend a vacation.

6. A rain fly, an extra layer of cloth, protects the people in the tent.

Grammar

4. Choosing a place to pitch a tent is difficult.

7. Knowing the danger of summer storms, we took raincoats with us.

5. One of the things to consider is the direction of the wind.

8. Our camp having been set up, we felt ready to enjoy the mountains.

Copyright © by Glencoe/McGraw-Hill

Lesson 34
Diagraming Sentences with Clauses

Use the following models as a guide in diagraming compound sentences and complex sentences with adjective, adverb, and noun clauses.

Selective breeding has been used for centuries to improve domesticated farm animals, and the results are seen everywhere. (compound sentence)

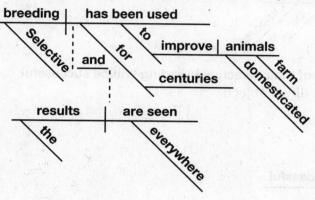

One example is sheep that give finer wool. (complex sentence with adjective clause)

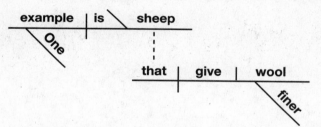

If farmers wish to improve their animals by selective breeding, they must keep careful records. (complex sentence with adverb clauses)

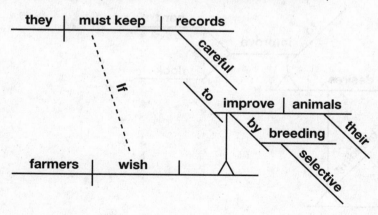

Copyright © by Glencoe/McGraw-Hill

Grammar

Which of many characteristics are desirable is an important decision. (complex sentence with noun clause as subject)

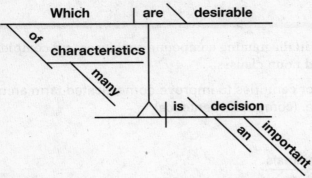

Livestock farmers hope that the results of their selective breeding will be successful. (complex sentence with noun clause as direct object)

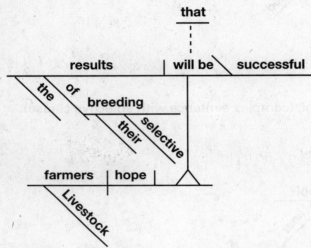

Successful livestock farmers can sell superior breeding stock to whoever desires to improve a herd or flock. (complex sentence with noun clause as object of preposition)

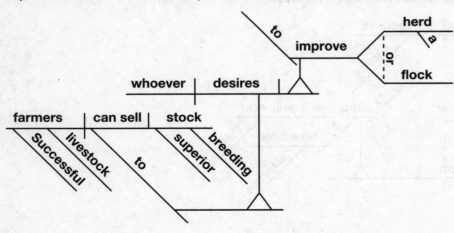

Copyright © by Glencoe/McGraw-Hill

▶ **Exercise 1** **Diagram each sentence.**

1. Members of the club may invite whomever they want to the awards banquet.

3. If Danielle does not study harder, her eligibility for the soccer team might be suspended.

2. That so many people were willing to volunteer for the project made it a success.

4. Even though the movie was quite long, it was very entertaining.

Copyright © by Glencoe/McGraw-Hill

Grammar

5. Send that birthday card to whoever has the best sense of humor.

7. Some young children who attend the preschool are very cautious, but others just do whatever they want.

6. People who live in glass houses should not throw stones.

8. How the raccoon got into the attic is another question.

Copyright © by Glencoe/McGraw-Hill

☑ Unit 5 **Review**

▶ Exercise 1 **Diagram each sentence.**

1. Gary, a music student, and Paul, our band director, consider Bach king.

2. The last drop of water having fallen from the canteen, the explorer let out a cry of despair.

3. Regaining his feet, the runner stumbled onward, and he soon found himself at the finish line.

4. Gatlinburg, a small town in the foothills, has grown quite large.

5. Whether Robin decides to attend the meeting is unimportant to whoever is in charge.

6. Catching the flag would prove that she deserved a spot with the flag corps.

Copyright © by Glencoe/McGraw-Hill

Cumulative Review Units 1–5

▶ **Exercise 1** Write *trans.* in the blank if the action verb is transitive or *intr.* if the action verb is intransitive.

_____trans._____   We heaped the stones in a pile by the door.

_____   **1.** The twins sang at the top of their lungs.

_____   **2.** Surely they have investigated the cause of the accident by now.

_____   **3.** I couldn't believe my eyes!

_____   **4.** What should we do now?

_____   **5.** The wind whipped through my too-thin jacket.

_____   **6.** Milan answered the phone with a gruff, "What?"

_____   **7.** Joshua collected the discarded pizza boxes.

_____   **8.** Mrs. Glimsher wrote me a letter about Kyle's broken wrist.

_____   **9.** Mary Lou paints like Picasso.

_____ **10.** Did anyone tell the Mozzels about the block party?

▶ **Exercise 2** Add an adjective clause or an adverb clause to each sentence.

The man had a phone in his car.

The man who talked incessantly had a phone in his car. _____

1. Howard has written a book. _____

_____

_____

2. The lampshade was shaped like a lily. _____

_____

_____

_____

3. The sky was clear. _____

_____

_____

_____

Copyright © by Glencoe/McGraw-Hill

4. Why don't we play a board game? _____

_____

_____

_____

5. The hotel lacked all but the barest necessities. _____

_____

_____

_____

6. More people attended this year's home show. _____

_____

_____

_____

7. Joe missed his cue. _____

_____

_____

_____

8. You'll have to replace that pitcher. _____

_____

_____

_____

9. That clarinetist is my sister. _____

_____

_____

_____

10. Someday I'd like to visit Aberdeen, Scotland. _____

_____

_____

_____

Copyright © by Glencoe/McGraw-Hill

▶ **Exercise 3 Diagram each sentence.**

1. The wagon drivers offered their oxen hay.

3. On the shores of Maine, her grandfather had built a home for his family.

2. Our plans having been decided, we made reservations.

4. The women and their daughters attended a weekend retreat in July.

Copyright © by Glencoe/McGraw-Hill

Grammar

Unit 6: Verb Tenses, Voice, and Mood

Lesson 35
Regular Verbs: Principal Parts

Verbs have four main parts—a base form, a present participle, a simple past form, and a past participle. A regular verb forms its past form and past participle by adding *-ed* or *-d* to the base form. A regular verb forms its present participle by adding *-ing* to the base form. Both the present and past participle forms require a helping verb.

Base Form: The umpire **yells** at the batter.
Present Participle: The umpire **is yelling** at the batter.
Past Form: The umpire **yelled** at the batter.
Past Participle: The umpire **has yelled** at the batter.

▶ **Exercise 1** Complete each sentence by writing the form of the verb indicated in parentheses.

All the students at school _____love_____ baseball. (base form of *love*)

1. Our team members _____ new uniforms for the championship game. (base form of *need*)

2. We are _____ against the Newton High Tigers. (present participle of *play*)

3. We certainly _____ to win the game. (base form of *expect*)

4. However, three of our best players have _____ themselves this year. (past participle of *injure*)

5. The expense of nine new uniforms almost _____ us. (past form of *ruin*)

6. To pay for them, the kids _____ cars for eight Saturdays in a row. (past form of *wash*)

7. Everyone _____ the sight of buckets and sponges. (past form of *hate*)

8. Apu said that his hands _____ like dried prunes. (past form of *look*)

9. The work is over; now we are _____ forward to the fun. (present participle of *look*)

10. The rally we held yesterday has _____ in boosting the team's morale. (past participle of *succeed*)

11. Akira, our best batter, has _____ to hit at least three home runs. (past participle of *promise*)

12. Ms. Concordia, our principal, is _____ tickets for the game. (present participle of *print*)

13. She is _____ about giving the team a special surprise if they win the game. (present participle of *talk*)

14. Jerome can _____ that the surprise will be a special guest at the victory dance. (base form of *guess*)

Copyright © by Glencoe/McGraw-Hill

15. He knows that Ms. Concordia's brother does _____ drums in a famous rock group. (base form of *play*)

16. Could she be _____ to ask the group to play at the dance? (present participle of *plan*)

17. In the last game our shortstop hit a line drive and _____ to first base as fast as he could. (past form of *gallop*)

18. Just before he got there he _____ over a small stone and was tagged out. (past form of *trip*)

19. Everyone is _____ that such accidents will not spoil this game. (present participle of *hope*)

20. By this time tomorrow we hope to be _____ a rousing victory. (present participle of *celebrate*)

▶ **Exercise 2 Identify the form of each verb in italics.**

focused   _____past_____

1. have *wondered*	_____	**11.** *shouted*	_____
2. are *jumping*	_____	**12.** *type*	_____
3. *borrowed*	_____	**13.** *rented*	_____
4. have *kneeled*	_____	**14.** were *climbing*	_____
5. *walk*	_____	**15.** is *shoveling*	_____
6. *modeled*	_____	**16.** had *painted*	_____
7. *illustrated*	_____	**17.** *investigate*	_____
8. have *caused*	_____	**18.** are *baking*	_____
9. *describe*	_____	**19.** has *leaked*	_____
10. was *escaping*	_____	**20.** *exploded*	_____

▶ **Writing Link Write a paragraph using at least seven of the italicized words in Exercise 2.**

_____

_____

_____

_____

_____

_____

_____

Copyright © by Glencoe/McGraw-Hill

Lesson 36
Irregular Verbs: Principal Parts

Irregular verbs form their past form and past participle in ways different from the *-ed* and *-d* additions used for regular verbs. See the examples below for the verb *be*.

Present Participle: You are **being** very stubborn.
Past Form: You **were** funny at the party last night.
Past Participle: You **have been** unusually quiet today.

The principal parts of some irregular verbs are shown below.

BASE FORM	PRESENT PARTICIPLE	PAST FORM	PAST PARTICIPLE
be (am, is, are)	being	was, were	been
begin	beginning	began	begun
break	breaking	broke	broken
bring	bringing	brought	brought
choose	choosing	chose	chosen
drink	drinking	drank	drunk
eat	eating	ate	eaten
fall	falling	fell	fallen
fight	fighting	fought	fought
fly	flying	flew	flown
go	going	went	gone
keep	keeping	kept	kept
lose	losing	lost	lost
run	running	ran	run
swim	swimming	swam	swum
wear	wearing	wore	worn
see	seeing	saw	seen

▶ **Exercise 1** Underline the verb in parentheses that correctly completes each sentence. Write whether the verb is a *base form, present participle, past form,* or *past participle.*

_____past form_____   The Olympic Games (begin, <u>began</u>) in Greece in 776 B.C.

_____   1. Reba has (swim, swum) in this event many times.

_____   2. Last year she (swam, swum) it in record time.

_____   3. The coach says that Tonelle is (dive, diving) her very best.

_____   4. Today Jane (wear, wore) her favorite bathing suit to practice.

_____   5. She has (saying, said) that it brings her good luck.

_____   6. Bob (think, thought) he wouldn't qualify for the high dive.

_____   7. However, we think he is (going, go) to win easily.

Copyright © by Glencoe/McGraw-Hill

Grammar

_____ **8.** Two years ago Timmy (win, won) the pole vault.

_____ **9.** The local newspaper has (wrote, written) about him often.

_____ **10.** A photo they (take, took) of him won a sports award.

_____ **11.** Have you (go, gone) to any of the events yet?

_____ **12.** I (gone, went) to watch the broad jump yesterday.

_____ **13.** Sam (tell, told) us that his right knee is sore.

_____ **14.** He hopes he has not (tore, torn) a muscle.

_____ **15.** He has (see, seen) a doctor about it already.

_____ **16.** I (think, thinking) the doctor recommended heat.

_____ **17.** Did you know that he has (have, had) an operation on that knee?

_____ **18.** We hope the twins (win, winning) a track scholarship to college.

_____ **19.** After the track meet, may I (ride, rode) home with you?

_____ **20.** I (drive, drove) here yesterday with my sister.

▶ **Exercise 2** **Write in the blank the verb form indicated. Use a disctionary if necessary**

past participle of *write* _____*written*_____

1. past form of *break* _____   **11.** past participle of *come* _____

2. present participle of *see* _____   **12.** past form of *fly* _____

3. base form of *lose* _____   **13.** past participle of *fall* _____

4. past form of *drink* _____   **14.** past participle of *fight* _____

5. past participle of *swim* _____   **15.** past form of *begin* _____

6. present participle of *bring* _____   **16.** past participle of *throw* _____

7. past form of *wear* _____   **17.** past form of *sleep* _____

8. base form of *run* _____   **18.** present participle of *keep* _____

9. past participle of *go* _____   **19.** past participle of *be* _____

10. present participle of *eat* _____   **20.** past form of *choose* _____

Copyright © by Glencoe/McGraw-Hill

Lesson 37
Tense of Verbs: Present, Past, and Future

Grammar

The **present tense** expresses an action that is repeated, ongoing, or always true. It also expresses an action that is happening right now. The present tense and the base form of a verb are the same, except for the third person singular (*he, she,* or *it*), which adds *-s* or *-es.* The verb *be* is an exception to this rule.

Andrea **plays** basketball for the school team. (repeated action)
She **dunks** the ball. (right now)
The school **has** two basketball teams. (always true)

The **past tense** expresses an action that has already occurred. In regular verbs the past tense is formed by adding *-ed* or *-d* to the base form. In irregular verbs the past tense takes a variety of forms. The verb *be* uses two past tense forms—*was* and *were.* The past tense is the same as the past form.

We **studied** hard for the test.
All the chickens **flew** the coop.
Jay **was** riding in my car.
We **were** pleased with our work.

The **future tense** expresses an action that will take place in the future. The future tense is formed by adding *will* to the base form.

I **will go** to the dance with Felipe.
My dad **will be** happy with my grades.

▶ **Exercise 1 Complete each sentence by writing the form of the verb in parentheses.**

Guillermo _____*began*_____ his experiment yesterday. (past tense of *begin*)

1. My grandmother _____ Tuesday. (future tense of *arrive*)

2. The Science Club _____ a new president. (past tense of *elect*)

3. The cat always _____ her catnip mouse. (present tense of *lose*)

4. Our class _____ next June. (future tense of *graduate*)

5. I _____ the movie two weeks ago. (past tense of *see*)

6. Roberto always _____ a funny joke to tell. (present tense of *have*)

7. Today he _____ a joke about a light bulb. (past tense of *tell*)

8. This afternoon I _____ my closet. (future tense of *rearrange*)

9. We _____ who wins the race. (future tense of *see*)

10. Maizie always _____ me her problems. (present tense of *tell*)

Copyright © by Glencoe/McGraw-Hill

11. I _____ in school almost all day. (past tense of *be*)

12. My sister _____ money for college. (future tense of *save*)

13. After weeks of looking, Jim _____ a job. (past tense of *find*)

14. She _____ the office about the meeting. (future tense of *notify*)

15. _____ you please _____ the door for me? (future tense of *open*)

16. The twins _____ almost always together. (present tense of *be*)

17. They _____ for three days to get here. (past tense of *drive*)

18. I _____ my new radio with me to the beach. (past tense of *bring*)

19. Consuelo _____ for the job tomorrow. (future tense of *interview*)

20. It _____ almost time to leave for class. (present tense of *be*)

21. I _____ never _____ his face. (future tense of *forget*)

22. Jacob _____ his jacket on a nail. (past tense of *hang*)

23. I think I _____ my car keys in the grass. (past tense of *lose*)

24. The French club _____ a debate tomorrow. (future tense of *hold*)

25. Our side _____ the mock trial. (past tense of *win*)

26. Who _____ the Declaration of Independence first? (past tense of *sign*)

27. I think he _____ about the surprise party. (present tense of *know*)

28. Alfonso _____ us paint the room. (future tense of *help*)

29. Shakespeare _____ many fine plays. (past tense of *write*)

30. Last week Beth _____ ten laps. (past tense of *swim*)

31. The gym _____ soon _____ new equipment. (future tense of *need*)

32. Arturo _____ almost all the potato salad. (past tense of *eat*)

33. I _____ my paycheck to the bank. (future tense of *take*)

34. His old car _____ down on the highway. (past tense of *break*)

35. The crowd of people _____ past us. (past tense of *run*)

36. Mom _____ about the boys. (present tense of *worry*)

37. My quarter _____ in the parking meter. (past tense of *jam*)

38. The conductor _____ us the right stop. (future tense of *tell*)

39. Grandma _____ me how to knit. (past tense of *teach*)

40. The batter _____ a swing at the ball. (past tense of *take*)

Copyright © by Glencoe/McGraw-Hill

Lesson 38
Perfect Tenses: Present, Past, and Future

Grammar

The **present perfect tense** is used either to express an action that took place at some indefinite time in the past or to express an action that began in the past and continues in the present. The present perfect tense is formed with the past participle of the verb and the helping verb *has* or *have.* This tense often includes adverb phrases.

She **has told** the teacher about her absence.
I **have given** you all my class notes.

The **past perfect tense** is used to show that one action in the past began and ended before another action in the past started. The past perfect tense is formed with the past participle of the verb and the helping verb *had.*

They **had left** the house by the time I arrived.

The **future perfect tense** is used to show that one action or condition in the future will begin and end before another event in the future starts. The future perfect tense is formed with the past participle of the verb and the helping verbs *will have.*

By the time we get there, the movie **will have started**.

▶ **Exercise 1** Draw two lines under each perfect-tense verb. Write whether the tense of the verb is *present perfect, past perfect,* or *future perfect.*

____present perfect____ Alison has never been to the Pacific Northwest.

_____ 1. Have you decided whether to take French next term?

_____ 2. By this time next year the child will have grown six inches.

_____ 3. They didn't go to the movie because they had already seen it.

_____ 4. Have you had trouble with the car before?

_____ 5. Before we spoke I didn't know there had been an accident.

_____ 6. I have tried to explain the problem many times.

_____ 7. My family has hunted in these woods for generations.

_____ 8. After tonight I will have heard the concert six times.

_____ 9. They were tired because the work had been especially hard.

_____ 10. Has Mr. O'Reilly graded our papers yet?

_____ 11. Digna has lived in this country for three years.

_____ 12. She had already demanded a raise from her boss.

_____ 13. I wanted to dance with her, but Bill had already asked her.

Copyright © by Glencoe/McGraw-Hill

_____ **14.** Ruth has voted for him before, but she won't again.

_____ **15.** The coaches have stressed that the players should be careful.

_____ **16.** The climbers had hoped to get to the top.

_____ **17.** We had waited a long time before we gave up and left.

_____ **18.** After this one I will have filled out ten applications.

_____ **19.** By the end of the day we will have picked a bushel of apples.

_____ **20.** They have played darts together many times.

_____ **21.** By next week they will have traveled a thousand miles.

_____ **22.** Mrs. Jones has requested us not to shout.

_____ **23.** The wind had never blown so fiercely.

_____ **24.** The pitcher has thrown the ball too hard.

_____ **25.** Julio will have invited Jessica to the party by now.

_____ **26.** By six o'clock Henry had showered and shaved.

_____ **27.** The students have decorated the gym with streamers.

_____ **28.** Akimi has wanted a car for a long time.

_____ **29.** Nayyer had worked as a waiter before.

_____ **30.** The car has had many flat tires.

_____ **31.** We have lived in this apartment for years.

_____ **32.** By the end of July, I will have mowed the lawn six times.

_____ **33.** Has the space shuttle landed yet?

_____ **34.** It was too late—the spy had discovered the secret.

_____ **35.** Scientists have uncovered many riddles of the universe.

_____ **36.** Has the caterer arrived with the refreshments?

_____ **37.** The bride has postponed the wedding.

_____ **38.** The ceremony had started before the superintendent got there.

_____ **39.** I am sure that when the buzzer sounds, Hobbes will have scored at least ten points.

_____ **40.** The police have asked us not to gather on the corner.

Copyright © by Glencoe/McGraw-Hill

Lesson 39
Tenses of Verbs

The **present tense** expresses an action that is repeated, always true, or happening right now.

I often **buy** muffins at this bakery.

The **past tense** expresses an action that has already occurred.

I **tossed** the ball in the air and **hit** it hard.

The **future tense** expresses an action that will take place in the future.

Sharon **will subtract** the numbers.

The **present perfect tense** expresses an action that took place at some time in the past or an action that began in the past and is still continuing.

Jake **has gathered** the flowers.

The **past perfect tense** shows that one action in the past began and ended before another action started.

He **had** already **come** inside by the time it started to rain.

The **future perfect tense** shows that an action in the future will begin and end before another action begins.

I **will have finished** my exam by the time yours begins.

▶ **Exercise 1** Draw two lines under each verb. Write in the blank the tense of the verb.

__past__   Dr. Della Chiesa told us a strange story yesterday.

_____ 1. There is an island in the Pacific called Guam.

_____ 2. As an animal specialist, he visits the island often.

_____ 3. By the 1960s, game wardens on Guam had noticed a decrease in the bird population.

_____ 4. However, no one found any bodies of dead birds.

_____ 5. By the 1980s, some species of birds had almost disappeared.

_____ 6. What had endangered so many birds to the point of extinction?

_____ 7. After much study, Julie Savidge, a biologist, reached some conclusions.

_____ 8. She ruled out disease and loss of habitat as the culprits.

_____ 9. Then she discovered a relationship between the disappearance of birds and the increase of brown tree snakes.

Copyright © by Glencoe/McGraw-Hill

Grammar

_____ **10.** Was there a connection between the two events?

_____ **11.** The brown tree snake is not native to Guam.

_____ **12.** It had probably sneaked onto the island on a plane or a boat.

_____ **13.** Dr. Savidge often discovered eggs and feathers in the snakes' stomachs.

_____ **14.** Further, the snake had proved its ferocity by its attacks on babies.

_____ **15.** Dr. Savidge concluded that the snake was responsible for the disappearance of the birds.

_____ **16.** It was hard to convince other scientists of the truth of her findings, but finally they agreed.

_____ **17.** Today biologists work to reestablish endangered bird populations on Guam.

_____ **18.** In the meantime, several brown tree snakes, hidden in air freight, have reached Hawaii.

_____ **19.** Fortunately, people captured them before they escaped into the forests.

_____ **20.** By the end of this century, many tropical birds will have disappeared due to the brown tree snake.

▶ **Exercise 2** **Write in the blank the tense of the verb indicated in parentheses.**

we ___will have ridden___ (future perfect of *ride*)

1. it _____ (present of *explode*)

2. I _____ (future perfect of *fight*)

3. they _____ (past perfect of *enjoy*)

4. he _____ (future of *choose*)

5. you _____ (future perfect of *fly*)

6. it _____ (past perfect of *break*)

7. they _____ (present of *write*)

8. I _____ (future perfect of *see*)

9. they _____ (past perfect of *throw*)

10. it _____ (future perfect of *spin*)

11. I _____ (past of *be*)

12. we _____ (future of *tune*)

Copyright © by Glencoe/McGraw-Hill

Lesson 40
Verbs: Progressive and Emphatic Forms

The **progressive form** of a verb expresses an action that is continuing at the time referred to in the sentence. The progressive form uses the present participle of the verb with the appropriate tense of the verb *be*.

Present Progressive:	They **are joking**.
Past Progressive:	They **were joking**.
Future Progressive:	They **will be joking**.
Present Perfect Progressive:	They **have been joking**.
Past Perfect Progressive:	They **had been joking**.
Future Perfect Progressive:	They **will have been joking**.

▶ **Exercise 1** **Complete each sentence by writing in the blank the verb form indicated in parentheses.**

I _____ am leaving _____ tomorrow, so I'll say good-bye now. (present progressive of *leave*)

1. They _____ at the meeting. (future progressive of *speak*)

2. By Tuesday they _____ for three weeks. (future perfect progressive of *travel*)

3. The horse _____ over the fence. (present progressive of *jump*)

4. The chorus _____ tonight. (future progressive of *sing*)

5. She _____ for his address. (past perfect progressive of *ask*)

6. They _____ when the phone rang. (past progressive of *eat*)

7. We _____ next. (future progressive of *perform*)

8. The dog _____ all day. (present perfect progressive of *sleep*)

9. Soon he _____ on his novel for six years. (future perfect progressive of *work*)

10. While you _____, we were swimming. (past progressive of *hike*)

11. I _____ as fast as I can. (present progressive of *run*)

12. Jaime _____ here on his way through town. (future progressive of *stop*)

13. Anita _____ when the phone rang. (past perfect progressive of *nap*)

14. They _____ very generous to us. (present progressive of *be*)

15. They _____ each other often. (present perfect progressive of *visit*)

16. Before their argument they _____. (past perfect progressive of *date*)

17. In June they _____ for a year. (future perfect progressive of *redecorate*)

18. The kids _____ into the pool. (past progressive of *dive*)

Copyright © by Glencoe/McGraw-Hill

19. _____ you _____ in the contest? (present progressive of *compete*)

20. I _____ my homework before Sunday night. (future progressive of *finish*)

The **emphatic form** adds emphasis to the verb. The emphatic form uses the base form of the verb with *do*, *does*, or *did*.

Present Emphatic: I **do need** a new dress.
                           Rhonda **does buy** a lot of new clothes.
Past Emphatic: You **did spend** too much on those shoes.

► **Exercise 2** **Complete each sentence by writing the correct emphatic form of the verb in parentheses.**

I _____*did turn*_____ my homework in on time yesterday. (*turn*)

1. No matter what you say, I _____ how to boil water. (*know*)

2. Sheila _____ instructions; the instructions were wrong. (*follow*)

3. I _____ the dishes last night. (*wash*)

4. Before you forget, _____ your grandmother for the check. (*thank*)

5. Whatever else he lacks, Carl _____ good manners. (*have*)

6. Allen _____ he gets the job. (*hope*)

7. I _____ glasses; I can not see well. (*need*)

8. Antoine _____ her your message before he left. (*give*)

9. Jess _____ a good job on the garden last spring. (*do*)

10. Sally _____ to go with us, but her dad says she can't. (*want*)

11. It's hard to believe, but he _____ that poem. (*write*)

12. Billy _____ to her; she just didn't hear him. (*speak*)

13. He _____ her, but he doesn't know how to tell her. (*like*)

14. I _____ you're a good cook; I'm just not hungry. (*think*)

15. Akira _____ for the test, but it was very difficult. (*study*)

16. If you go to the store, _____ me a *Sports Illustrated*. (*get*)

17. Oh, _____ him before he finds out from someone else. (*tell*)

18. It took a lot of courage, but she _____ from the high board. (*dive*)

19. It didn't show much, but John _____ himself at the party. (*enjoy*)

20. I'd love a cake, and _____ it chocolate. (*make*)

Copyright © by Glencoe/McGraw-Hill

Lesson 41
Verbs: Compatibility of Tenses

When two or more events take place at the same time in a sentence, the verb tenses must be the same.

Incorrect: When Holly **applied** for the job, she **gives** several references.
Correct: When Holly **applied** for the job, she **gave** several references.

Sometimes one event occurs before or after another event in a sentence. In these cases it is appropriate to shift tenses.

Incorrect: By the time Cindy **arrived,** Jason left.
Correct: By the time Cindy **arrived,** Jason **had left.**

Here the tense shifts from past (*arrived*) to past perfect (*had left*) to show that Jason left before Cindy arrived.

▶ **Exercise 1** **Complete each sentence with the correct tense of the verb in parentheses.**

We stopped by your apartment, but you _____ were _____ not home. (*be*)

1. We planned a picnic, but the rain _____ us to postpone it. (*force*)

2. Orlando will walk the dog just before he _____. (*leave*)

3. Winter's snows have melted, and spring _____ on the way. (*be*)

4. No one knows how much the candidate _____ on her election. (*spend*)

5. If you study hard, I'm sure you _____ the test. (*pass*)

6. Diana lent me this dress, and I _____ to be careful with it. (*promise*)

7. By the end of the trial, the suspect _____ his name. (*clear*)

8. Anita drove her little brother to the dentist's office and _____ for him. (*wait*)

9. Alicia tried out for the part, but Sandra _____ it. (*get*)

10. I knew you wanted that book, so I _____ it for you. (*buy*)

11. Because you don't understand Spanish, I _____ for you. (*translate*)

12. Anthony found some arrowheads when he _____ in the field. (*dig*)

13. I didn't know you _____ her to the prom. (*invite*)

14. Our class had decided that we _____ to put on a rock opera. (*want*)

15. By day's end the farmer _____ almost all of his land. (*plow*)

16. Helena spoke calmly, but her eyes _____ her anger. (*reveal*)

Copyright © by Glencoe/McGraw-Hill

Grammar

17. If you look closely you _____ the nucleus of the amoeba. (*see*)

18. The Coast Guard went to the rescue, but the boat _____ already. (*sink*)

19. She asked him to be careful with the key, but he _____ it. (*lose*)

20. Did you say that you spoke to him before he _____ school? (*leave*)

▶ **Exercise 2** **Draw two lines under each verb or verb phrase. The second verb or verb phrase in each sentence is incorrect. In the blank, write the correct tense of the second verb or verb phrase.**

Lenny <u>loved</u> baseball, so he <u>had decided</u> to read about it.   **decided**

1. Many people believe that television had displayed too much violence.   _____

2. Lenny hoped to join a team, and he wants it to be the Oilers.   _____

3. When we entered the theater, the usher had shown us to our seats.   _____

4. Cricket is a game that used innings and umpires.   _____

5. While Juan peeled the potatoes, Luba shells the peas.   _____

6. I read in a book that Lewis and Clark try to teach the Nez Percé "the game of base."   _____

7. If the weather is mild, the school held the graduation ceremony outside.   _____

8. As the ice thawed, a puddle of water has formed.   _____

9. The Knicks' first official game was with the New York Baseball Club; they will lose.   _____

10. My dad made spaghetti sauce and had asked me to try it.   _____

11. Lou Gehrig was a fine player; he hits four home runs in one game.   _____

12. Satchel Paige was a porter before he becomes a great pitcher.   _____

13. My grandma always sits in her favorite chair when she did her knitting.   _____

14. Frisky ran out the door and howls at the moon.   _____

15. Ted Williams played for the Red Sox; he is one of their best players.   _____

16. Many people collect baseball cards because it was a lot of fun.   _____

17. By the time I finished my homework, my favorite show ended.   _____

18. Whenever Luisa goes camping, she borrowed a sleeping bag from Mitch.   _____

19. Panda bears sleep a lot because it was hard work eating bamboo for fourteen hours a day!   _____

20. I feel like playing baseball; where was my mitt?   _____

Copyright © by Glencoe/McGraw-Hill

Lesson 42
Voice of Verbs

Action verbs can be used in two ways—in the active voice and in the passive voice. A sentence has a verb in the **active voice** if the subject performs the action. A sentence has a verb in the **passive voice** if the action is performed on the subject. The passive voice is formed by using the past participle of the verb with a form of the verb *be*.

Angelina **drove** the pickup. (active voice)
The pickup **was driven** by Angelina. (passive voice)

The passive voice can give variety to your writing. In general, however, the active voice is more interesting, more direct, and makes for livelier writing.

▶ **Exercise 1** Draw two lines under each verb or verb phrase. Write *A* above the verb if it is active and *P* if it is passive.

                    P   A
We <u>were amazed</u> when Bella <u>played</u> the solo.

1. Ben dropped the ball, and the other team picked it up.

2. Stella is liked by the whole class.

3. My dog bit the mail carrier, who was treated at the urgent care center.

4. Audrey ate a piece of cake and was given another.

5. Krista wrote this postcard, but it wasn't mailed until yesterday.

6. The drums were played by Stan.

7. The cake for the party will be baked by Harry's dad.

8. Andy milked the cows, and Sue gathered the eggs.

9. First prize was won by Trudy, and Jamal won second prize.

10. The scientist split the atom.

11. Captain Kidd buried the treasure, and no one could find it.

12. Ethiopia was ruled by Haile Selassie.

13. Mozart wrote many wonderful sonatas.

14. Carmen painted a portrait of her aunt, and it was given to her uncle.

Copyright © by Glencoe/McGraw-Hill

15. Captain Morse will fly the plane to Iceland.

16. Carlos dropped the spaghetti, so our dog ate it.

17. Dr. Washington gave the lecture, but few were listening.

18. The carpenters built the house, and it was finished ahead of schedule.

19. The sled was pulled by horses.

20. The project will be created by a team of students.

▶ **Exercise 2** Write *A* above the verb if it is in the active voice and *P* if it is in the passive voice. Then rewrite each active-voice sentence in the passive voice and each passive-voice sentence in the active voice.

　　　　　　　　　　　　　　　　　　P
The washing machine was fixed by the repair person. ___The repair person fixed the washing machine.___

1. A beachcomber found a gold coin. _____

2. The paper was typed by Felicia. _____

3. Abby will drive the tractor. _____

4. The problem was solved by Andre. _____

5. The scarf was knitted by my mom. _____

6. Dr. DiFalco examined the cat. _____

7. The operator placed the call. _____

8. My horse will win the race. _____

9. Cinderella will sweep the hearth. _____

10. The pennant was won by the Red Sox. _____

11. The plumber fixed the leaky faucet. _____

12. The baby spilled the oatmeal. _____

Copyright © by Glencoe/McGraw-Hill

Lesson 43
Mood of Verbs

Verbs express one of three moods—the indicative mood, the imperative mood, or the subjunctive mood.

The indicative mood makes a statement or asks a question. This is the mood most frequently used.

She **picks** up the flute and **plays** it.

The imperative mood expresses a command or makes a request.

Pick up the flute and **play** it.

In formal English the subjunctive mood is used to express indirectly a demand, recommendation, suggestion, or statement of necessity. In this case, the subjunctive uses the imperative form of the verb.

We demand [*or* recommend *or* suggest] that he **leave** town.
It is essential that the law **be** changed.

The subjunctive mood also states a condition or a wish that is contrary to fact. This use of the subjunctive always requires a past form and often follows the word *if.* The subjunctive mood uses *were,* not *was.*

If she **were** engaged, she would have told me.
I wish I **were** an astronaut.

▶ **Exercise 1 Write *ind.* in the blank if the verb in italics is indicative, *imp.* if it is imperative, or *subj.* if it is subjunctive.**

___imp___   Please *be* careful with the car.

_____ **1.** Robin wishes that she *could* fly a plane.

_____ **2.** Lincoln *spoke* eloquently at Gettysburg.

_____ **3.** My father asked that I *explain* where I had been.

_____ **4.** I *am writing* a paper about the U.S. justice system.

_____ **5.** Next, *fry* the onions and garlic in olive oil.

_____ **6.** Is it necessary that I *be* here tomorrow morning?

_____ **7.** He *is leaving* tomorrow at ten o'clock.

_____ **8.** Please *explain* the problem to Kim.

_____ **9.** He treats her as if she *were* a child.

_____ **10.** We *spent* a wonderful day climbing Mt. Washington.

Copyright © by Glencoe/McGraw-Hill

_____ **11.** *Describe* the accident as accurately as you can.

_____ **12.** If I *were* his mother, I would not give him the car keys.

_____ **13.** I wish I *knew* half as much about cars as you do.

_____ **14.** *Eat* up; there's much more.

_____ **15.** Who *will volunteer* to be on the public relations committee?

_____ **16.** Jerold *stormed* angrily out of the room.

_____ **17.** If I *had graduated* last spring, I would have applied for the job.

_____ **18.** *Try* to get here before the storm starts.

_____ **19.** *Invite* them to the party if you want to.

_____ **20.** *Did* Sami *finish* writing his term paper?

▶ **Exercise 2 Complete each sentence with the indicative, imperative, or subjunctive form of the verb in parentheses.**

   If I _____were_____ you, I would study for the test. (*be*)

1. He usually _____ a long time at the store. (*take*)

2. Rob wishes that he _____ play the drums. (*can*)

3. Sheila _____ to learn to play the flute. (*want*)

4. The blue dress _____ much too expensive. (*be*)

5. If he _____ the movie, he would say so. (*like*)

6. Please _____ your room before Saturday. (*clean*)

7. Is it necessary that he _____ so fast? (*drive*)

8. I wish I _____ going to Boston with you. (*be*)

9. It is essential that your parents _____ here. (*be*)

10. I recommend that she _____ this book. (*read*)

11. If I _____ glasses, I would get them. (*need*)

12. The doctor recommends that she _____ eight hours of sleep. (*get*)

13. It's essential that the water _____ to a full boil. (*come*)

14. After all, it's not as if she _____ an expert. (*be*)

15. If I _____ as badly as he does, I'd never open my mouth. (*sing*)

16. The club demanded that the chairperson _____. (*resign*)

Copyright © by Glencoe/McGraw-Hill

☑ Unit 6 **Review**

▶ **Complete each sentence by writing the tense, mood, or voice of the verb in parentheses.**

I ___have asked___ her several times to go out with me. (present perfect tense of *ask*)

1. Jill _____ her car this morning. (past tense of *wash*)

2. The hiking club _____ Mt. Washington. (present participle of *climb*)

3. Jake _____ forward to seeing you. (present tense of *look*)

4. Yesterday Diana _____ in the marathon. (past tense of *run*)

5. Until now I _____ he would win. (past tense of *think*)

6. Jim _____ with his friends. (present perfect tense of *go*)

7. You _____ to him after class. (past progressive tense of *speak*)

8. George _____ to Greece with his family. (future tense of *travel*)

9. He _____ us to help him with his project. (past tense of *beg*)

10. The movie _____ in one minute. (present tense of *begin*)

11. They _____ for the concert. (present perfect tense of *leave*)

12. I didn't know whether you _____ milk. (past perfect tense of *buy*)

13. By then you _____ my letter. (future perfect tense of *get*)

14. They _____ here. (present progressive tense of *eat*)

15. By noon they _____ for two hours. (future perfect progressive tense of *study*)

16. Eduardo _____ permission. (past emphatic form of *ask*)

17. I wish he _____ here now. (subjunctive mood of *be*)

18. The poem _____ by Alonzo. (future tense, passive voice of *read*)

19. Esther _____ by a spider. (past tense, passive voice of *bite*)

20. It is essential that you _____ here. (subjunctive mood of *be*)

Copyright © by Glencoe/McGraw-Hill

Grammar

Cumulative Review: Units 1–6

▶ **Exercise 1** Draw one line under each adjective and two lines under each adverb. Draw an arrow from the adjective or adverb to the word it modifies. Ignore the articles *a, an,* and *the.*

We often listen attentively to the guest speaker.

1. Diego almost always walks to school.

2. Most cats wash themselves very gracefully.

3. Today Jenny will enter a singing contest at the nearby school.

4. Ruth works hard in the new vegetable garden.

5. The friendly team, as they drove south, waved enthusiastically to the home crowd.

6. This morning, I burned my hand on the piping hot pan.

7. Go away and let me read this French book alone.

8. Those are the most unusual three stamps I ever have seen!

9. I will leave you and Amy here until you are ready to behave properly.

10. Yesterday, various small birds were singing near the cherry tree.

11. Often, if I know a test will be hard, I study longer than I usually do.

12. Almost every piece of stereo equipment was on sale at the Jefferson mall near the ball field.

13. Come here so we can sit closer to the stage and see the actors better.

14. I will not wear that dress to the junior prom!

15. My family ate less yesterday because we had less food.

16. She never felt so bad as when she did badly on the job interview.

▶ **Exercise 2** Draw one line under each subject complement, and write *pred. nom.* (predicate nominative) or *pred. adj.* (predicate adjective) in the blank. Circle each object complement, and write *noun, pronoun,* or *adjective* in the blank.

pred. adj., noun   Sandy is allergic to fur, so she called her cat Taboo.

_____ 1. The soloist seemed nervous during the first act.

Copyright © by Glencoe/McGraw-Hill

_____ 2. I find playing on a team good experience.

_____ 3. Cole considers my guitar his.

_____ 4. The homemade spaghetti tasted delicious.

_____ 5. Sumi is the captain of the field hockey team.

_____ 6. The student council elected Raul president.

_____ 7. The cinnamon made the bread wonderful.

_____ 8. The English teacher called Sholeh's creative project extraordinary.

_____ 9. Mrs. Jabar was the director of the school play.

_____ 10. The Bastille in Paris became the symbol of tyranny during the French Revolution.

_____ 11. Fireworks are very dangerous to play with.

_____ 12. Mr. Kleiber is my guidance counselor.

_____ 13. I call the jacket mine even though it is really my dad's.

_____ 14. The movie plot sounds intriguing!

_____ 15. The bad weather made her trip miserable.

_____ 16. Why do you look so cheerful today?

_____ 17. I thought the man a phony until I saw his badge.

_____ 18. The language dolphins use to communicate remains a mystery to scientists.

_____ 19. Recycling is extremely important to the environment.

_____ 20. The continuous rainfall rendered irrigation unnecessary.

▶ **Exercise 3** **Draw one line under each prepositional phrase and two lines under each participial phrase. Circle each gerund phrase. Identify the sentence by writing *simple, compound, complex,* or *compound-complex* in the blank.**

____compound____ I kept admiring the car at the dealership, but needing money, I didn't buy it.

_____ 1. Most members of the junior class and a few members of the senior class got together and made plans for the upcoming junior-senior prom.

_____ 2. Tina enjoys participating in extra-curricular clubs, but they involve a major time commitment.

_____ 3. We go to our exercise class when we get home from school.

Copyright © by Glencoe/McGraw-Hill

Grammar

_____ **4.** Anticipating the bell, I finished my homework and packed my book bag.

_____ **5.** Consumers must be wary about the commercials on television.

_____ **6.** Swimming at our school has become very popular since our school got a new pool.

_____ **7.** Here is the sports section that you left in the living room.

_____ **8.** Moisha, feeling feverish and exhausted, tried to take a nap, but she was awakened by the doorbell.

_____ **9.** The word processor that we bought in New York is broken, and we don't know how it happened.

_____ **10.** Repairing things is not my dad's strength although he does like to try.

_____ **11.** Pancakes with lots of syrup and butter make eating breakfast a pleasure.

_____ **12.** When the loggers from town had finished, what had once been a dense forest thriving beautifully was now an arid wasteland.

_____ **13.** The science teacher could identify nine different species of ants in the corner of his backyard.

_____ **14.** My sister, who is a sophomore in college, is coming home for spring break, and my parents and I are meeting her at the airport.

_____ **15.** Singing and playing the guitar are my favorite hobbies, but I also enjoy collecting shells at the beach.

_____ **16.** In *Oliver Twist* by Charles Dickens, Oliver asks for more gruel.

_____ **17.** Walking to school every day gives me time to organize my day.

_____ **18.** The man who wrote this letter to the editor is obviously dissatisfied with the new waste-water treatment plant.

Copyright © by Glencoe/McGraw-Hill

Unit 7: Subject-Verb Agreement

Lesson 44
Subject-Verb Agreement

A verb must agree with its subject in person and number. In the present tense, add -s or -es to the base form for the third-person singular.

SINGULAR
She **jumps.**
He **watches.**

PLURAL
They **jump.**
They **watch.**

In verb phrases, the helping verbs *be, have,* and *do* change form to agree with third-person subjects.

SINGULAR
It **is** green.
He **was** sick.
She **is skiing.**
He **has fallen** down.
Does she **like** to ski?

PLURAL
They **are** green.
They **were** sick.
They **are skiing.**
They **have fallen** down.
Do they **like** to ski?

▶ **Exercise 1 Underline the verb in parentheses that agrees with the subject.**

Many people (is, <u>are</u>) disgusted by insects.

1. However, understanding insects (helps, help) people enjoy them.

2. For example, the cricket (is, are) a fascinating creature.

3. Everyone (has heard, have heard) the cricket's song.

4. The cricket's musical organs (is, are) on the base of its wings.

5. Scientists (calls, call) them stridulating organs.

6. *Stridulate* (comes, come) from a Latin word meaning "to creak."

7. Crickets (sings, sing) by scraping their wings together.

8. Most insect musicians (is, are) males.

9. Scientists (assumes, assume) that they sing to attract females.

10. (Does, Do) you know that cockroaches have probably been on this planet longer than human beings?

11. Surely this (means, mean) that the insect has extraordinary powers of survival.

12. The roach (was not designed, were not designed) to live indoors.

Copyright © by Glencoe/McGraw-Hill

13. However, its instincts (helps, help) it to adapt to indoor living.

14. Also, its flattened shape (aids, aid) in its success as a household pest.

▶ **Exercise 2** **Choose the verb in parentheses that agrees with the subject. Write your choice in the blank.**

Many horror movies _____deal_____ with giant insects. (deals, deal)

1. The movie *Them* _____ a story about giant ants. (tells, tell)

2. Supposedly, the ants' gigantism _____ by nuclear radiation. (was caused, were caused)

3. An entire army _____ to wipe out the ants. (was needed, were needed)

4. Thousands _____ fighting the monstrous creatures. (was killed, were killed)

5. People _____ fascinated by stories of strange and impossible events. (seems, seem)

6. Maybe these stories _____ us face fears that are more real. (helps, help)

7. Most children _____ to the fear caused by looking at photographs of alarming insects. (thrills, thrill)

8. I _____ forcing myself to look at such photographs in magazines. (remembers, remember)

9. Strangely enough, being frightened _____ fun. (was, were)

10. Of course, an insect's picture _____ not the same as the real thing. (is, are)

11. Nevertheless, perhaps these exercises _____ our ability to face truly frightening events. (strengthens, strengthen)

12. What _____ horror movies' present popularity reveal about our need to cope with a variety of frightening circumstances? (does, do)

13. We _____ by terrorism and strange diseases. (is threatened, are threatened)

14. Environmental changes _____ havoc in some areas of the world. (is wreaking, are wreaking)

15. Natural catastrophes _____ suffering and damage. (causes, cause)

16. Maybe scary movies _____ us to cope better with these events. (enables, enable)

17. Old horror movies _____ so clumsily made that you could see the zippers in the monsters' costumes. (was, were)

18. Today's movie monsters _____ more lifelike. (seems, seem)

19. _____ you have a favorite horror movie? (does, do)

20. If you _____ you don't have one, I will be very surprised. (says, say)

Copyright © by Glencoe/McGraw-Hill

Lesson 45
Intervening Prepositional Phrases

The verb must agree with the subject of the sentence, not with the object of a preposition. Thus, the subject of a sentence is never contained in a prepositional phrase.

The **collection** of rare stamps **was** very valuable. (The subject is *collection,* a singular noun. *Of rare stamps* is a prepositional phrase with a plural object. The verb *was* agrees with the singular subject *collection.*)

The **puppies** in the basket **have** brown fur. (The subject is *puppies,* a plural noun. *In the basket* is a prepositional phrase with a singular object. The verb *have* agrees with the plural subject *puppies.*)

▶ **Exercise 1** **Underline the verb in parentheses that agrees with the subject.**

The bouquet of flowers (<u>is</u>, are) for Amanda.

1. Apartments in this city (is required, are required) to have smoke alarms.

2. A convoy of trucks (is roaring, are roaring) down the highway.

3. This list of names (is, are) very important.

4. A dealer in rare books (was asked, were asked) to look at the collection.

5. All the students in the school (is wearing, are wearing) green today.

6. The bush of roses in full bloom (was, were) a beautiful sight.

7. Spies for our government (was arrested, were arrested) in France.

8. The members of the Senate committee (walks, walk) solemnly into the room.

9. Applicants for this job (is expected, are expected) to speak both English and Spanish.

10. A busload of tourists (was taking, were taking) photographs.

11. The view of the mountains (was spoiled, were spoiled) by the building.

12. That group of stars (is called, are called) the Big Dipper.

13. Some explorers of the New World (was looking, were looking) for the Fountain of Youth.

14. The musicians in the orchestra (is taking, are taking) their seats.

15. The bag of marbles (belongs, belong) to my little sister.

16. A box of warm coats (was delivered, were delivered) to the shelter.

17. The green areas on the map (indicates, indicate) parks.

18. Many secrets of the universe (has, have) yet to be discovered.

19. Life forms beneath the sea (seems, seem) mysterious.

Copyright © by Glencoe/McGraw-Hill

20. The grove of birch trees (is shining, are shining) in the sun.

21. The pot of flowers (looks, look) lovely on the table.

22. Sounds of distant music (floats, float) through the air.

23. Students who major in computer science (has, have) good prospects for employment.

24. Any traveler in distant lands (has, have) to keep an open mind.

25. Employees at Grump's Department Store (gets, get) a half-hour for lunch.

26. The leaves on the maple tree (is turning, are turning) bright red.

27. Cars driving through the tunnel (turns, turn) their lights on.

28. The houses along Pine Street (has, have) tidy yards.

29. Mr. Alonzo, the baker of these pastries, (does, do) fine work.

30. The sailors on the ship (rejoices, rejoice) at seeing land.

31. The apples beneath the tree (bakes, bake) well in pies.

32. Several teaspoons of cinnamon (was added, were added) to the mix.

33. The socks under the bed (was found, were found) by the puppy.

34. Shouts from the crowd (is frightening, are frightening) the baby.

35. People on the beach (was building, were building) sand castles.

36. Teams from our school (dominates, dominate) most athletic events.

37. Rising mists from the moor (casts, cast) an aura of mystery over the scene.

38. Her frequent changes of residence (is confusing, are confusing) the post office.

39. Survivors of the war (is marching, are marching) in the parade.

40. A shipment of cookies (is arriving, are arriving) at the grocery store.

▶ **Writing Link** **Write sentences that contain the following intervening prepositional phrases:** *of these video games, with the tractor, under the car's massive engine,* **and** *at the ballet.*

_____

_____

_____

_____

_____

_____

Copyright © by Glencoe/McGraw-Hill

Lesson 46
Agreement with Linking Verbs

In sentences with linking verbs, the verb agrees with the subject, not the predicate nominative.

Roses and lavender make a lovely bouquet. (The verb *make* agrees with the subjects, *roses and lavender,* not the predicate nominative, *bouquet.*)

Unfortunately, the **result** of the discussion **was** more disagreements. (The verb *was* agrees with the subject, *result,* not the predicate nominative, *disagreements.*)

▶ **Exercise 1** Underline the verb in parentheses that agrees with the subject.

Highways 101 and 101A (is, <u>are</u>) the most direct route to the airport.

1. Branches from pine trees (makes, make) a good shelter for a garden.

2. The accidents (was, were) a tragedy.

3. The robins' nest (is, are) a mass of twigs.

4. The children (seems, seem) the image of their father.

5. The bird's bright wings (was, were) a beautiful sight.

6. Eyes (appears, appear) as a symbol in many artists' work.

7. Before our eyes the piles of lumber (is becoming, are becoming) a house.

8. The warm, sunny days (was, were) a great gift to the tomato plants.

9. The dancers' costumes (was, were) a symphony of color.

10. The students (is working, are working) together as a team.

11. Dishonest people (is, are) a disgrace to any profession.

12. Large numbers of books (forms, form) a library.

13. The ugly statues (was, were) a monument to bad taste.

14. The musicians in their tuxedos (was, were) a sight to behold.

15. The focus of a teacher's life (is, are) the students.

16. The lakes in this area (is, are) a haven for many tourists.

17. Their different backgrounds (was, were) a great gulf between them.

18. The smiling children (seems, seem) the picture of happiness.

19. The chorus's songs (was, were) a delight to the ears.

20. They say that the eyes (is, are) a window to the soul.

Copyright © by Glencoe/McGraw-Hill

▶ **Exercise 2** Draw one line under the simple subject. Draw two lines under the verb in parentheses that agrees with it.

The <u>whereabouts</u> of the necklace (remains, <u>remain</u>) a mystery.

1. Final exams (was, were) a disaster.

2. Peanut butter and bananas (makes, make) a great sandwich.

3. Those mountain peaks (is, are) a great challenge to a climber.

4. The participants (is keeping, are keeping) their comments to a minimum.

5. The thousands of dollars they spent (was, were) a terrible waste.

6. The search planes (is, are) the only hope for the stranded hikers.

7. The explosion (was caused, were caused) by sparks.

8. Stars on a dark night (is, are) a splendid sight.

9. The dress (is, are) several inches too short.

10. The children's closets (is, are) a mess.

11. Your furtive glances (has betrayed, have betrayed) your guilt.

12. Hot dogs and beans (was, were) my father's favorite meal.

13. His twin daughters (is, are) the apple of his eye.

14. The stock market (is posting, are posting) great gains today.

15. The comedian's jokes (was, were) a riot.

16. The test scores (represents, represent) the students' best effort.

17. The unfair trials (was, were) a travesty of justice.

18. The lights twinkling on the water (seems, seem) like stars in the sky.

19. Building wooden models of ships (is, are) my hobby.

20. Rude remarks from the children (continues, continue) to be a problem.

▶ **Writing Link** Write several sentences about your preference for indoor or outdoor activities. Check that the verb in each sentence agrees with the subject.

_____

_____

_____

_____

_____

_____

Copyright © by Glencoe/McGraw-Hill

Lesson 47
Agreement in Inverted Sentences

Grammar

In most sentences the subject comes before the verb. However, some inverted sentences begin with a prepositional phrase followed by the verb and then the subject. The verb in such sentences must always agree with the subject, not with the object of the prepositional phrase.

Up into the sky fly the birds.   **Up into the sky flies the bird.**

In sentences that begin with *here* or *there*, do not confuse either word with the subject. Look for the subject following the verb.

Here is my driver's license.   **There are many cars on this highway.**

Questions are inverted sentences. In such constructions, a helping verb often comes before the subject.

Does Jamie have a pencil?   **Do all the students have books?**

▶ **Exercise 1** Draw a line under the simple subject. Choose the verb or helping verb in parentheses that agrees with the subject and write it in the blank.

In her hand she _____carries_____ a stone. (carries, carry)

1. _____ the magician making scarves disappear? (is, are)

2. From the rafters _____ the decorations. (hangs, hang)

3. Up the staircase _____ the students. (surges, surge)

4. Into the arena _____ the elephant. (ambles, amble)

5. Onto his knees _____ the young man. (sinks, sink)

6. "Amanda, _____ you love me?" he asks. (does, do)

7. Around her neck _____ a golden chain. (hangs, hang)

8. On the clothesline _____ the clean sheets. (hang, hangs)

9. From her ears _____ sparkling earrings. (dangles, dangle)

10. Beneath the tree _____ the brown and white cows. (lies, lie)

11. Through the streets _____ the competitors. (runs, run)

12. From the crowd _____ an ear-splitting cheer. (comes, come)

13. Onto the horse's back _____ the rider. (bounds, bound)

14. Onto the floor _____ the spaghetti. (falls, fall)

15. Across the floor _____ the meatball. (rolls, roll)

Copyright © by Glencoe/McGraw-Hill

16. Here _____ the band down the street. (comes, come)

17. Into the glass _____ the magic potion. (falls, fall)

18. There _____ a bug on your shirt. (is, are)

19. Over the fences _____ the horse. (leaps, leap)

20. There _____ many ways to get to Des Moines. (is, are)

▶ **Exercise 2** **Write in the blank the form of the verb in parentheses that agrees with the subject.**

Here _____ *is* _____ the story the old woman told to me. (*to be*)

1. Every spring up _____ the announcements about the class rummage sale. (*to go*)

2. From every attic _____ junk. (*to descend*)

3. In front of Jason's house _____ five huge boxes. (*to sit*)

4. To the gym _____ carloads and carloads of stuff for the sale. (*to go*)

5. Out _____ the tables to hold the goods. (*to come*)

6. Through the gym _____ students and teachers to examine the sale items. (*to troop*)

7. Up to Jason's table _____ Ronda. (*to walk*)

8. Down _____ Ronda fifty cents for a can opener. (*to plunk*)

9. "There _____ several more can openers in this box," says Jason. (*to be*)

10. "_____ they work better than this one?" asks Ronda. (*to do*)

11. "There _____ not much demand for broken can openers," says Jason. (*to be*)

12. Behind a broken lamp _____ an old book. (*to sit*)

13. Inside the book _____ several photographs. (*to be*)

14. In one photograph _____ Jason's grandparents on their honeymoon. (*to be*)

15. On their faces _____ an expression of love and hope. (*to be*)

16. In their hearts _____ great hopes for the future. (*to reside*)

17. Before them _____ out their whole life together. (*to stretch*)

18. Through the book _____ a prospective buyer. (*to thumb*)

19. "There _____ some old photographs in this book," he says. (*to be*)

20. Across the street _____ a friendly philosopher with a unique perspective on life. (*to live*)

Copyright © by Glencoe/McGraw-Hill

Lesson 48
Agreement with Special Subjects

A **collective noun** names a group. In a sentence, a collective noun is singular when it names the group as a whole. It is plural when it refers to individual members of a group.

Singular:	The **club** holds a dance.	The **team** wins the game.
Plural:	The **class** volunteer time.	The **audience** cheer and clap.

Some nouns ending in *-s,* such as *mumps, measles,* and *mathematics,* take singular verbs. Other nouns ending in *-s,* such as *scissors, pants, binoculars,* and *eyeglasses,* take plural verbs. Many nouns that end in *-ics* are either singular or plural, depending on the context.

Singular: **Mumps** is usually a disease of childhood.
Plural: The **scissors** need to be sharpened.
Singular: **Ethics** is the study of principles of conduct.
Plural: That person's **ethics** leave a lot to be desired.

A noun of amount can refer to a single unit, in which case it is singular. It can also refer to several individual units, in which case it is plural.

Singular: Two **weeks** is not enough time to see Europe.
Plural: Your five **days** of probation are up.

▶ **Exercise 1** Underline the simple subject. Fill in the blank with the verb or helping verb in parentheses that agrees with the subject in the context of the sentence.

The <u>audience</u> _____*rises*_____ to applaud the soloist. (rises, rise)

1. Twenty-two dollars _____ too much to pay for a scarf. (is, are)

2. The band _____ practicing tonight. (is, are)

3. Most of us _____ voting for Geraldine. (is, are)

4. _____ mathematics your favorite subject? (is, are)

5. The scissors _____ sharpening. (needs, need)

6. Much of the garden _____ filled with roses. (was, were)

7. The group _____ on how to spend the money. (votes, vote)

8. The herd of deer _____ scattering. (is, are)

9. Three-quarters of the cake _____ been eaten. (has, have)

10. My family _____ vacationing together. (is, are)

11. The audience _____ fighting over the handkerchief. (was, were)

12. At what time _____ the news come on? (does, do)

Copyright © by Glencoe/McGraw-Hill

13. A computer company _____ offered to donate software. (has, have)

14. Chad's family _____ not agree on where to spend the holidays. (does, do)

15. The public _____ fascinated by the trial. (seems, seem)

16. The audience _____ moved by the actor's speech. (was, were)

17. There _____ 365 days in a year. (is, are)

18. Thirty-eight cents _____ on the table. (is, are)

19. Good binoculars _____ a lot of money. (costs, cost)

20. Checkers _____ Samantha's favorite board game. (is, are)

21. Social studies _____ us how different cultures live. (teaches, teach)

22. Our two weeks in Canada _____ flown by. (has, have)

23. Four years _____ the length of the president's term in office. (is, are)

24. The majority of the voters _____ to want a new highway. (seems, seem)

25. The chess team _____ organizing a dance. (is, are)

26. *Two Years before the Mast* _____ a fine novel. (is, are)

27. Two cups of raisins _____ plenty for the cake. (is, are)

28. The orchestra _____ wonderful tonight. (sounds, sound)

29. Her eyeglasses _____ broken. (is, are)

30. Two-thirds of the money _____ to Joel. (belongs, belong)

31. The band _____ not playing in time to the music. (was, were)

32. The litter of puppies _____ born on Tuesday. (was, were)

33. The PTA _____ holding a fund-raiser tonight. (is, are)

34. Gymnastics _____ a lot of flexibility. (requires, require)

35. The committee _____ arguing over the money. (is, are)

36. The Ski Club _____ for Sugarloaf on Saturday. (leaves, leave)

37. The labor union _____ on a president next week. (votes, vote)

38. Twenty dollars _____ a cheap price for the telescope. (seems, seem)

39. Ten miles _____ not too far to drive to work. (is, are)

40. Three-quarters of the exam _____ essay questions. (is, are)

Copyright © by Glencoe/McGraw-Hill

Lesson 49
Agreement with Compound Subjects

Some sentences have more than one subject. A **compound subject** that is joined by *and* or *both . . . and* is usually plural. However, some compound subjects have two parts that make up one unit. These take a singular verb.

Singular: **Bacon** and **eggs** is my favorite breakfast.
Plural: The **dog** and **cat** are playing.
Plural: Both **Anna** and **Mindy** work at the hospital.

Compound subjects joined by *or, nor, either . . . or,* or *neither . . . nor* always have a verb that agrees with the closer subject.

Singular: Either **Carlo** or **Max** has the book.
Singular: Neither **eggs** nor **bacon** is on the menu.
Plural: Neither the **garden** nor the **lilacs** are in bloom.

When a compound subject is preceded by *many a, every,* or *each,* the subject takes a singular verb.

Many a **hiker** and **climber** has gotten lost in these mountains.
Every **door** and **window** has been locked.
Each **nook** and **cranny** is being searched.

▶ **Exercise 1** **Draw a line under the compound subject. Choose the verb or helping verb in parentheses that agrees with the subject and write it in the blank.**

Every <u>hill</u> and <u>mountain</u> _____is_____ covered with snow. (is, are)

1. Each student and teacher _____ a name badge. (has, have)

2. Many a horse and rider _____ fallen on this jump. (has, have)

3. Hot dogs and beans _____ a popular meal in Boston. (is, are)

4. Both my mom and stepdad _____ coming to the concert. (is, are)

5. Neither Grace nor John _____ to go. (wants, want)

6. Either Meg or the twins _____ to meet you at the library. (plans, plan)

7. Neither the mirror nor the glasses _____ broken. (was, were)

8. Neither the horses nor the cow _____ been fed. (has, have)

9. The needle and thread _____ in the sewing box. (is, are)

10. Both my uncles and my aunt _____ called. (has, have)

11. Either a bird or a whistle _____ making that sound. (is, are)

12. Neither ice cream nor cookies _____ a low calorie snack. (is, are)

Copyright © by Glencoe/McGraw-Hill

Grammar

13. Many a tourist and traveler _____ visited our city. (has, have)

14. Every street, avenue, and boulevard _____ a new sign. (needs, need)

15. Each broken computer and printer _____ been fixed. (has, have)

16. My socks and sneakers _____ wet. (is, are)

17. Both fruit and vegetables _____ a healthy snack. (makes, make)

18. Fish and chips _____ popular in England. (is, are)

19. Either the robin or the blue jays _____ eating the seeds. (is, are)

20. Neither my brother nor my friends _____ been invited to the party. (has, have)

21. Either Jake or Alexis _____ a ride home. (needs, need)

22. Neither the donkey nor the horses _____. (bites, bite)

23. Both taxis and buses _____ on this corner. (stops, stop)

24. Neither Jack nor Beth _____ to talk on the phone. (likes, like)

25. Every car and truck _____ a toll on the highway. (pays, pay)

26. Each bush and flower _____ covered with dew. (is, are)

27. Neither frogs nor salamanders _____ in this pond. (lives, live)

28. Not every nurse and doctor _____ her or his job. (likes, like)

29. Soup and salad _____ a tasty lunch. (makes, make)

30. The matches and candle _____ on the desk. (is, are)

31. Both Andrea and Jaime _____ to day care. (goes, go)

32. Vitamins and minerals _____ strong bodies. (builds, build)

33. Neither Deb nor Sandy _____ late for work. (was, were)

34. Every newspaper and magazine _____ interesting stories. (contain, contains)

35. Every photograph and painting _____ damaged. (was, were)

36. In the movie, every criminal and bandit _____ the dust. (bites, bite)

37. Warm milk and toast _____ me to sleep. (puts, put)

38. Both Edwina and Fred _____ their mom's car. (drives, drive)

39. Neither Ed nor the boys _____ much to say. (has, have)

40. Many a horse and cow _____ lived in this barn. (has, have)

Copyright © by Glencoe/McGraw-Hill

Grammar

Lesson 50
Intervening Expressions

Certain expressions seem to create a compound subject, but do not. *Accompanied by, as well as, in addition to, plus,* and *together with* are expressions that introduce phrases that tell about the subject. However, the subject remains singular and takes a singular verb.

▶ **Exercise 1** **Draw a line under the subject. Then write the form of the verb in parentheses that agrees with the subject. Use the present tense of the verb.**

The brook, as well as the lake and the pond, _____freezes_____ in winter. (*freeze*)

1. Aspirin, besides a good night's sleep, _____ a headache. (*help*)

2. The dog, as well as the cat, _____ a good bath. (*need*)

3. Andy, accompanied by Jessie and Jill, _____ tomorrow. (*leave*)

4. Nebraska, as well as Montana and Idaho, _____ severe winters. (*get*)

5. Aileen, in addition to her brothers and sisters, _____ dark hair. (*have*)

6. A headache, accompanied by sniffles and sneezing, _____ a symptom of the flu. (*be*)

7. Toby, plus Andrea and Ali, _____ for the job today. (*interview*)

8. The violin, in addition to the guitar and the viola, _____ a stringed instrument. (*be*)

9. Gold, as well as iron and steel, _____ a lot. (*weigh*)

10. Fruit, accompanied by sugar and milk, _____ good. (*taste*)

11. Jenny, besides Pete and Terry, _____ the secret. (*know*)

12. Dan, plus Margaret and Fred, _____ the piano. (*play*)

13. The baby, besides her mom and dad, _____ happy. (*look*)

14. Sara, in addition to Gena, _____ at Grump's. (*shop*)

15. The bike, as well as the car, _____ a flat tire. (*have*)

16. The detective, as well as the police officer, _____ on the scene. (*arrive*)

17. My stepdad, together with my mom, _____ often. (*travel*)

18. The plant, along with the garden, _____ to be watered. (*need*)

19. Fur, in addition to feathers, _____ against cold. (*insulate*)

20. The knife, as well as the scissors, _____ very sharp. (*be*)

21. Jean, accompanied by her friends, _____ skiing every winter. (*go*)

Copyright © by Glencoe/McGraw-Hill

22. The carpenter, as well as the bricklayer, _____ special tools. (*use*)

23. Milk, besides meat and beans, _____ a source of protein. (*be*)

24. The television show, as well as the movie, _____ at eight o'clock. (*begin*)

25. Jodie, besides Kim, _____ high school. (*attend*)

26. The house, besides the barn, _____ a paint job. (*need*)

27. The tall woman, as well as the man beside her, _____ in the choir. (*sing*)

28. The group, accompanied by the teacher, _____ today. (*leave*)

29. Mr. Phillips, aided by his son, _____ tomatoes. (*raise*)

30. Krista, as well as her sisters, _____ frequently. (*telephone*)

31. The cave, along with the tree, _____ shelter. (*offer*)

32. The tulip, besides the daffodil, _____ in spring. (*bloom*)

33. My mother, as well as my sister, _____ her job. (*love*)

34. The movie star, accompanied by her hairdresser, _____ on the set. (*be*)

35. The cake, as well as the pie, _____ chocolate. (*contain*)

36. The door, as well as the window, _____. (*squeak*)

37. Math, besides English, _____ her favorite subject. (*be*)

38. Bette, together with Anthony, _____ in that pool. (*swim*)

39. The puppy, as well as the kitten, _____ soundly. (*sleep*)

40. The captain, accompanied by the sailors, _____ the ship. (*abandon*)

▶ **Writing Link** Write a paragraph about your favorite restaurant. Write at least four sentences that contain intervening expressions.

_____
_____
_____
_____
_____
_____
_____
_____
_____

Copyright © by Glencoe/McGraw-Hill

Lesson 51
Indefinite Pronouns as Subjects

Many subjects are indefinite pronouns. A verb must agree with an **indefinite pronoun** used as a subject.

Singular: **Nobody** in the group is to blame.
Singular: **Neither** is ready.
Singular: **One** of my friends speaks Greek.
Plural: **Both** of my sisters are in the play.
Plural: **Many** of the students play tennis.

Some pronouns can be either singular or plural, depending on the nouns to which they refer.

Singular: **Some** of the cake is gone.
Plural: **Some** of the houses need paint.

Indefinite pronouns fall into three groups:

Always Singular:	each	everyone	nobody	anything
	either	everybody	nothing	someone
	neither	everything	anyone	somebody
	one	no one	anybody	something
Always Plural:	several	few		both	many
Singular or Plural:	some	all	any	most, none

▶ **Exercise 1** Draw one line under the indefinite pronoun subject. Draw two lines under the correct form of the verb.

<u>Some</u> of the people of the Stone Age (was, <u>were</u>) hunters and gatherers.

1. Many of the ruins found (is, are) from the Stone Age.

2. Several of the ruins (is, are) in Ireland.

3. Many of the archaeologists (travels, travel) afar to study ruins.

4. Almost everyone (agrees, agree) that archaeology is fascinating.

5. Some of these ancient people (was, were) farmers.

6. One of the important questions (is, are) whether agriculture was imported from the Old World to the New World.

7. Some of the evidence (suggests, suggest) that American cotton came from Africa.

8. One of the archaeologists (believes, believe) that this happened without human intervention.

Copyright © by Glencoe/McGraw-Hill

9. Some of the ancient graves (contains, contain) mummified remains.

10. Many of the graves (reveals, reveal) wonderful art treasures.

11. Some of the treasures (consists, consist) of jewelry.

12. Many of the early tools discovered (was, were) very efficient.

13. Some of the early stone axes (is, are) still very sharp.

14. Almost nothing (is, are) known about ancient stone tombs.

15. One of the most intriguing puzzles (is, are) their construction.

16. Some of these tombs (was, were) erected in Scotland.

17. Nobody (knows, know) how these huge tombs were built.

18. Many of these archaeological mysteries (entices, entice) students.

▶ **Exercise 2 Draw one line under the indefinite pronoun subject. Draw two lines under the correct form of the verb.**

Each of the leads (was, were) eventually abandoned by the detective.

1. Few of my friends (has, have) been to Europe.

2. Not everyone (knows, know) that Elvis is dead.

3. (Is, Are) there anything good on television tonight?

4. Nobody (has, have) won the contest yet.

5. Neither of the twins (is, are) at home.

6. All of the coats (is, are) on sale.

7. A few of the members (has, have) called in sick.

8. Everything in the produce department (is, are) fresh.

9. Several of the apples (has, have) bruises.

10. Many of my relatives (is, are) coming to the family reunion.

11. Nothing (sleeps, sleep) as soundly as a cat.

12. Someone (was, were) knocking on the door.

13. One of the doctors (is, are) still in the office.

14. (Has, Have) anyone confessed to the crime?

15. Both of my pets (has, have) won ribbons.

16. Almost anybody (is, are) a better chess player than I am.

Copyright © by Glencoe/McGraw-Hill

Lesson 52
Agreement in Adjective Clauses

When the subject of an adjective clause is a relative pronoun, the verb in the clause must agree with the antecedent of the relative pronoun.

Carla is one of the students who speak Spanish.

In the preceding example the antecedent of *who* is *students,* not *one,* because other students besides Carla speak Spanish. Since *students* is plural, *who* is considered plural, and the verb in the adjective clause, *speak,* must also be plural.

Arlo is the only one of my brothers who has a scar.

In the preceding example the antecedent of *who* is *one,* not *brothers,* because only one brother has a scar. Since *one* is singular, *who* is considered singular, and the verb in the adjective clause, *has,* must also be singular.

▶ **Exercise 1 Draw one line under the antecedent of each relative pronoun. Draw two lines under the correct form of the verb.**

Jaime is the only <u>one</u> of my relatives who (<u>plays</u>, play) the fiddle.

1. Wheat is one of the crops that (supports, support) farmers.

2. *Jurassic Park* is one of the movies that (was, were) directed by Steven Spielberg.

3. The dog is one of the animals that (was, were) domesticated by early civilizations.

4. Broccoli is one of the vegetables that (contains, contain) calcium.

5. Harold is the only one of us who (likes, like) that movie.

6. *Stampede* is one of the English words that (comes, come) from Spanish.

7. The hammer is one of the tools that (is, are) useful around the house.

8. The parrot is one of the birds that (mimics, mimic) human speech.

9. The chimpanzee is one of the many animals that (uses, use) tools.

10. The wooly mammoth is one of the Ice Age mammals that (is, are) extinct.

11. Bettina is the only one of my sisters who (is, are) on the Dean's list.

12. Vitamin A is one of the vitamins that (is, are) good for the eyes.

13. Cortez was one of the Spaniards who (was, were) explorers of the New World.

14. Betty is one of the volunteers who (works, work) in a hospice.

15. Dan is the only one of the chefs who (makes, make) a good soufflé.

16. Beans is one of the vegetables that (has, have) a lot of protein.

Copyright © by Glencoe/McGraw-Hill

17. Wood is one of the materials that (is, are) used to build houses.

18. New Year is one of the holidays that (falls, fall) in the winter.

19. Jake is the only one of the athletes who (has, have) won three medals.

20. Frost is one of the poets who (has, have) won the Pulitzer Prize.

21. Jim is one of my friends who (is, are) interested in archaeology.

22. The washing machine is one of the things that (needs, need) to be fixed.

23. London is one of the English cities that (is, are) tourist meccas.

24. Dr. Smith is one of the scientists who (is, are) studying vaccines.

25. The dormitory is one of the buildings that (was, were) damaged in the earthquake.

26. *A* is one of the letters that (makes, make) up the alphabet.

27. This is one of the streets that (leads, lead) to Boston.

28. Ms. Cole is one of the teachers who (advises, advise) the students.

29. Grump's Department Store is one of the places that (hires, hire) students.

30. Accounting is one of the professions that (requires, require) math skills.

31. *The Scarlet Letter* is one of the novels that (was, were) written by Hawthorne.

32. Huskies are one of the animals that (enjoys, enjoy) working.

33. Edna is the only one of my friends who (remembers, remember) my birthday.

34. *1984* is the only one of the books that (is, are) overdue.

35. The Porsche is one of the cars that (is, are) very expensive.

36. The loon is one of the birds that (nests, nest) beside water.

37. The *Edmund Fitzgerald* is one of the boats that (was, were) wrecked on Lake Superior.

38. The waterlily is one of the plants that (grows, grow) in the pond.

39. *The Merchant of Venice* is one of the plays that (was, were) performed by our class.

40. Ariela is one of the people who (owes, owe) me money.

41. Tennis is one of the sports that (interests, interest) me.

42. Aunt Louisa is the only one of my relatives who (performs, perform) in front of an audience.

43. Blue is one of the colors that (blends, blend) with the decor of this room.

44. Walden Pond is one of the places that (inspires, inspire) Jerome.

45. Chicken cordon bleu is the only one of the entrees that (appeals, appeal) to April.

Copyright © by Glencoe/McGraw-Hill

✓ Unit 7 **Review**

▶ **Exercise 1** Underline the subject of each sentence. Then choose the verb in parentheses that agrees with the subject and write it in the blank.

<u>Paula</u> _____runs_____ every day after school. (runs, run)

1. Ben and Consuelo often _____ duets. (sings, sing)

2. His fit of sneezing _____ the class. (is disrupting, are disrupting)

3. The job _____ up a lot of his spare time. (takes, take)

4. Two hundred boxes of cards _____ by the club. (was sold, were sold)

5. His frequent fevers _____ a worry to his parents. (was, were)

6. Gathering clouds _____ a storm. (foretells, foretell)

7. Her pets _____ a great joy to her. (is, are)

8. Final exams _____ the last hurdle before graduation. (is, are)

9. Down the mountain _____ the skiers. (speeds, speed)

10. In her pocket _____ several acorns. (was, were)

11. Two dollars _____ not a big tip for this meal. (is, are)

12. The group _____ not _____ on which movie to see. (does agree, do agree)

13. Every student _____ to study. (needs, need)

14. Both Eliza and George _____ to cook. (loves, love)

15. The rock, as well as the waves, _____ the ship. (threatens, threaten)

16. Ireland, besides England, _____ many ancient ruins. (has, have)

17. Some of my brothers _____ sheep. (raises, raise)

18. One of the climbers _____ reached the top. (has, have)

19. Each of the actors _____ a bow. (takes, take)

20. A few of the vacationers _____ to go home. (wants, want)

21. There _____ the perfect used car. (sits, sit)

22. Mr. Martinez often _____ the symphony orchestra. (conducts, conduct)

23. Under the couch _____ the missing shoe. (lies, lie)

24. The point of all of Grandfather's stories _____ to seize the day. (is, are)

Copyright © by Glencoe/McGraw-Hill

Cumulative Review: Units 1–7

▶ **Exercise 1** Write in the blank the part of speech of each italicized word. Use these abbreviations: *N* (noun), *V* (verb), *pro.* (pronoun), *adj.* (adjective), *adv.* (adverb), *prep.* (preposition), *conj.* (conjunction), and *int.* (interjection).

___N___   Kelly and *Mike* attended several football games.

_____ **1.** Chloe ran *to* the door to meet her long-lost cousin.

_____ **2.** Jasmine could hear *crickets* chirping all night.

_____ **3.** After spending the day at the zoo, *they* felt like buying an exotic pet.

_____ **4.** The flowers in the vase on her desk *withered* and died.

_____ **5.** Mother *carefully* taught us about the consequences of spreading rumors.

_____ **6.** *Well,* how did you think the movie would end?

_____ **7.** Let's build a *sand* castle while the tide is out.

_____ **8.** The last song will be a ballad *or* an anthem.

_____ **9.** The *parade* begins in half an hour.

_____ **10.** Have *you* tried Leon's new computer game?

_____ **11.** *Wow!* Look at that firecracker explode!

_____ **12.** Our community theater *mounted* a production of Philip Barry's funniest play.

_____ **13.** Gwen planted pansies, tulips, *and* lavender in her flower garden this year.

_____ **14.** Anne *often* goes shopping on Saturday, but she visits the malls on other days as well.

_____ **15.** A *lovely* rainbow appeared in the sky after the harsh summer storm.

_____ **16.** Jessica has *never* ridden a train before, so she is quite excited about this trip.

_____ **17.** A sailboat glided on the clear, sparkling waters *of* the lake.

_____ **18.** *Everyone* enjoys having time to relax.

_____ **19.** Did you read the *interview* with the author of that new book in today's newspaper?

_____ **20.** Margaret *volunteers* at the conservatory on weekends.

_____ **21.** *Gee,* I never noticed how much Tim and Tom look alike.

_____ **22.** Stars twinkled *in* the sky like diamonds set against a dark blue velvet background.

_____ **23.** Al is learning how to play the trombone so that he can accompany Bill, *who* plays saxophone.

_____ **24.** We were all sad when we heard that Martha has *officially* left the team.

Copyright © by Glencoe/McGraw-Hill

► **Exercise 2** **Underline each subordinate clause. Write *adj.* in the blank if it is an adjective clause, *adv.* if it is an adverb clause, or *N* if it is a noun clause.**

adj. The person who wrote this poem has a sensitive soul.

_____ **1.** The server who waited on us was friendly and efficient.

_____ **2.** When Dr. Yee reached the border, she heard several car horns blowing.

_____ **3.** Whatever the rest of the family decides is fine with me.

_____ **4.** The instructor said to marinate the vegetables before we added them to the rest of the mixture.

_____ **5.** A band that Marty knows has agreed to play at the school dance.

_____ **6.** Ms. Jenkins gave the job to Gloria, who is an excellent seamstress.

_____ **7.** Nathan will watch whichever television show has the most jokes.

_____ **8.** What the volleyball team would really like is more time to practice.

_____ **9.** After she started going to school, little Emily stopped watching *Lucy's Toy Shop*.

_____ **10.** Where Uncle Bob's house is located remains a mystery.

_____ **11.** The optometrist who examined Paul's eyes says Paul needs glasses.

_____ **12.** Rosalyn takes her camera with her wherever she travels.

_____ **13.** Do you know who is coming to the dinner party?

_____ **14.** The place where Ria first met Reggie will always be special to her.

_____ **15.** Until spring arrives, Suzanne is going to do most of her exercising indoors.

_____ **16.** The dress that Maureen bought for the dance is a beautiful shade of aquamarine.

_____ **17.** The player who won the chess tournament hails from Bangor, Maine.

_____ **18.** Whoever sent the gift forgot to send a card.

_____ **19.** Zack will order whatever is listed first on the menu.

_____ **20.** When Tina graduates from high school, she plans to attend the University of Notre Dame.

► **Exercise 3** **Draw two lines under the verb in parentheses that best completes each sentence.**

The road to my friend's house (is, are) not long.

1. Stacy always (appreciates, appreciate) her mother's sound advice.

2. On top of the television (sits, sit) the remote control.

3. Here (resides, reside) the best golfer on the East Coast.

4. The story of Curt's adventures in Washington (amuses, amuse) us every time we hear it.

Copyright © by Glencoe/McGraw-Hill

Grammar

5. (Waits, Wait) until you see how this music video ends.

6. The books in this library (circulates, circulate) frequently.

7. Those pictures that Renata ordered (looks, look) wonderful.

8. Everybody (hopes, hope) to win the lottery someday.

9. After practice, Hal usually (walks, walk) to the yogurt shop on Maple Street.

10. Over the music (floats, float) one soft, beautiful voice.

11. Claudia's fingers (flies, fly) across the keyboard with the speed of a gazelle.

12. Steve and Lydia (attends, attend) the impressionist exhibit at the art museum.

13. Lucas's name (is, are) in the *Toledo Blade* today.

14. After Sally, Crystal (is, are) the next skater scheduled to perform.

15. Racing to reach the airplane, Rafi (jumps, jump) over a pile of suitcases.

16. This year's variety show (includes, include) several never-before-seen acts.

17. The antique cars at the auto show still (runs, run) fairly well.

18. That chemistry experiment (requires, require) careful preparation.

19. Across the street (is, are) two restaurants, a bank, and a travel agency.

20. Great ideas (begins, begin) with simple thoughts.

21. Gretchen, Courtney, and I (sings, sing) in the show choir.

22. The interior decorators at that firm (develops, develop) the most appealing rooms.

23. Three words in Joe's essay (seems, seem) to be misspelled.

24. A picnic in the park (sounds, sound) delightful to me.

25. Here (stands, stand) the persons waiting to get into the concert.

26. The heart of the matter (was, were) really a question of pride.

27. Through the gathering darkness (glows, glow) a handful of candles.

28. Everyone (watches, watch) the big game with excitement.

29. Daffodils (dots, dot) the verdant meadow.

30. A persistent moan (echoes, echo) in the empty house.

31. Several coins (is, are) tossed into the Italian fountain.

32. Bees (hovers, hover) around the brightest flowers.

33. Into the stadium (proceeds, proceed) loyal fans.

34. Neither rain nor snow (prevents, prevent) the work from going forward.

Copyright © by Glencoe/McGraw-Hill

Unit 8: Using Pronouns Correctly

Lesson 53
Case of Personal Pronouns

Personal pronouns are pronouns that refer to persons or things. The case, or form, of a personal pronoun may be nominative, objective, or possessive, depending on its function in the sentence.

CASE	SINGULAR PRONOUNS	PLURAL PRONOUNS	FUNCTION IN SENTENCE
Nominative	I, you, she, he, it	we, you, they	subject or predicate nominative
Objective	me, you, her, him, it	us, you, them	direct object, indirect object, or object of preposition
Possessive	my, mine, your, yours, his, her, hers, its	our, ours, your, yours, their, theirs	replacement for possessive noun(s)

They thought that John went home. (nominative)
Sherry bumped **him** by accident. (objective)   The best entry was **yours**. (possessive)

Use the **nominative case** for a personal pronoun in a compound subject. Use the **objective case** for a personal pronoun in a compound object.

Theresa and **she** had the highest scores in the class.
Alpesh invited Corey and **me** to the track meet.

Use the **possessive case** to show possession. Never spell possessive pronouns with an apostrophe. *It's* is a contraction of *it is.* Do not confuse *it's* with the possessive pronoun *its*.

The book is **hers**. The victory is **ours**.
It's about time for the program. **Its** value is beyond comprehension.

▶ **Exercise 1 Underline the pronoun in parentheses that best completes each sentence.**

Many people dedicated (them, <u>their</u>) lives to developing the digital computer.

1. One pioneer, John W. Mauchly, spent much of (he, his) life developing computer technology.

2. While a student at Ursinus College, (he, him) constructed an analog computer to analyze weather data.

3. This early machine did (it's, its) job well, but slowly and with virtually no flexibility.

4. In 1941, Mauchly joined the Moore School of Electrical Engineering at the University of Pennsylvania, where (he, him) refined digital technology.

5. (He, Him) collaborated with others at the school to build the first large electronic computer, ENIAC.

Copyright © by Glencoe/McGraw-Hill

Grammar

6. (They, Their) built this huge machine to produce ballistic trajectory tables.

7. Along with John von Neumann, (they, them) followed with EDVAC, the world's first programmable computer.

8. Seeing the commercial possibilities for (them, their) invention, they formed a corporation to build computers.

9. As the research neared (its, it's) fruition, (they, their) corporation was absorbed by the giant company Remington Rand.

10. Remington Rand, with Mauchly on (its, it's) staff, added Grace Murray Hopper to the team.

11. Admiral Hopper devoted (she, her) energy to pioneering the use of compilers.

12. A compiler translates a program from (its, it's) original form that humans can read to a form that computers can access.

13. Spending most of (her, she) career in the U.S. Navy, Admiral Hopper nevertheless contributed greatly to the development of a computer business programming language known as COBOL.

14. Businesses rushed to utilize the new technology because they knew it would expand productivity for (they, them).

▶ **Exercise 2** **Label each italicized pronoun *nom.* (nominative), *obj.* (objective), or *poss.* (possessive).**

                                                                  obj.
Since my friend Juana Alvarez moved, I have received three letters from *her.*

1. The Alvarez family spends much of *its* time utilizing computer on-line services.

2. More of *their* productive time is spent with a computer than ever before because of the expanded services of on-line systems.

3. What makes *them* different from standard bulletin board system (BBS) features?

4. Unlike local bulletin board systems, commercial services offer a wide variety of serious information to serve *their* clientele.

5. Mr. Alvarez uses *his* computer to find up-to-the-minute stock market quotations and financial news that concerns *him.*

6. Mrs. Alvarez spends part of *her* day contacting clients through the electronic mail section.

7. When *she* works on *her* school reports, Juana's favorite feature is the reference library.

8. "*I* really save time because the computer can find *my* topics in a few seconds," she said.

9. Gilberto has found that, through the Internet, *he* can access large libraries to locate materials that will suit his needs.

10. "Our computer modem has given *us* an added dimension in *our* lives," stated Mrs. Alvarez.

Copyright © by Glencoe/McGraw-Hill

Lesson 54
Pronouns with and as Appositives; After *Than* and *As*

Grammar

A pronoun placed after a noun or another pronoun to identify, explain, or rename it is an **appositive pronoun**. When the appositive pronoun explains or identifies a subject or a predicate nominative, use the **nominative case**. When the pronoun explains or defines a direct object, an indirect object, or an object of a preposition, use the **objective case**.

The woman in the white jeans, **she,** was an eyewitness to the accident.
André presented the trophies to the winners, Juan and **me.**

In elliptical adverb clauses using *than* and *as,* use a pronoun in the case that would be used if the missing words were fully stated.

Marsha received higher scores than **he.** (Marsha received higher scores than **he** received.)
The article complimented James and Doreen as much as **them.** (The article complimented James and Doreen as much as it complimented **them.**)

▶ **Exercise 1** Underline the correct pronoun. Write the case (*nom.* for nominative and *obj.* for objective) in the blank. Some sentences may have more than one pronoun to identify.

_____nom., obj._____ The Norton sisters, Karen and (she, her), helped (they, them) with the planning.

_____ 1. The losers, Raji and (I, me), bought pizza for Ben and Clara.

_____ 2. The membership cards have arrived for the new members, Kisha and (he, him).

_____ 3. Because I hadn't studied, the test gave (I, me) more problems than usual.

_____ 4. "The culprit is (I, me)," admitted Ashford.

_____ 5. Everyone donated a dollar to buy a present for (she, her).

_____ 6. Dowana, more than (I, me), worked hard to make the team.

_____ 7. Mr. Grover spent as much time with the beginners as with (they, them).

_____ 8. (He, him), Alberto Ramirez, won every free-throw contest.

_____ 9. Better than (he, him), try asking Darcy for help with your math questions.

_____ 10. Consuelo and Betty sang (they, them) a lullaby so the babies would go to sleep.

_____ 11. Camping without electricity was less of a problem for (she, her), than (they, them).

_____ 12. After the meeting, the sisters, Angie and (she, her), went out for pizza.

_____ 13. Because he made the team, his dad bought (he, him) a new pair of cross-training shoes.

_____ 14. The winners of the cheerleader spirit contest were (we, us), the juniors.

Copyright © by Glencoe/McGraw-Hill

_____ **15.** Because Katarina twisted her ankle, Rhoda carried (she, her) to the car.

_____ **16.** Teresa, as well as (she, her), won two tickets to *The Phantom of the Opera*.

_____ **17.** Since I was unfamiliar with the neighborhood, Mr. Chin drew a map for (I, me).

_____ **18.** The scratching of the limb against the house gave Mark and (I, me) a terrible start.

_____ **19.** (They, Them), Mable and Otto, run the 440 faster than Kara and (I, me).

_____ **20.** If it weren't for Jamal and (she, her), the school paper would not get printed.

_____ **21.** Ms. Adkins managed to motivate (they, them), Sheila and Alpesh.

_____ **22.** The new owners of the bait shop are (they, them), Mr. and Mrs. Giles.

_____ **23.** The newspaper interviewed Alan as well as (she, her).

_____ **24.** (She, Her), Andrea Thompson, is our representative on the student council.

_____ **25.** Mattie, rather than (he, him), volunteered to be chairman of the ethics committee.

_____ **26.** The team chose Chun as its captain rather than (he, him).

_____ **27.** The waitress served (I, me) the wrong entrée.

_____ **28.** The only applicants who met the qualifications were Candy and (I, me).

_____ **29.** Famous guests at the banquet included Archie Griffin, Steve Young, and (he, him).

_____ **30.** The results of the poll elated Paul as much as (she, her).

_____ **31.** Several people took advantage of the offer besides Chuck and (she, her).

_____ **32.** The entire student body cheered the runners, Maria and (he, him), to victory.

_____ **33.** The nod went to Gary rather than (she, her).

_____ **34.** Miklos, as well as (he, him), is saving money for basketball camp.

_____ **35.** Three of the players, Adzo, Alejandra, and (I, me), scored in the double digits.

_____ **36.** Deciding which article to run was difficult for the editors, Joel and (she, her).

_____ **37.** Of the three we know, Ito, Cal, and (he, him), the most popular is Ito.

_____ **38.** (She, Her), a professional athlete, holds clinics for our school every summer.

_____ **39.** Both of the game's stars, Sanjay and (he, him), were playing with injuries.

_____ **40.** Kaleena upset (he, him) with her catty remarks.

Copyright © by Glencoe/McGraw-Hill

Lesson 55
Reflexive and Intensive Pronouns

Hisself and *theirselves* are incorrect forms. Never use them.

The hermit had spent thirty years by **himself**.
The parents **themselves** supplied the extra labor.

Always use a reflexive pronoun when the pronoun refers to the person who is the subject of the sentence.

Incorrect: He saved **him** a lot of trouble.
Correct: He saved **himself** a lot of trouble.
Incorrect: She found **her** an apple for a snack.
Correct: She found **herself** an apple for a snack.

Never use a reflexive pronoun when it does not refer to the same person as the subject.

Incorrect: Shelley and **myself** were born in October.
Correct: Shelley and **I** were born in October.
Incorrect: Aaron and **yourself** are the only ones who can drive.
Correct: Aaron and **you** are the only ones who can drive.

▶ **Exercise 1 Write _C_ in the blank if the sentence is correct. If the pronoun in italics is incorrect, write the correct pronoun in the blank.**

_____I_____ Douglas and *myself* caught seven fish before breakfast.

_____ **1.** Achim spends much time praising *hisself*.

_____ **2.** May Lien earned *her* a lot of money.

_____ **3.** Emil bought four hamburgers for Rolf and *him* to share.

_____ **4.** Carlene, Andy, and *myself* are the new Student Council representatives.

_____ **5.** The guests eagerly helped *themselves* to the tempting buffet.

_____ **6.** Koko surprised *herself* and managed to remain calm in the face of the insults.

_____ **7.** Kobla and *himself* are the only ones who got a perfect score.

_____ **8.** Here are three chairs for Kim, Frances, and *you*.

_____ **9.** During the volleyball tournament, Carey's team called *themselves* the Sparkling Spikers.

_____ **10.** The orchestra raised a thousand dollars for *it* by selling pizza.

_____ **11.** June tagged along with Fernando and *myself*.

_____ **12.** The Ortas are our neighbors. Our family and *they* are good friends.

Copyright © by Glencoe/McGraw-Hill

_____ **13.** Gerald managed to solve the mystery all by *himself*.

_____ **14.** Every day, Billy found *himself* more enthused with the club's progress.

_____ **15.** Carmen and *you* saved the game by scoring fourteen points each in the last quarter.

_____ **16.** Erika and Toni made *them* new outfits for the party.

_____ **17.** The choir members took great pride in *theirselves* and their accomplishments.

_____ **18.** My parents bought theater tickets for the Murphys and *them*.

_____ **19.** When the old company closed, Mr. Williams found *him* a new job with the Skye Products Corporation.

_____ **20.** Did you remember to bring sweaters for Wanda and *yourself*?

▶ **Exercise 2** **Write a pronoun in the blank that correctly completes the sentence.**

Estella was proud of _____herself_____ for winning the MVP Award.

1. Get _____ another piece of pie.

2. Elizabeth allowed _____ two hours to study for the math final.

3. Ms. Swenson and _____ are the only persons I have known that are named *Inge*.

4. We managed to decipher the poorly written instructions for _____.

5. Will you straighten the desktop as a favor to Marla and _____?

6. The roles of the faculty members were played by our teachers _____.

7. A country which is independent has the freedom to govern _____.

8. Kent earned _____ the right to compete in the district finals.

9. In order to get a copy of the new postal cancellation, I sent a letter to _____.

10. Enrique and _____ are the most popular singers in the whole school.

11. People who cannot organize _____ cannot organize others.

12. Cathy allowed no one but _____ to read her diary.

13. Kenji reserved seats for _____ and Cheryl.

14. I usually write poetry for _____ and no one else.

15. Rosa seldom gave _____ credit for any of the contributions she made to the French Club.

16. The Changs and _____ vacationed in North Dakota.

17. Since he can't reach the top shelf, will you put this box up there for _____?

18. Though he tried to concentrate, Chuck found _____ daydreaming during the speech.

Copyright © by Glencoe/McGraw-Hill

Lesson 56
Who and Whom in Questions and Subordinate Clauses

Use the nominative case pronouns *who* and *whoever* when the pronoun is the subject of the sentence, the subject of a clause, or a predicate nominative in a sentence or a clause.

Who will be the next president? (subject of the verb *will be*)

He knows **who** his true friends are. (subject of the noun clause *who his true friends are*)

Mr. Adams knew **who** came in late. (subject of noun clause *who came in late*)

Use the objective case pronouns *whom* and *whomever* when the pronoun is a direct object, an indirect object, or an object of a preposition.

Mavis wants to know **whom** you saw at the mall. (direct object of noun clause *whom you saw at the mall*)

The president, **whomever** we select, will have a difficult job. (direct object of *select*)

With **whom** did Bill go to the fair? (object of the preposition *with*)

▶ **Exercise 1** **Underline the pronoun in parentheses that best completes each sentence.**

Tom Sawyer, (who, <u>whom</u>) most people love, is an amusing character.

1. One of America's finest writers was Mark Twain, (who, whom) was born in November 1835.

2. Mark Twain, (who, whom) was born Samuel Langhorne Clemens, was the fourth of five children.

3. The family's poverty was obvious to (whoever, whomever) made their acquaintance.

4. When he was four, his father, (who, whom) was a hard worker but a poor provider, moved the family to Hannibal, Missouri.

5. When his father died, the boy, (who, whom) was twelve, was apprenticed to a printer.

6. Sam's older brother, Orion, (who, whom) bought the *Hannibal Journal,* gave him his first experience with typesetting and writing.

7. (Whoever, Whomever) struck Sam's fancy became the subject of his witty characterizations.

8. The people (who, whom) Sam spoofed often made trouble for Orion.

9. Orion, (who, whom) was often frustrated with his brother, knew that the satire sold papers.

10. In 1857, young Clemens apprenticed himself to a riverboat pilot (who, whom) he had come to respect.

11. Sam, (who, whom) had received his pilot's license, tried this new trade for two and a half years.

Copyright © by Glencoe/McGraw-Hill

12. The author, (who, whom) called these years the happiest of his life, later wrote about piloting in *Life on the Mississippi.*

13. The young man, (who, whom) wanted nothing to do with the Civil War, went with his brother to Nevada to do some mining.

14. Soon Clemens, (who, whom) had begun using the pen name Mark Twain, was writing for the *Enterprise* in Virginia City.

15. His contributions were popular with (whoever, whomever) would read them.

16. In 1864 Mark, (who, whom) fortune still eluded, went to San Francisco where he worked on several newspapers.

17. He often made time to listen to (whoever, whomever) had tall tales to tell.

18. A miner, (who, whom) Twain met in Calaveras County, provided him with a "jumping frog" story that the author set down in words.

19. Twain, (who, whom) was called the "Wild Humorist of the Pacific Slope," achieved a measure of national fame with this story.

20. Traveling to the Hawaiian Islands, the Mediterranean, and the Holy Land, he was a correspondent (who, whom) wrote glittering pieces for his employers.

21. *Innocents Abroad* was a revision of these experiences that secured the fame of the author, upon (who, whom) fortune seemed to smile at last.

22. In 1869, he married Olivia Langdon, (who, whom) was from Elmira, New York.

23. Olivia, (who, whom) modified many of Mark's exaggerations, sometimes improved their readability but often weakened the writing.

24. Twain, (who, whom) bought a publishing house in Hartford, Connecticut, earned much money from writing, lecturing, and publishing.

25. The writer, (who, whom) now rode the crest of popularity, abandoned journalism for literature.

26. The next few years, 1872–1889, were productive for this man (who, whom) had come so far.

27. William Dean Howells, (who, whom) was editor of the *Atlantic Monthly,* became one of Twain's closest friends.

28. Howells also became his literary adviser, upon (who, whom) Twain depended heavily.

29. The author, (who, whom) was unused to a secure lifestyle, spent his money on high living and unsuccessful investments.

30. (Who, Whom) could have guessed that his heavy investments in both a typesetting machine and a publishing house would fail?

Copyright © by Glencoe/McGraw-Hill

Grammar

Lesson 57
Agreement in Number and Gender and with Collective Nouns

An antecedent is a word or group of words to which a pronoun refers or that a pronoun replaces. A pronoun must agree with its antecedent in both number (singular or plural) and gender (masculine, feminine, or neuter). The antecedent may be a noun, another pronoun, or a phrase or clause acting as a noun.

The Taylors landscaped **their** yard in an unusual way. (plural pronoun)
Kimiko regained **her** confidence after a few putting lessons. (singular feminine pronoun)
The cheetah licked **its** chops. (singular neuter pronoun)

Traditionally, a masculine pronoun is used when the gender of the antecedent is unknown or may be either masculine or feminine. As language changes, some people prefer using gender-neutral wording. To avoid using only the masculine, the examples show three ways to reword the sentence.

The *doctor* makes **his** rounds every day. (*Doctor* may be masculine or feminine, but the pronoun here is masculine.)

The *doctor* makes **his** or **her** rounds every day. (Both genders of the pronoun are included.)

Doctors make **their** rounds every day. (Both the antecedent and the pronoun are plural.)

Doctors make rounds daily. (The pronoun is eliminated.)

When the antecedent of a pronoun is a collective noun, the number of the pronoun depends upon whether the collective noun is used as singular or plural.

The class had **its** first meeting yesterday. (*Class* is used as a single unit; therefore, the singular pronoun is used.)

The legislature take **their** vacations during the summer months. (This sentence refers to separate acts of the members; therefore, the plural pronoun is used.)

▶ **Exercise 1** Write a pronoun in the blank that agrees with the antecedent; then underline the antecedent.

Felipe left ____his____ report on the kitchen table.

1. The Carmonas all have _____ mother's eyes.

2. Each member must pledge _____ loyalty to the group.

3. Ms. Arnold coached the cheerleaders as _____ practiced their routines.

4. The emergency squad offers _____ services to all in need.

5. Akiko changed for _____ date before she ate dinner.

Copyright © by Glencoe/McGraw-Hill

Grammar

6. Lemuel and I researched _____ family tree.

7. The Panthers play _____ opening game tonight.

8. When Juan and I left school, _____ went straight to soccer practice.

9. Mr. Copas and Seán never tire of talking about _____ record catch of trout.

10. If you will give me a list of things you need, I will get _____.

11. Billy and Carol are amazing. I've never seen two people work together better than _____.

12. Sasha and Trina work every day after school because _____ family needs the money.

13. Just before we graduated, our class gave _____ entire treasury to purchase some new computers for the school.

14. Norman and Natasha spent a lot of money on _____ skiing gear.

15. Camille wrote _____ deepest feelings in the diary; _____ contents were private.

16. The girl on the phone said _____ name was Jane, but _____ sounded exactly like Maria.

17. Orville worked hard at accomplishing _____ goals.

18. The tennis player had trouble controlling _____ serves.

19. When my dad and his three brothers were children, _____ all shared one bicycle.

20. Congress passed forty-seven bills during _____ last session.

▶ **Exercise 2** Circle any pronoun in italics that does not agree with its antecedent. Write its correct form in the blank. If the italicized pronoun agrees with its antecedent, write *C* in the blank.

____their____ The candidates used the poll results to estimate *his* support base.

_____ 1. Albert and Teresa featured a live rabbit in *their* science project.

_____ 2. The musicians performed *his* program at the municipal auditorium.

_____ 3. Marlene spent the evening studying for *his* math test.

_____ 4. Most members of the Spanish club recommend it to *their* friends.

_____ 5. Bill organized *its* schedule to allow for extra leisure time.

_____ 6. My sisters and I finished our homework, and then *she* watched television.

_____ 7. Neither of the Jones girls played *her* best.

_____ 8. The team is proud of *their* record.

_____ 9. Does anyone have an extra battery in *their* locker?

_____ 10. Hakeem is never too busy to help *his* friends.

Copyright © by Glencoe/McGraw-Hill

Lesson 58
Agreement in Person

A pronoun must agree in person with its antecedent.

Incorrect: Henri lives in Tampa where **you** can sunbathe all year long.
Correct: Henri lives in Tampa where **he** can sunbathe all year long.
Incorrect: They like camping because **you** can be close to nature.
Correct: They like camping because **they** can be close to nature

▶ **Exercise 1 Rewrite the sentence to eliminate the inappropriate use of** *you* (*your*)**. Substitute a pronoun that agrees with the antecedent or a suitable noun.**

Tom attended the outdoor drama where you could enjoy the summer weather.

Tom attended the outdoor drama where he could enjoy the summer weather.

1. Maria climbed to the top of the hill where you could see Tennessee.

_____

2. Maude and Clarice found a little boutique where you get terrific bargains on hypoallergenic

makeup. _____

_____

3. Bill likes the library because there you can satisfy your curiosity on any subject.

_____

4. Achim had no knowledge of your basic rights as a citizen.

_____

5. Martina stayed away from parties where you couldn't wear casual clothes.

_____

6. Every member knew that the tradition was well established before you were born.

_____

7. The stars seemed so close that you could reach up and grab one.

_____

8. We went to the theater early so you would have a better chance of getting good seats.

_____

9. Our goal is to make everyone feel that you truly have equal opportunity.

_____

Copyright © by Glencoe/McGraw-Hill

Grammar

10. Rosie proved that, with the right attitude, you could accomplish nearly anything.

_____

11. Dan and Luisa are going to the track banquet where you receive the awards you earned during

the season. _____

_____

12. Ed was happy for the new bus route because you don't have to walk all the way through the

subdivision. _____

_____

13. Mary and Al go to the YMCA three days a week because you can work out for three dollars a

session. _____

_____

14. The Morgans were eager for their vacation because you could get away from the bustle of their

busy shop. _____

_____

15. Yoruba and Steve checked their answer sheets carefully because you wouldn't get a second

chance. _____

_____

16. Basketball clinics are valuable since you always need to improve your skills.

_____

17. Jeannine finally realized that you can't get a top grade without some personal effort.

_____

18. For the trip to London, you will stop over in New York.

_____

19. To learn about their ancestors, you can attend a family reunion.

_____

20. Anya and Ramona took a compass on their hike because you can use it to find your way if you

become lost. _____

_____

Copyright © by Glencoe/McGraw-Hill

Lesson 59
Agreement with Indefinite Pronoun Antecedents

When a pronoun's antecedent is an indefinite pronoun, the pronoun must agree in number with it.

Neither of the girls spent **her** entire allowance.
Several members missed **their** chance to speak with the president.

When no gender is specified, it is traditional to use a masculine pronoun with an indefinite antecedent. If gender-neutral wording is desired, use both masculine and feminine, reword the sentence to make the antecedent plural, or omit the personal pronoun entirely.

TRADITIONAL: Every one of the students should prepare **his** own homework.
GENDER-NEUTRAL: All of the students should prepare **their** own homework.
                            Every one of the students should prepare the homework.

▶ **Exercise 1** **Write a pronoun in the blank that agrees with the indefinite antecedent. Underline the indefinite pronoun antecedent.**

<u>Neither</u> of the girls left _____her_____ umbrella on the bus.

1. All of the Turner children have labeled _____ notebooks on the outside.

2. When Muriel graduates, another of the girls will take _____ place as president.

3. Any of the stock boys will be happy to lend _____ assistance.

4. None of the sopranos has _____ music memorized.

5. Some of our teachers keep _____ records in a computer.

6. I want to speak with each of the boys: Deon, Karl, and _____.

7. A few of the football players hung their heads because _____ had lost the game.

8. All of the NHL players risk injury to _____ legs in every game.

9. Each of the mothers had _____ own special way of handling her child.

10. All of the members are required to keep _____ uniforms clean and neat.

11. When all of the girls had gone home, only one had forgotten _____ project list.

12. Both of us had reached the point of frustration with _____ brothers.

13. Of all the girls on the track team, no one chose high hurdles as _____ specialty.

14. Each of them is responsible for _____ own property.

15. Either of the boys may choose thermodynamics as the theme for _____ science project.

Copyright © by Glencoe/McGraw-Hill

Grammar

Grammar

16. Some of the girls perceived that remark as damaging to _____ pride.

17. Many of the NBA players plan for _____ future by reinvesting much of their salary.

18. Any of the waitresses works hard to improve _____ tips.

19. Everyone hopes _____ audition went well.

20. Somebody in the girls' locker room is laughing so loudly that _____ voice can be heard in the hallway.

21. Both of his friends enjoyed _____ dinner.

22. A few of the guys spent _____ lunch hour practicing their lines for the play.

23. Will any of the women on the staff cast _____ vote against this proposal?

24. The others saw the importance of _____ role in the project.

25. Of all the boys, not one failed to report to _____ interview on time.

26. All of Amy's friends admitted to feeling lonely at some time in _____ lives.

27. Everybody has _____ strong points.

28. Both of the writers saw _____ essays in print.

29. Each of the parents held secret dreams for the success of _____ children.

30. Nobody has any excuse for trying less than _____ best.

31. Every one of the women has earned _____ spot on the golf tour.

32. Both of them received _____ shipments in an amazingly short time.

33. Most of the horse show judges have spent years refining _____ talent.

34. Neither of the siblings vents _____ feelings in a visible manner.

35. Someone in the balcony lost _____ coat.

36. Each chose Will Smith as _____ favorite comedian.

37. None of the girls went to the prom without _____ makeup and _____ hairbrush.

38. None of the cross-country runners finished with _____ best time.

39. Each of the servers bussed the tables in _____ area.

40. All of the guys had computer games on _____ wish lists.

▶ **Writing Link** **Write two sentences using indefinite pronouns that have indefinite antecedents.**

_____

_____

_____

Copyright © by Glencoe/McGraw-Hill

Lesson 60
Clear Pronoun Reference

Do not use the pronouns *this*, *that*, *which*, and *it* without a clearly stated antecedent.

Unclear: Nina will sing at the assembly, **which** I always enjoy.
Clear: I always enjoy Nina's singing at the assembly.

Sometimes a pronoun will seem to have more than one antecedent. In such instances, reword the sentence to make the antecedent clear or omit the pronoun.

Unclear: Raji had the wrestling advantage over Bob because he was heavier. (*Raji* or *Bob* could be the antecedent of *he*)
Clear: Raji, because he was heavier, had the wrestling advantage over Bob. (*Raji* is the antecedent of *he*)
Clear: Heavier than Bob, Raji had the wrestling advantage. (pronoun is eliminated)

The pronouns *you* and *they* should not be used as indefinite pronouns. Instead, name the performer of the action.

Indefinite: When the Hallelujah Chorus is performed, **you** should rise.
Clear: When the Hallelujah Chorus is performed, **the audience** should rise.
Clear: When the Hallelujah Chorus is performed, **everyone** should rise.

▶ **Exercise 1** Rewrite each sentence so that the antecedent of the pronoun in parentheses is clear. You may choose to eliminate the pronoun in some cases.

The Tigers played the Lions last Friday and (they) scored eleven runs.

The Tigers scored eleven runs when they played the Lions last Friday.

1. Ellen brought a copy of the new schedule of activities that (they) are offering this summer at the city parks. _____

2. The swimming pool has been enlarged by twenty feet (which) is larger than any other in the state. _____

3. Not only will there be baseball and basketball, but (you) can play soccer, too.

_____

4. Ollie noticed that five team sports were on the list, (which) are open to all ages.

_____

5. Cal has different interests from Mario because (he) prefers individual sports.

_____

Copyright © by Glencoe/McGraw-Hill

Grammar

Grammar

6. For people like Cal, (they) have fourteen individual sports on the list.

_____

7. Jogging, hiking, and weight training are available if (you) don't want to be competitive.

_____

8. The program includes a full schedule of non-sporting activities (which) has something for

everyone. _____

_____

9. Eastgate Park offers (you) a small plot to raise flowers or vegetables.

_____

10. Those with artistic tastes may choose from twenty craft workshops and fine arts classes which

(they) offer at Mill Street Park. _____

_____

11. Sharon joined her cousin Gillian in the pastels class because (she) didn't want to attend

without someone she knew. _____

_____

12. The leather tooling class required a fee for supplies (which) was on Wednesday mornings.

_____

13. Performing opportunities are available at all the parks (which) have professional leadership.

_____

14. A concert band, a chorus, and an orchestra will make weekly appearances (that) involve scores

of participants. _____

_____

15. The drama group will perform three one-act plays (which) is already rehearsing.

_____

16. Four professional groups are scheduled for concerts (that) are on tour.

_____

17. Of course, all the traditional facilities like playgrounds and picnic areas (that) are popular are

still available. _____

_____

18. The shelter houses are in such demand that (you) have to reserve them a month in advance.

_____

Copyright © by Glencoe/McGraw-Hill

✓ Unit 8 **Review**

▶ **Exercise 1** **Write a pronoun in the blank to correct the inappropriate pronoun in italics.**

his or her
_____ _or his or her_ Each absentee got _their_ assignment from Brenda.

_____ 1. The cookies were donated by Antoinette and _she._

_____ 2. The guests, Armand and _her,_ were very poised.

_____ 3. All the ballerinas keep _herself_ physically fit.

_____ 4. Curt misses Florida because _they_ can walk on the beach anytime.

_____ 5. Sara had a better free-throw percentage than _her._

_____ 6. Anyone can join provided _they_ attends the meetings.

_____ 7. Mary Ann liked the new hobby shop because _you_ can find everything easily.

_____ 8. The rules change was approved by all of _we_ on the committee.

_____ 9. The aptitude test will be given to _we_ juniors during third period.

_____ 10. Each of the students liked working on the community clean-up project because it gave _them_ a sense of accomplishment.

_____ 11. Alonzo gave the keys to the boys, Rabi and _he._

_____ 12. The league champions are _us,_ the Wildcats.

_____ 13. To _who_ was the prize awarded?

_____ 14. Our class spent four days helping the victims _whom_ were displaced by the flood.

_____ 15. Our ancestors succeeded because _we_ worked hard.

_____ 16. All of the boys completed _his_ homework on time.

_____ 17. Steve got _hisself_ a new CD player.

_____ 18. The team _itself_ washed the dirty jerseys.

_____ 19. Karl got better grades than Melissa because _she_ studied harder.

_____ 20. Every team deserved a letter, said Mr. Giles, even _them._

Copyright © by Glencoe/McGraw-Hill

Grammar

Cumulative Review: Units 1–8

▶ **Exercise 1** Label each italicized word with its part of speech: *N* (noun), *V* (verb), *adj.* (adjective), *adv.* (adverb), *pro.* (pronoun), *prep.* (preposition), or *con.* (conjunction).

    prep.   N
With a loud crash, the vase fell to the *floor.*

1. His *leaving* caused a *lot* of comment.

2. *After* the rain shower, the *entire* world seemed refreshed.

3. Is *Ethan Frome* fiction *or* biography?

4. Brunhilda, a character in *Wagnerian* operas, *was* the beautiful leader *of* the Valkyries.

5. I found Ms. Lopez *extremely* well *prepared* for the debate.

6. Running and weight *lifting* are Alpesh's *favorite* activities.

7. *Both* the advisers spoke with *Brooklyn* accents.

8. Do you understand that there will be more *responsibility* placed *on those* who can handle it?

9. The pigeons *outside* his window awakened Geraldo with *their soft* cooing.

10. The Walkers' new van *runs* on diesel *fuel.*

11. The *entire* surprise party came off *without* a hitch.

12. *Because of* a disease called *blight,* chestnut trees have become *very* rare.

13. *Your* gear *should include* the following: *extra* socks, a first-aid kit, *and* a rain poncho.

14. After *thirty* years of marriage, Renaldo is *still* happy when *he* returns to his wife after a day at work.

15. The MVP award went to *her,* the girl *with* the *red* hair.

16. Durrell *is being scouted* by three major *colleges* because of his outstanding passing ability.

17. Can a person from *our* tiny community understand the pressures of life in the city?

18. *Interestingly* enough, Jo *wrote* the story that appeared in the newspaper, *but* she hasn't seen a printed copy yet.

19. Kahlil ate *two* eggs *besides* the pancakes.

20. Please hand me the jars, *those* with the green *labels.*

Copyright © by Glencoe/McGraw-Hill

▶ **Exercise 2 Draw two lines under the correct verb form.**

Carey and Mel (is, <u>are</u>) the funniest persons in our class.

1. (Do, Does) the Honeywells live here?

2. The addax, an example of an endangered animal, (is, are) native to Africa.

3. Everyone who attended (is, are) impressed with Mr. Honer's speaking ability.

4. Jesse, along with the Chin sisters, (devote, devotes) much of his time to studying.

5. Connie, Jaleel, and Pearl (advocate, advocates) a generous approach to the situation.

6. Neither the Cadburys nor Mr. Skidmore (own, owns) a riding lawn mower.

7. Physics (is, are) his favorite science course.

8. Al or they (has, have) many resources that will help you with your project.

9. "We can use additional volunteers," (remark, remarks) Paul.

10. Most of the squadron (believe, believes) that the new equipment will improve performance.

11. All of the team (look, looks) forward to the rematch with Westport.

12. The Carillos and Hector (subscribe, subscribes) to that magazine.

13. (Is, Are) the employees taking their vacations in July?

14. The reporters from the newspaper (work, works) very hard to meet deadlines.

15. The board of education (provide, provides) transportation for all field trips.

16. The senator's politics (change, changes) from day to day.

17. Few of the class (arrange, arranges) their schedules with efficiency.

18. Ms. Wu, who is on the staff of school counselors, (provide, provides) an interesting
    introduction to their program.

19. Cryonics (is, are) a new frontier for many forms of life science.

20. The football player (hope, hopes) for a better season next year.

▶ **Exercise 3 Draw a line under the word in parentheses that best completes each sentence.**

The mother was proud of her children, for (who, <u>whom</u>) she had sacrificed much.

1. Will you help Addie and (I, me)?

2. The highest producers, Rafael and (he, him), were treated to lunch.

3. The president of the school board (himself, hisself) visited the class.

4. Blame the sophomores rather than (we, us).

5. Anita bought (her, herself) a new pair of shoes for the party.

Copyright © by Glencoe/McGraw-Hill

Grammar

6. Mr. Taylor, (who, whom) he had trusted, proved to be unreliable.

7. In speech class, the class told about (its, their) hobbies.

8. The Millers often go to the lake where (you, they) can relax and revitalize themselves.

9. Anyone who wants to participate must have (his *or* her, their) physical exam by next week.

10. I bought bouquets for Karin and (she, her).

11. Give this to the first chair flautist, (she, her).

12. Ariel, as well as (he, him), was late for the ballgame.

13. To finance their banquet, the French Club raised two hundred dollars for (them, themselves).

14. Juanita called Kareem, (who, whom) is the chairman of the committee.

15. Each member of the volleyball team received (its, her) award at the dinner.

16. Because (you, he) loves nature, Yoshin is always ready to go camping.

17. Many of our class (is, are) involved in some type of community service program.

18. I can't tell (who, whom) wrote this.

19. The army (is, are) an important part of our nation's defense.

20. Because she is new, Mr. Alvaraz gave Jenny a written copy of (his, her) duties.

Copyright © by Glencoe/McGraw-Hill

Unit 9: Using Modifiers Correctly

Lesson 61
Modifiers: Three Degrees of Comparison

Adjectives and adverbs have three degrees of comparison. The positive form is the base form, the form used as an entry word in a dictionary. It is never used to make a comparison. The comparative form compares two things or people. The superlative form compares three or more things or people.

Alonso is **smart**. He learns **quickly**. (positive)
Alonso is **smarter** than I am. He learns **more quickly** than I do. (comparative)
He is the **smartest** student here. He learns the **most quickly** of all. (superlative)

Most one-syllable adjectives use -*er* or -*est* for the comparative and superlative forms. Spelling changes occur in some of these comparative and superlative forms. Most two-syllable adjectives form the comparative and superlative the same way; however, if -*er* or -*est* sounds awkward, use *more* or *most*. Also use *more* and *most* to form the comparative and superlative of adjectives of three or more syllables.

brave, brav**er**, brav**est**   sad, sad**der**, sad**dest**   pretty, prett**ier**, prett**iest**
hesitant, **more** hesitant, **most** hesitant
comfortable, **more** comfortable, **most** comfortable

Most adverbs of more than one syllable and all adverbs ending in -*ly* use *more* and *most* to form the comparative and superlative degrees.

often, **more** often, **most** often   tightly, **more** tightly, **most** tightly

▶ **Exercise 1** Write in the blank the correct form (positive, comparative, or superlative) of the adjective or adverb in parentheses.

The old plane is _____smaller_____ than the new one. (small)

1. Few activities were _____ to Americans in the early 1900s than flying. (exciting)

2. However, African Americans found it _____ to gain access to the new technology than their white counterparts did. (hard)

3. Due to racial bias, African Americans found access to flight training the _____ of all. (difficult)

4. Many tried to use flying to achieve a _____ status in society. (high)

5. The _____ avid fliers were able to fly in Europe. (fortunate)

6. People in Europe were _____ in the area of racial relations. (tolerant)

Copyright © by Glencoe/McGraw-Hill

Grammar

7. Oddly enough, even in the early part of the twentieth century, African American women pilots were just as _____ as African American male pilots. (famous)

8. Bessie Coleman took flying _____ than most of her contemporaries, and she learned to fly in France. (seriously)

9. People came to see her stunt flying—the _____ the better, they felt. (dangerous)

10. Coleman was one of the _____ fliers of her generation. (adventurous)

▶ **Exercise 2** **Underline the modifier in parentheses that best completes each sentence.**

Another young pilot was (more eager, most eager) to succeed than many of his

contemporaries.

1. Eugene Bullard, America's first African American aviator, learned to fly in France because America was (more racially, most racially) segregated than Europe.

2. Bullard had already learned German during a stay in Berlin, so he learned French even (more quickly, most quickly) than he might have otherwise.

3. He joined the French Foreign Legion and went into action after (hasty, most hasty) training.

4. Bullard hated the killing and said in his autobiography, "Every time the sergeant yelled 'Feu!' I got (sicker, sickest)."

5. Injured in the Battle of Verdun in 1916, Bullard recovered (slowly, most slowly) at a hotel that had been turned into a hospital.

6. Bullard adopted French ways and even would slip into French speech as he grew (more excited, most excited) about an issue.

7. Bullard learned that soldiers with (serious, seriouser) injuries that kept them from trench warfare could still learn to fly.

8. He trained with the French Air Service and was then assigned to Avord, the (larger, largest) air school in France.

9. Despite Bullard's skill, the Lafayette Flying Corps, which included the (more famous, most famous) American aviators flying for France, did not assign him to duty.

10. Eventually he did fly in combat and won the Croix de Guerre, France's (higher, highest) military honor.

Copyright © by Glencoe/McGraw-Hill

Lesson 62
Modifiers: Irregular Comparisons

Grammar

Some common modifiers have irregular comparative forms.

POSITIVE	COMPARATIVE	SUPERLATIVE
good, well, bad, badly, ill	better, worse	best, worst
far (distance)	farther	farthest
far (degree, time)	further	furthest
little, many, much	less, more	least, most

▶ **Exercise 1** **Write in the blank the correct form of the modifier in parentheses.**

The hiker came down with the _____worst_____ case of poison ivy ever. (bad)

1. Janine's performance in the play was _____ than Marilyn's. (good)

2. This is the _____ cold I've ever had. (bad)

3. Cory is _____ curious than Stella about biology. (much)

4. Helen's kite went up _____ of them all. (far)

5. She hurt her knee even _____ in her second fall on the ice. (badly)

6. *The Alien's Revenge* was the _____ movie in the festival. (good)

7. The aliens traveled _____ back in time than they had planned to. (far)

8. Carla's band got the _____ cheers of all the entrants. (many)

9. Dolores adapted _____ to the new school than Gerardo did. (well)

10. With several intact levees, Oakdale had the _____ flooding of all the small towns along the river. (little)

11. Sarah had _____ time for baby-sitting than Clara had. (much)

12. This book on Antarctic travel is the _____ exciting I've read. (much)

13. The house looks in _____ shape than it did before the storm. (bad)

14. The students' enthusiasm for the party was _____ than I expected. (little)

15. Gustavo spelled the _____ of all the competitors. (well)

16. Diana felt _____ of all after her team lost. (badly)

17. The baby ducks swam _____ each day. (far)

18. Officials feared the flu outbreak would be the _____ one yet. (bad)

19. Mr. Carver is _____ than he was yesterday. (ill)

Copyright © by Glencoe/McGraw-Hill

20. Holly explores astronomy _____ than I do. (far)

21. Is the band's new song _____ than its last one? (good)

22. The spring flood was the _____ in years. (bad)

23. Grandmother gets _____ joy from my letters than from my phone calls. (much)

24. The garage is the _____ our cat ever goes from the house. (far)

25. I feel _____ than I did yesterday. (badly)

26. Jake puts his _____ energy into his music. (good)

27. I have nothing _____ to say. (far)

28. We picked six quarts of berries, the _____ ever. (many)

29. Mary completed her exercises in _____ shape than the rest of us. (good)

30. What's the _____ we have to spend to get a new dishwasher? (little)

31. I got _____ answers right than wrong. (many)

32. Yolanda showed the _____ maturity of all. (much)

33. Both players limped, but Brad's limp was _____. (bad)

34. I study _____ of all without the television on. (well)

35. Bankers suffered _____ than farmers in the Depression. (little)

36. The team played the _____ game of the season. (bad)

37. The _____ I hiked, the more my blister hurt. (far)

38. That company has the _____ ads on TV. (bad)

39. I usually feel _____ with the flu than with a cold. (bad)

40. The doctor looked _____ into the man's medical history. (far)

▶ **Writing Link** **Write a paragraph comparing two television programs. Use at least two modifiers that have irregular comparative forms.**

_____

_____

_____

_____

_____

_____

_____

Copyright © by Glencoe/McGraw-Hill

Lesson 63
Modifiers: Double and Incomplete Comparisons

Grammar

A word's comparison forms can use -er and -est or more(less) and most(least), but not both.

Incorrect: The lake is more larger than the pond.
Correct: The lake is **larger** than the pond.
Incorrect: The sequoia is the most largest tree.
Correct: The sequoia is the **largest** tree.

Use other or else to make your comparisons complete or clear.

Unclear: The town department store is larger than any building.
Clear: The town department store is larger than any **other** building.
Unclear: The scientist has more awards than anyone.
Clear: The scientist has more awards than anyone **else**.

Be sure your comparisons compare things that are alike.

Unclear: Rosa's hair is curlier than her mother. (Rosa's hair is being compared
                    incorrectly with her mother in her entirety.)
Clear: Rosa's hair is curlier **than that of her mother**.
Clear: Rosa's hair is curlier **than her mother's hair**.

▶ **Exercise 1** **Circle each double or incomplete comparison. Write *C* in the blank if the sentence is correct.**

_____   Jackie is (more smarter) than anyone else in class.

_____ **1.** The moon is less brighter than the sun.

_____ **2.** The sun is the most brightest object in our solar system.

_____ **3.** It even reflects off Pluto, which is farther away than any other planet.

_____ **4.** Pluto is also smaller than any planet.

_____ **5.** Jupiter is the most largest planet.

_____ **6.** Earth is the largest of all the rocky inner planets.

_____ **7.** The inner planets are less gassier than the outer planets, which are mostly gas.

_____ **8.** Since all the planets were formed at about the same time, it is hard to say which ones

           are more older than the others.

_____ **9.** Venus has a thick atmosphere that is more poisonous than Earth.

_____ **10.** On the other hand, Mars has a thinner atmosphere than that of Earth.

_____ **11.** The most loveliest sights in the solar system are the ring systems around some of the

           planets.

Copyright © by Glencoe/McGraw-Hill

_____ **12.** Of all the planets, Saturn has the most extensive system of rings.

_____ **13.** Because they are so large, Saturn's rings reflect more sunlight and are much more shinier than the rings of Jupiter.

_____ **14.** Our moon looks bright to us because it is much more closer to Earth than the stars.

_____ **15.** Saturn has the most moons of any planet.

▶ **Exercise 2** **Write the correct form of each double or incomplete comparison in the blank. If the comparison is correct write *C* in the blank.**

_____C_____ Our sun is the most important heavenly body for us on Earth.

_____ **1.** However, the sun is smaller and less hotter than many other stars.

_____ **2.** The sun is, of course, the most closest to Earth of all stars.

_____ **3.** Even though the star Proxima Centauri is 4.3 light years away from our sun, it is still closer than any star.

_____ **4.** Astronomers have learned how to tell which stars are more farther away than other stars.

_____ **5.** If several stars have the same magnitude, or true brightness, the star that is the most faintest is the farthest away.

_____ **6.** The most brightest of all stars are supernovas.

_____ **7.** These are huge stars that explode at the end of their lives, and shine brighter than anything else around them for many months.

_____ **8.** After a supernova explodes, the remaining matter falls inward to become the most densest of all stars, a neutron star.

_____ **9.** Even though a neutron star is small, its dense makeup makes it more heavier than any other star.

_____ **10.** Some supernovas collapse inward to form a black hole, where the gravity is stronger than other stars.

_____ **11.** The sun can never be a supernova, because such a star must be much more massive than the mass of our sun.

_____ **12.** The sun will expand and become a red giant eventually, and its surface temperature will become more lower than its temperature at present.

_____ **13.** As the sun expands, in several billion years, the surface of Earth will become the most hottest it has ever been.

_____ **14.** Star color is one way astronomers can tell which stars are the hottest and the most coolest.

_____ **15.** Yellow stars, like our sun, are cooler than stars that are white or blue-white.

Copyright © by Glencoe/McGraw-Hill

Grammar

Lesson 64
Using *Good* or *Well*; *Bad* or *Badly*

Good is always used as a adjective. *Well* is used as an adverb telling how something is done, or as an adjective meaning "in good health."

The Rangers played a **good** game. (adjective)
The house looks **good** after its paint job. (adjective following linking verb)
I can't see **well** from here. (adverb)
I ate too much and now I don't feel **well**. (adjective meaning "in good health")

Bad is always an adjective. *Badly* is an adverb and follows an action verb.

The umpire made a **bad** call. (adjective)
It looks **bad** for the defendant. (adjective following linking verb)
The actress played that part **badly**. (adverb following an action verb)

▶ **Exercise 1** Write *good, well, bad,* or *badly* in the blank to complete each sentence.

Sue hoped her guests would have a _____ good _____ time at the party.

1. At the relay, our team got off to a _____ start.

2. Cecilia felt she had never completed a test so _____.

3. Sean asked Carol to point out the _____ spots on his newly painted car.

4. Connie felt _____ about her part in discovering the comet.

5. If I wake up and don't see the sun, I usually feel _____.

6. We can't hear this videotape very _____.

7. The teacher talked to us about our _____ behavior.

8. The new car performed _____ in the safety test drive.

9. Jay says his brother is not feeling _____ enough to play.

10. That colorful jacket looks _____ on Abel.

11. The episode of *Space Travelers* tonight was very _____.

12. Janine is afraid she will not fit in _____ at her new school.

13. Robert reacted very _____ when he failed the exam.

14. I don't usually like pasta, but this dish is really _____.

15. Homer always behaves _____, even in stressful situations.

16. I hope the politician will give a _____ speech for once.

17. I've had unpleasant medicine before, but this stuff is _____!

Copyright © by Glencoe/McGraw-Hill

Name _____ Class _____ Date _____

18. Is this investment a _____ one?

19. How _____ do you know the new student?

20. Sandra really hopes she will be _____ enough to go to the game.

▶ **Exercise 2** Circle each incorrect use of *good, well, bad,* or *badly*. Write the correct word in the blank. If the sentence is correct, write *C*.

_____badly_____   He was hurt (bad) in the accident.

_____   **1.** Jason thinks he has to do good in every subject he studies.

_____   **2.** The paper reported that the team played bad.

_____   **3.** The swimming team really look well in their bright swimsuits.

_____   **4.** Mika wants bad to win the spelling trophy.

_____   **5.** She has earned good grades all through high school.

_____   **6.** The coming storm looked badly, so we headed for home.

_____   **7.** Alana was hurt badly in her fall from the horse.

_____   **8.** This painting will fit good in that space.

_____   **9.** Sean cannot play chess very good.

_____   **10.** I'm sorry things are going so bad for you.

_____   **11.** I want to do well on the next test so I will study hard.

_____   **12.** The witness testified badly because he was nervous.

_____   **13.** You look good after your long bout with the flu.

_____   **14.** The injury looked badly at first, but it was only skin deep.

_____   **15.** Clancy does not feel very well about refusing to help his brother study.

_____   **16.** Cory was shaking bad after going out in the cold without a coat.

_____   **17.** Amaretto cheesecake is a very good dessert.

_____   **18.** I thought the mediation meeting went very good.

_____   **19.** The fresh fruit went badly before we were able to eat it.

_____   **20.** I don't know your sister very good.

_____   **21.** Kent is a good piano player.

_____   **22.** Sammi plays the oboe good.

_____   **23.** At least Myra's cake wasn't as badly as this soufflé.

_____   **24.** It is well to plan ahead.

Copyright © by Glencoe/McGraw-Hill

Lesson 65
Double Negatives

Grammar

A **double negative** is two negative words in the same clause. Use only one negative word to express a negative idea. You can usually correct a double negative by using one positive form.

NEGATIVE	POSITIVE
neither, never, no, nobody	either, ever, any, anybody
none, no one, nothing, nowhere	anyone, anything, anywhere

Incorrect: I haven't seen **no** stars tonight. (Two negatives – *not* and *no*)
Correct: I haven't seen **any** stars tonight. (Positive *any* replaces negative *no*)
Correct: I have seen **no** stars tonight. (One negative form – *no*)
Incorrect: She **never** goes **nowhere**. (Two negatives – *never* and *nowhere*)
Correct: She **never** goes **anywhere**. (Positive *anywhere* replaces negative *nowhere*.)
Correct: She goes **nowhere**. (One negative form – *nowhere*)

▶ **Exercise 1** Circle each phrase containing a double negative. Rewrite the phrase correctly following the sentence. Most sentences can be corrected in more than one way. Write *C* if the sentence is correct.

There (isn't no) animal on Earth that humans envy as much as birds. _isn't any/is no_____

1. There isn't no better time for birding than spring. _____

2. I don't like nothing as much as welcoming the migrating birds as they come north. _____
_____

3. Many of my friends don't know nothing about identifying birds. _____
_____

4. I wasn't getting nowhere with birdwatching myself until I bought a good field guide. _____

5. I couldn't tell any difference between a Canada warbler and a magnolia warbler, for example.
_____

6. There isn't no better way to tell them apart than to focus on their "necklaces," the markings
around their yellow necks. _____

7. The short "necklace" on the Canada warbler isn't nothing like the long hanging "necklace" on
the magnolia warbler. _____

8. To be sure you can see both birds up close, there is no better investment than a good pair of
binoculars. _____

Copyright © by Glencoe/McGraw-Hill

Grammar

9. Before I had a book and binoculars, I could not name none of the rarer birds that fill our skies

each spring. _____

10. I couldn't identify nothing except our familiar robin, blue jay, and crow. _____

_____

11. Now there isn't nothing like the thrill of sighting a bluebird or a yellow-billed cuckoo. _____

_____

12. On weekends, I don't study nothing but my bird book. _____

13. At first I didn't expect any success as a bird-watcher. _____

14. I couldn't tell no difference between the various kinds of lake ducks. _____

_____

15. Because I have the book, I won't never forget the difference between the red-headed and red-

bellied woodpeckers. _____

16. Though both have red head markings, downy woodpeckers don't have no long bills like hairy

woodpeckers. _____

17. I haven't seen no pileated woodpecker yet. _____

18. For a while I wasn't getting nowhere with identifying the many warblers. _____

_____

19. But finally I realized that there is nothing I'd rather do in the early morning than see which

birds are around. _____

20. Unfortunately, my sister will stop at nothing to try to confuse me with her birdcalls. _____

_____

▶ **Exercise 2** Circle each double negative and correct it following the sentence. Write *C* if the
sentence is correct.

There (aren't no) animals more interesting than birds. _____ aren't any/are no

1. Because humans can't never fly, at least by themselves, birds fascinate us. _____

_____

2. Humans do not have a body shape like a bird's skeleton. _____

3. With its long straight neck, beak, and legs, a bird doesn't let nothing get in the way of its

streamlined travel. _____

4. Birds' bones are hollow and don't carry no extra weight. _____

Copyright © by Glencoe/McGraw-Hill

5. And without its strategically placed feathers, a bird wouldn't get nowhere in the air. _____
_____

6. If you look at a plane, you can see that it looks like nothing so much as a big bird. _____

7. It seems that human beings are determined that there isn't nothing we can't do if we set our

minds to it. _____

8. Some birds don't never fly. _____

9. Penguins' strong wings don't take them nowhere in the air. _____
_____

10. A swan swims and hasn't no reason to fly. _____

11. Ostriches don't fly because they are such swift runners. _____

12. Birds haven't no way to store much energy, so they must eat much of the time. _____
_____

13. There aren't no activities that use as much energy as flying and maintaining a constant body

temperature. _____

14. So there are few times during a bird's waking hours when it is not seeking food or eating.
_____

15. Birds and reptiles haven't no differences in the area of reproduction. _____

16. They both lay eggs, which don't never hatch until the young are ready. _____

17. Birds' beaks aren't nothing like one another. _____

18. Some birds break into seeds and nuts with beaks that are like nothing so much as a chisel.
_____

19. Ducks don't have no reason for a sharp beak, because their flat beaks filter food from the water.
_____

20. Nature doesn't give nothing to a bird, or any creature, that is not useful in some way. _____
_____

▶ **Exercise 3** **Place a check in the blank next to each sentence that uses negatives correctly.**

____✔____ The scientific name for owls is not heard very often, but they are known as *strigiformes.*

_____ 1. Owls haven't never been studied as closely as other birds.

_____ 2. They are not known for their friendliness.

Copyright © by Glencoe/McGraw-Hill

_____ 3. In fact, some people have feared owls even though the owls never did them no harm.

_____ 4. Superstitions have arisen around these creatures, but I never believed none of them.

_____ 5. Owls are not noisy when they move about; their secretive nature has made it difficult for scientists to study them.

_____ 6. There is hardly no place in the world where they cannot be found.

_____ 7. Owls do not usually hunt for no food during the day.

_____ 8. They do not generally live in no groups, either.

_____ 9. These birds of prey are loners, but they are not without their usefulness.

_____ 10. At night, barn owls do not hesitate to capture any rodents lurking around a farm.

_____ 11. However, owls are not known for their nest-building talents.

_____ 12. Sometimes they don't build none of the nest themselves; they simply use a nest that a hawk or a crow has abandoned.

_____ 13. You won't find oval eggs in their nests because owl eggs are nearly round.

_____ 14. No more than twelve eggs will be laid at one- or two-day intervals.

_____ 15. Females aren't never the only ones to care for the nest; males do, too.

_____ 16. Neither males nor females will allow another animal or a human to intrude upon their nest.

_____ 17. You couldn't find nowhere to hide if one of them thought you were attacking its young.

_____ 18. Young owls are not pushed out of the nest as soon as the young of other kinds of birds.

_____ 19. Owls are not as closely related to hawks as they are to nighthawks and whippoorwills.

_____ 20. I didn't never realize there are 525 different kinds of owls.

_____ 21. The burrowing owl is not the smallest—that would be the elf owl.

_____ 22. The elf owl isn't no more than six inches long.

_____ 23. Most great gray owls grow to no less than thirty inches in length.

_____ 24. I haven't nowhere seen anything as unnerving as the stare of one of these birds.

_____ 25. Owls' eyes are not on either side of their head, like most birds, but pointed forward.

_____ 26. This isn't the only reason their gazes seem so piercing.

_____ 27. Owls cannot never move their eyes in their sockets the way humans do.

_____ 28. An owl cannot see a moving object unless it moves its entire head.

_____ 29. No wonder nothing is no stronger than the glare of an owl.

_____ 30. Nobody thinks of other birds as being smarter; the owl's wide-eyed stare has helped it gain a reputation for wisdom.

Copyright © by Glencoe/McGraw-Hill

Lesson 66
Misplaced and Dangling Modifiers

Misplaced modifiers modify the wrong word, or seem to modify more than one word in a sentence. Correct such a construction by moving the modifier as close as you can to the word it modifies.

Misplaced: The campers slipped on the mossy rocks **crossing the river**.
Clear: The campers **crossing the river** slipped on the mossy rocks.

Some **dangling modifiers** do not seem to modify any word in the sentence. To correct this, use a word that the dangling modifier can modify.

Dangling: **Canoeing all day**, a break was needed.
Clear: **Canoeing all day**, the campers needed a break.

The word *only* must be placed before the word or group of words it modifies in order for the sentence to be clear.

Unclear: Stella **only** takes trumpet lessons in the summer.
Clear: Stella takes **only** trumpet lessons in the summer. (She takes no other lessons except trumpet.)
Clear: Stella takes trumpet lessons **only** in the summer. (She takes trumpet lessons at no other time except in the summer.)
Clear: **Only** Stella takes trumpet lessons in the summer. (No one else takes trumpet lessons except Stella.)

▶ **Exercise 1 Circle each misplaced or dangling modifier. Write in the blank the word that the dangling or misplaced modifier should modify. If the sentence is correct, write *C* in the blank.**

_____audience_____   (Laughing at all his jokes,) Stan was happy with the audience.

_____   1. Waiting for the game to begin, Karen's heart pounded.

_____   2. Invented in California, millions of people worldwide now thrill at the sport of skateboarding.

_____   3. Rising at dawn, the sun led the hikers across the prairie.

_____   4. Proposing a new law, the congresswoman documented the need for stricter safety regulations.

_____   5. Each week on his paper route, customers pay Dan for delivery.

_____   6. Regina fashioned sculptures of the fairgoers made of clay.

_____   7. Searching frantically, the family's lost dog was found.

_____   8. Lakeisha saw several distant farmhouses and barns climbing the tree.

Copyright © by Glencoe/McGraw-Hill

_____ 9. Whimpering under the couch, the storm frightened our dog.

_____ 10. Hunched over his books, Kwasi studied long into the night for the test.

_____ 11. Sneaking up on her brother, an apple fell on Hannah's head and made her cry out.

_____ 12. Flying over the prairie, the antelope were frightened by the plane's noise.

_____ 13. The witnesses said they saw a man rushing from the jewelry store with a black hat.

_____ 14. After waiting for hours, the ticket seller said we would have to wait for the next showing.

_____ 15. Cleaning my room, I found my favorite socks.

_____ 16. Running neck and neck, the contestants crossed the finish line at the same time.

_____ 17. Listening to the news, the reporter described the scene of an accident I had just driven past.

_____ 18. Pitching a no hitter, the crowd cheered Marcy as she left the field.

_____ 19. Dad gave a new bicycle to Jeff with ten speeds.

_____ 20. Aimed at the Pole Star, the cold weather made my telescope hard to manipulate.

▶ **Exercise 2** **Place a carat (ʌ) and write the word *only* where it should be properly placed to match each meaning in parentheses.**

     only
 Marsha talked to Lilla ʌ at the party. (Marsha did not talk to Lilla except at the party.)

1. Rafi paid ten dollars for the purple sweater. (Rafi bought the last purple sweater available.)

2. Rafi paid ten dollars for the purple sweater. (Rafi got a sweater for a sale price.)

3. Rafi paid ten dollars for the purple sweater. (No one else had the money to buy the sweater.)

4. Rock hunting is the main hobby of my cousin. (My cousin has several hobbies besides rock hunting.)

5. Rock hunting is the main hobby of my cousin. (The speaker has just one cousin.)

6. Hal is allowed to camp out overnight on weekends. (No one else is allowed to camp out overnight on weekends.)

Copyright © by Glencoe/McGraw-Hill

7. Hal is allowed to camp out overnight on weekends. (Hal is not allowed to camp out overnight during the rest of the week.)

8. Hal is allowed to camp out overnight on weekends. (Hal must study during the day on weekends.)

9. Mickey played Peter Pan when she attended Columbus High School. (Mickey did not play Peter Pan anyplace besides Columbus High School.)

10. Mickey played Peter Pan while she attended Columbus High School. (Mickey did not play any other role while she attended Columbus High School.)

11. Mickey played Peter Pan while she attended Columbus High School. (No one else played Peter Pan except Mickey.)

12. Jody turned in a ten-page report for science class. (Jody did not turn in a ten-page report for any other class.)

13. Jody turned in a ten-page report for science class. (No one else turned in a ten-page report.)

14. Jody turned in a ten-page report for science class. (Jody's report for science class was too short.)

15. I wrote Grandma three letters this semester. (I usually write more often to Grandma.)

16. I wrote Grandma three letters this semester. (No one else wrote three letters to Grandma.)

17. I wrote Grandma three letters this semester. (I did not write three letters to anybody except Grandma.)

18. Marty likes to develop his own pictures. (Marty doesn't like to develop anyone else's pictures.)

19. Marty likes to develop his own pictures. (No one else likes to develop his or her own pictures.)

20. Graham takes the train when he has a lot of extra time to travel. (Graham takes the plane when he doesn't have a lot of time.)

▶ **Exercise 3** **Place a check in the blank next to each sentence that uses modifiers correctly.**

_____✔_____   Racing to catch the bus, Tina tripped over an uneven sidewalk.

_____ **1.** The third contestant walked down the runway wearing a tuxedo.

_____ **2.** A bird with red feathers perched on a branch of the maple tree.

_____ **3.** Greg jogs only on Saturdays and Sundays. (Greg never jogs on weekdays.)

_____ **4.** Samantha only says she is ready to leave. (No one but Samantha is ready to leave.)

_____ **5.** Cameron slipped on the ice waiting for his ride.

_____ **6.** Hoping the sky would clear, more gray clouds appeared on the horizon.

Copyright © by Glencoe/McGraw-Hill

Grammar

_____ 7. The grandfather clock chimed the hour in the hall.

_____ 8. Eating his pie with incredible speed, Jordan won the contest at the county fair.

_____ 9. Only Maureen would have written a poem like that. (No one but Maureen would have written such a poem.)

_____ 10. Two books on display at the library looked interesting to me, so I checked them out.

_____ 11. Dr. Rodriguez thinks only I might need glasses. (Dr. Rodriguez thinks of nothing else.)

_____ 12. The man walked across the street in a black fedora.

_____ 13. Singing the ballad for the first time, Frank's phrasing was remarkably accurate.

_____ 14. Cleaning her room, Melanie's lost necklace was discovered behind the bed.

_____ 15. A tour guide showed us the pandas in a leopard-print shirt.

_____ 16. Grandpa plants only tomatoes and lettuce in his garden. (Grandpa plants nothing but tomatoes and lettuce.)

_____ 17. Katrina will ski this mountain filled with determination.

_____ 18. The vase containing yellow roses brightened the room considerably.

_____ 19. Mr. Lee only knows two of the students in the algebra class. (Mr. Lee doesn't know all of the students.)

_____ 20. Gasping for breath, the hill slowed the runner down.

_____ 21. The child playing in the treehouse is Amanda's niece.

_____ 22. Helping Mom put away the groceries, I saw that she had bought my favorite dessert.

_____ 23. Gordon only works in the hardware store during the summer. (Gordon alone works in the hardware store.)

_____ 24. Only the passengers with small children are allowed to board. (No one but those with children can board.)

_____ 25. The car belongs to Kendra with the green exterior.

▶ **Writing Link** **Write two or three sentences about a new food you have tried recently. Use at least one modifier, correctly placed.**

_____

_____

_____

_____

_____

_____

Copyright © by Glencoe/McGraw-Hill

☑ Unit 9 **Review**

▶ **Exercise 1** **Underline the word or phrase in parentheses that best completes each sentence.**

The airplane is (<u>quicker</u>, quickest) than the train.

1. Zahara is (more talented, most talented) than Celia.

2. This is the (better, best) meal you've ever served.

3. The street was so (icy, iciest) we had to hold hands.

4. Devon is (silly, sillier) than anyone else in class.

5. We paid the (less, least) amount for the green dishes.

6. If you trade seats with me, you will be able to see (better, best).

7. We cried the (more, most) at the story of the lost dog.

8. This track star jumped (farther, further) than anyone else.

9. That is the (more ridiculous, most ridiculous) statement I've ever heard.

10. Because it did not deal with the real issues, the mayor's speech seemed (bad, badly) to us.

11. Carry this box; it's (light, lighter) than yours.

12. Now the table is (wobblier, wobbliest) than it was before.

13. Sal didn't do as (good, well) as he had hoped in the game.

14. That is the (worse, worst) joke I've ever heard!

15. Zina sings (bad, badly) and out of tune, but she doesn't care.

16. I am much (less, least) patient than my brother.

17. Sheila stumbled (bad, badly) and sprained her ankle.

18. I made Grandpa (more comfortable, most comfortable) with a pillow.

19. She wants to explore the Middle Ages (farther, further) than we have done in class.

20. Homer is the (more restless, most restless) of all.

21. I think *My Cousin Vinny* is the (funnier, funniest) movie ever made.

22. Patrick has the flu and doesn't feel (good, well) today.

23. Liz didn't have (any, no) tissues with her.

24. This small car gets (good, better) gas mileage than that luxury sedan.

25. I'm (sleepier, sleepiest) today than I should be.

Copyright © by Glencoe/McGraw-Hill

Cumulative Review: Units 1–9

▶ **Exercise 1** Underline the word in parentheses that best completes each sentence. Write *adj.* in the blank if the word is an adjective or *adv.* if it is an adverb.

adj.   The play we saw last night was a (<u>powerful</u>, powerfully) drama.

_____ **1.** Your brother sings (wonderful, wonderfully).

_____ **2.** The bathtub always looks (clean, cleanly) after I've used it.

_____ **3.** The cougar moved (quiet, quietly) through the forest after its prey.

_____ **4.** Can't you make your room be more (neat, neatly)?

_____ **5.** Is that a (real, really) diamond?

_____ **6.** My, that movie certainly was (terrible, terribly).

_____ **7.** The puppy watched (hungry, hungrily) while the kitten ate.

_____ **8.** I didn't know you could ski so (good, well).

_____ **9.** She is coughing (bad, badly) because of her cold.

_____ **10.** The lost campers were found (safe, safely) in the cave.

_____ **11.** The explorers peered (cautious, cautiously) over the rim of the volcano.

_____ **12.** After the storm, the water tasted (bad, badly) for a week.

_____ **13.** Thad is very (studious, studiously) about his courses.

_____ **14.** When you read poetry aloud, try to speak very (distinct, distinctly).

_____ **15.** The cricket sprang (sudden, suddenly) into the air.

_____ **16.** This pie tastes very (good, well).

_____ **17.** Jadzia feels very (strong, strongly) about the kind treatment of animals.

_____ **18.** She tries not to feel (envious, enviously) at her friends' successes.

_____ **19.** Are you (serious, seriously)?

_____ **20.** This bread is no longer (fresh, freshly).

_____ **21.** More (important, importantly), using the computer for this project will save us money.

_____ **22.** The TV advertisement made me (real, really) hungry.

_____ **23.** The new guidance counselor is extremely (friend, friendly).

_____ **24.** We (almost, most) caught a ten-pound fish!

_____ **25.** Turn (right, rightly) at the stop sign.

Copyright © by Glencoe/McGraw-Hill

▶ **Exercise 2** Circle each clause. Write in the blank whether the clause is an adjective clause (*adj.*) or an adverb clause (*adv.*).

___adv.___   We were late for the party (because we had a flat tire.)

_____ 1. After the party was over, we walked home.

_____ 2. This is the astronomy book that has the best photos.

_____ 3. Is that the building that you described?

_____ 4. This vase, which you broke, cannot be replaced.

_____ 5. Since I changed schools, I am getting better grades.

_____ 6. Here are the themes, which I have corrected.

_____ 7. Mrs. Ortiz is the one who phoned us.

_____ 8. If you look closely, you will see a bluebird.

_____ 9. The train came into view as it rounded the curve.

_____ 10. The team captains can choose the goal that they want to defend.

_____ 11. Is this the lake where you saw that huge turtle?

_____ 12. That was the stormy day when everyone went home early.

_____ 13. I hope the comic will perform again before we leave.

_____ 14. Although I don't like him, I was polite to Mr. Carver.

_____ 15. Sila, who lives next door, is climbing our tree.

_____ 16. I found your jacket in the room where we store the junk.

_____ 17. I'll plan to meet you for dinner unless I hear from you.

_____ 18. I recognized Velma because I had seen her at the game.

_____ 19. Rex is the dog that rescued the two children.

_____ 20. Grandma sat where she could see the birdfeeder.

_____ 21. That is the chair where President Carter sat.

_____ 22. Mrs. Sharvy, who plays bridge every day, needs a new deck of cards.

_____ 23. Saturday was the day when Cole was supposed to mow the lawn.

_____ 24. We laughed when the clown honked his nose.

_____ 25. The noise of the stereo was so loud that Rayna couldn't hear the phone.

Copyright © by Glencoe/McGraw-Hill

Grammar

► **Exercise 3** **Circle each double negative, double or incomplete comparison, and dangling or misplaced modifier. If the sentence is correct, write *C* in the blank.**

_____ (Hoping to surprise her friend,) the gift was sent by mail.

_____ 1. Speaking before a large group, the crowd made Kevin nervous.

_____ 2. Cruising at the same speed, the sleepy driver fought to keep awake.

_____ 3. Waiting patiently for the phone call, the sudden ring startled Ben.

_____ 4. Sean is closer to Joe than any classmate.

_____ 5. We shouldn't never have left the windows open.

_____ 6. The man leaped from the fire escape in the gray suit.

_____ 7. These pants are more tighter than they used to be.

_____ 8. Carrying a flaming dessert, the family awaited the waiter with anticipation.

_____ 9. Doesn't no one have the time?

_____ 10. Creeping around the building, the spy ran into the police.

_____ 11. His shoes are sturdier than Joe.

_____ 12. The actor in the red cape entered from stage right.

_____ 13. Hiking for several hours, the campers were exhausted and dirty.

_____ 14. Shooting a basket while running, the referee called a foul on the Eagles player.

_____ 15. I don't have no way to get to the meeting.

_____ 16. Winning every trophy in her class, the crowd cheered the runner.

_____ 17. This is the most messiest room I've ever seen!

_____ 18. Reggie found several rocks on his hike for his collection.

_____ 19. She shouldn't never have taken the test without studying.

_____ 20. I don't ever want to take such a hard test again.

_____ 21. Sheila couldn't have been more happier.

_____ 22. Baking in the oven, I smelled the cookies.

_____ 23. Frightened by the movie, Tricia was unable to fall asleep.

_____ 24. Pedro's computer is a newer model than Graham.

_____ 25. "Don't nobody move," the FBI agent exclaimed.

Copyright © by Glencoe/McGraw-Hill

*U*sage

Unit 10: Usage Glossary

Lesson 67
Usage: *a* to *altogether*

---

a, an *A* is used before words beginning with a consonant or "yew" sound. *An* is used before words beginning with a vowel sound.

a computer   **a** unicorn   **an** apple   **an** otter   **an** honor

a lot *A lot,* meaning "a large amount," should never be used as one word.

There's **a lot** of ice.

a while, awhile *A while* is part of a prepositional phrase and is usually preceded by *in* or *for. Awhile* is a single word used as an adverb.

Take a break for **a while**.   The dog barked **awhile**.

accept, except *Accept* is a verb that means "to receive" or "to agree to." *Except* is a preposition meaning "but" or a verb meaning "leave out."

Will you **accept** this gift? (verb)   Paint everything **except** the garage. (preposition)
The trial will **except** the informant from the charges. (verb)

adapt, adopt *Adapt* means "to adjust." *Adopt* means "to take something for one's own."

Can lizards **adapt** to a cold climate?   The city will **adopt** a new charter.

advice, advise *Advice* is a noun that means "recommendation." *Advise* is a verb that means "to give advice or counsel."

I need your **advice**.   I need you to **advise** me on this problem.

▶ **Exercise 1 Underline the word in parentheses that best completes each sentence.**

Sheila plans to (adapt, <u>adopt</u>) the first-aid practices she learned in health class.

1. It is (a, an) useful thing to know first aid for emergencies.

2. The best (advice, advise) for serious injuries is to call for help immediately.

3. You may need to keep the person comfortable for (awhile, a while).

4. Never move an injured person, (accept, except) to prevent more injury.

5. (A, An) victim of shock may engage in quick and shallow breathing.

6. Professionals (advice, advise) that injured persons should always be treated for shock.

7. Help shock victims (adapt, adopt) a position with the legs raised.

8. You may need to keep a shock victim warm for (awhile, a while).

Copyright © by Glencoe/McGraw-Hill

Usage

9. While you wait for (a, an) ambulance, reassure the injured person.

10. (Advice, Advise) him or her that help is on the way.

---

affect, effect *Affect* is a verb meaning "to cause a change in." *Effect* is a noun that means "result" or a verb that means "to bring about."

Your opinion won't **affect** my choice.
The rain will **effect** an increase in the crop yield and have an **effect** on grain prices.

ain't *Ain't* is unacceptable in speaking and writing. Use *I am not, she is not,* etc.

I **am not** going to explain this again!

all ready, already *All ready* means "completely ready." *Already* is an adverb that means "before" or "by this time."

I'm **all ready** to go.   We've **already** started.

all right, alright It is preferable to write this expression as two words.

I felt **all right** before I ate the huge sundae.

all together, altogether *All together* means "in a group." *Altogether* is an adverb that means "completely" or "on the whole."

Let's go **all together** to Sal's.   I am **altogether** in agreement with you.

▶ **Exercise 2** Write the correct word in the blank to replace each word or phrase in italics. If the word or phrase is correct, write *C* in the blank.

_____is not_____ Whatever he has, it *ain't* frostbite.

_____ **1.** Frostbite *effects* fingers, toes, ears, nose, and other areas.

_____ **2.** Rubbing frostbitten skin with snow *ain't* a good idea.

_____ **3.** However, it is *alright* to cover the area with a warm hand.

_____ **4.** It is *all together* important to get the victim inside quickly.

_____ **5.** It is not *all right* to use very hot water to soak the skin.

_____ **6.** It is *all together* a bad idea to treat frostbite with heat sources such as heating pads or hot water bottles.

_____ **7.** Too much heat has severe *affects* on the skin, too.

_____ **8.** The cold has *all ready* injured the skin.

_____ **9.** Now the excess heat can *affect* the skin with blisters.

_____ **10.** Cover the blisters with bandages to *effect* healing.

Copyright © by Glencoe/McGraw-Hill

Usage

Lesson 68
Usage: *allusion* to *could of*

---

allusion, illusion *Allusion* means "an indirect reference." *Illusion* means "a false idea."

The mayor made an **allusion** to his plan, but his dreams of success were an **illusion**.

anywheres, everywheres Do not use an -*s*; Use *anywhere, everywhere*.

Uncle Ed will travel **anywhere**. He really has been **everywhere**.

bad, badly *Bad* is an adjective; *badly* is an adverb.

I hurt my knee **badly** in my **bad** fall.

being as, being that Use *because* or *since* in formal speech or writing.

Because it rained, we stayed in.　　　　**Since** you came early, we will eat now.

beside, besides *Beside* means "next to." *Besides* means "in addition to" or "also."

The cat slept **beside** the bed.　　　　**Besides** Aunt Char, Mom will be there.

between, among Use *between* to refer to two persons or things. Use *among* to refer to more than two persons or things.

Six members argued **among** themselves. The quarrel was **between** Mike and Han.

▶ **Exercise 1**　**Write the correct word in the blank to replace each word or phrase in italics.**

_____illusion_____　　It's an *allusion* that Earth is a solid planet.

_____　**1.** Continental drift is a theory that is now believed *everywheres*.

_____　**2.** If you put North and South America *besides* each other, they would fit together.

_____　**3.** *Being as* at one time only one continent may have existed, all the continents would have fit together.

_____　**4.** When Alfred Wegener suggested this theory, people reacted *bad*.

_____　**5.** How could the huge continents have moved *anywheres* at all?

_____　**6.** However, Wegener showed other evidence *beside*.

_____　**7.** There was a similarity *between* the many species of animal and plant fossils on the continents of Africa, South America, Australia, and Asia.

_____　**8.** He also made *illusion* to the one-time presence of glaciers in Australia.

_____　**9.** *Being as* glaciers can exist only in cold climates, Australia may once have been farther north.

_____　**10.** Still, people *everywheres* doubted the continental drift theory.

Copyright © by Glencoe/McGraw-Hill

Usage

borrow, lend, loan *Borrow* means "to take something with the intention of returning it." *Lend* means "to give something with the intention that it will be returned." *Loan* is a noun.

You may **borrow** my CD if you will **lend** me your tape. I have your video game on **loan**.

bring, take *Bring* means "to carry from a distant place to a closer one." *Take* means "to carry from a nearby place to a more distant one."

Take this hoe to Mr. Lin's and **bring** back our shovel.

can, may *Can* indicates the ability to do something. *May* indicates permission or the possibility of doing something.

Since I **can** already speak Spanish, you **may** borrow my Spanish book.

can't hardly, can't scarcely These are double negatives. Use *can hardly* or *can scarcely*.

I **can hardly** believe your story. You **can scarcely** expect me to believe it.

continual, continuous Use *continual* to describe action that occurs regularly but with pauses. Use *continuous* to describe action that occurs with no interruption.

Jean hated the **continuous** noise of the crowd and the **continual** punching of the boxers.

could of, might of, must of, should of, would of These are incorrect. Use the helping verb *have* with *could, might, must, should,* and *would.*

You **could have** warned me, and then I **would have** remembered her birthday.

▶ **Exercise 2** Write the correct word or words in the blank to replace each word or phrase in italics. If the word or phrase is already correct, write *C* in the blank.

_____must have_____ Scientists *must of* discovered more facts besides Wegener's proofs.

_____ 1. They *can't hardly* believe what they found.

_____ 2. They saw that molten rock oozes *continuously* from the seafloor.

_____ 3. It cools, hardens, and is *brought* away from the openings, or rifts.

_____ 4. This, said scientists, *can* explain how continents move.

_____ 5. If the seafloor moved, Earth's crust *could of* moved, too.

_____ 6. This movement *lends* credence to the theory of plate tectonics, which suggests that Earth is broken into large plates.

_____ 7. Geologists *may* tell that when two continental plates collide, they push up material and form mountain ranges.

_____ 8. In fact, the Himalayas are *continually* rising by five centimeters each year.

_____ 9. When one plate dives under another one, volcanoes *can* erupt.

_____ 10. Where plates slide alongside one another, the land *can't hardly* avoid earthquakes.

Copyright © by Glencoe/McGraw-Hill

Lesson 69
Usage: *different from* to *regardless*

different from, different than In general, use the first expression.

Tonight's newscaster is **different from** last night's.

doesn't, don't *Doesn't* forms the contraction of "does not" and is used with *he, she, it,* and other singular nouns. *Don't* forms the contraction of "do not" and is used with *I, you, we, they,* and all plural nouns.

We **don't** like Mark's new car. He **doesn't** care what we think.

emigrate, immigrate *Emigrate* means "to move from one country to another," and *immigrate* means "to enter a country to settle there." Use the phrases *emigrate from* and *immigrate to* or *into*.

Jani's family **immigrated** to the United States in 1910.
They **emigrated** from Russia.

farther, further *Farther* is used with physical distance. *Further* is used to show time or degree.

The glacier moved **farther** down the slope each day.
Scientists are doing **further** studies of glaciers.

fewer, less Use *fewer* with nouns that can be counted. Use *less* with nouns that cannot be counted and with figures that represent a single amount or quantity.

There are **fewer** icicles and **less** ice on the roof than last year.
Not many people can run a mile in **less** than four minutes. (*Four minutes* represents a single period of time, not individual minutes.)

▶ **Exercise 1** Underline the word in parentheses that best completes each sentence.

This popcorn is (different from, different than) the kind we had last week.

1. My pickup has (fewer, less) wheels than that larger truck.

2. Many people (emigrated, immigrated) to the United States in the early 1900s.

3. I thought the shed was (farther, further) into the woods than this.

4. Patricia (doesn't, don't) like that new video.

5. I need to think (farther, further) about this important decision.

6. Did your family (emigrate, immigrate) from China?

7. The school is holding (fewer, less) dances this year than last year.

8. Vanesa's haircut is (different from, different than) her mother's.

Copyright © by Glencoe/McGraw-Hill

9. I'd like to spend (fewer, less) than ten dollars for the present.

10. They (doesn't, don't) think we can win the championship.

---

good, well *Good* is an adjective. *Well* is an adverb. When referring to health, use *well*.

Sam felt **good** about how **well** he had performed at the concert.   I don't feel **well**.

had of Use only *had* with a past participle.

I wish you **had** told me you were going to be late.

hanged, hung Use *hanged* to mean "put to death by hanging." Use *hung* in all other cases.

The military **hanged** deserters.   We **hung** from the tree by our knees.

in, into, in to *In* means "inside" or "within" and *into* indicates movement or direction from outside to inside. *In to* combines an adverb with a preposition and is different from both.

Jack was working **in** his room when a stranger walked **into** the house.
Bring the employees **in to** meet the new boss.

irregardless, regardless Always use *regardless*. To use *ir-* and *-less* together forms a double negative.

Regardless of what you think, I am going to enter the contest.

▶ **Exercise 2 Underline the word in parentheses that best completes each sentence.**

Many soldiers were (<u>hanged</u>, hung) during the Civil War.

1. Stack the groceries (in, into, in to) the pantry.

2. I wish you (had of, had) written to me about your award.

3. Mother is feeling particularly (good, well) since her retirement.

4. The soaked dog barked to come (in, into, in to) the house.

5. The voters will choose their favorite candidate (irregardless, regardless) of the polls.

6. This new paint really gives a (good, well) finish.

7. We (hanged, hung) the colorful textile above the fireplace.

8. (Irregardless, Regardless) of our differences, we can work together.

9. She took the new student (in, into, in to) meet the principal.

10. Because Maya drew (good, well), she was asked to design the yearbook cover.

Copyright © by Glencoe/McGraw-Hill

Usage

Lesson 70
Usage: *this kind* to *reason is because*

this kind, these kinds Use the singular *this* and *that* to modify *kind, type, sort.* Use the plural *these* and *those* to modify *kinds, types, sorts.*

This kind of apple is tart, but **those kinds** are sweet.
That type of computer is expensive, while **these types** are cheaper.

lay, lie *Lay* means "to put" or "to place" and takes a direct object. *Lie* means "to recline" or "to be positioned" and never takes a direct object.

Lay this video next to the VCR. Never mind, the cat wants to **lie** there.
I **laid** your clothes on the bed. Then the dog **lay** down on top of them.

learn, teach *Learn* means "to receive knowledge or skill." *Teach* means "to impart knowledge or skill."

She wants to **learn** to dive. Her brother will **teach** her after school.

leave, let *Leave* means "to go away." *Let* means "to allow or permit."

Do you have to **leave** now? **Let** me convince you to stay awhile.

like, as if *Like* introduces a prepositional phrase. *As* and *as if* introduce subordinate clauses.

This looks **like** a good movie. It looks **as if** it would be funny.
He hoped he wouldn't forget his lines **as** he had done before.

▶ **Exercise 1** **Underline the word in parentheses that best completes each sentence.**

This pie tastes (like, <u>as if</u>) it's stale.

1. My little brother will never (learn, teach) the correct way to program the VCR.

2. Did you (lay, lie) your cap on the sidewalk?

3. (Leave, Let) the firefighters through!

4. (This kind, These kinds) of skateboard is the most dangerous.

5. You look (like, as) a vampire in that getup!

6. Can you (learn, teach) me to use the graphics display?

7. It seems (like, as if) I already read this chapter.

8. You can (leave, let) the package inside the screen door.

9. After the hike, I was so exhausted I wanted to (lay, lie) on the grass.

10. I hate (this kind, these kinds) of buttons!

Copyright © by Glencoe/McGraw-Hill

loose, lose Use *loose* to mean "free" or "not fitting tightly." Use *lose* to mean "to misplace" or "to fail to win."

Fasten that **loose** shutter, or you might **lose** it in the high wind.

passed, past *Passed* is the past tense and past participle of *to pass. Past* is used as an adjective, adverb, preposition, or noun.

The racers **passed** the finish line. (verb)
Where have you been the **past** week? (adjective)
The mice crept **past** the sleeping cat. (preposition)
The car went **past** so fast I couldn't identify it. (adverb)
Morley recalled the victories from the **past**. (noun)

precede, proceed *Precede* means "to go or come before." *Proceed* means "to continue" or "to move along."

I **preceded** Kim into the hall and then **proceeded** to the head table.

raise, rise *Raise* means "to cause to move upward" and takes an object. *Rise* means "to get up" and does not take an object.

I watched the colt **raise** its head from sleep and then **rise** from its bed.

reason is because This phrase is repetitious. Use either *reason is that* or *because.*

The **reason** I called **is that** I will be late. I called **because** I knew you'd worry if I didn't.

▶ **Exercise 2 Underline the word in parentheses that best completes each sentence.**

Bill has lost weight these (passed, <u>past</u>) few months.

1. I was so tired I could hardly (raise, rise) my head.

2. Jeb hoped he would not (loose, lose) the present.

3. The reason I was angry (was because, was that) you laughed at me.

4. (Raise, Rise) the shades when the sun goes down.

5. Was that the ice cream truck that just went (passed, past)?

6. I hope that we all (passed, past) that course.

7. The rock band was (preceded, proceeded) by a comic act.

8. Ajay's filling came (loose, lose), so he went to the dentist.

9. It will be hard for the spy to get (passed, past) the sentry.

10. The farmers fear they will (loose, lose) their crops in the drought.

11. If you can (raise, rise) early enough, you can go fishing with us.

12. The reason he took the bus (is because, is that) his car is in the shop.

Copyright © by Glencoe/McGraw-Hill

Lesson 71
Usage: *respectfully* to *whom*

respectfully, respectively *Respectfully* means "with respect." *Respectively* means "in the order named."

Please act **respectfully** when you meet the ambassador.
Jean and Bill are sister and brother, **respectively**.

says, said *Says* is the third-person singular of the verb "to say." *Said* is the past tense of "to say."

Last week you **said** that you wanted to hike up Bald Mountain.
Whenever anyone **says** that, I know it's time to lace up my boots.

sit, set *Sit* means "to put oneself in a sitting position" and usually does not take an object. *Set* means "to put or place" and usually takes an object. When used to indicate the setting sun, *set* does not take an object.

Where should I **sit**?   Where should I **set** this box of cookies?

than, then *Than* is a conjunction used in a comparison. It is also used to show exception. *Then* is an adverb that means "at that time," "soon afterward," "at another time," "for that reason," or "in that case."

Sal is taller **than** Jill.   Other **than** Marcia, no one left.
The band had played by **then**.   She slept all night and **then** felt rested.

this here, that there Do not use *here* and *there* after *this* and *that*.

Do you like **this** painting?   I like it a lot better than **that** one!

who, whom Use *who* as the subject of a sentence. Use *whom* as the direct object of a verb or the object of a preposition.

Who messed up my desk?   **Whom** did you see?   To **whom** should I send this?

▶ **Exercise 1** Underline the word in parentheses that best completes each sentence.

When Jacob (said, <u>says</u>) something, you can trust him to mean it.

1. The invitation (respectfully, respectively) requests our presence at the wedding of our

   friend's daughter.

2. The dogs keep the wild creatures away, other (then, than) the brave raccoon who lives part-time

   in the garage.

3. Do you know what (this here, this) tool is called?

4. Why are the leaves dying on (that there, that) tree?

Copyright © by Glencoe/McGraw-Hill

Usage

5. Mrs. Contreras and Mr. Salazar are our history and Spanish teacher, (respectfully, respectively).

6. Don't (sit, set) that dish on the new table or it will leave a scratch.

7. The Student Council president cleared her throat and (than, then) began to speak.

8. Yesterday Horace (said, says) he went to Dewey High School before he transferred here.

9. Do you know (who, whom) painted that picture?

10. Last summer I was thinner (than, then) I am now.

11. (Set, Sit) the plant next to the window where it can get enough light.

12. (Whom, Who) do you trust with your CD player?

13. Dalila climbed the hill and (then, than) set up her camera.

14. Don't skate on (that there, that) bumpy surface, or you'll fall.

15. When you (said, says) you would teach me how to play chess, I took you at your word.

▶ **Exercise 2** Write the correct word in the blank to replace each word or phrase in italics. If the word or phrase is correct, write *C* in the blank.

_____ then _____   The diver leaped into the air and *than* plunged into the pool.

_____ **1.** Don't *set* there; the paint's still wet.

_____ **2.** Amad visited my family last summer, but I was on vacation *than*.

_____ **3.** *Whom* is the cat's owner?

_____ **4.** The dog found a comfortable spot and *than* curled up in a ball.

_____ **5.** Can I *sit* this bowl on the glass table?

_____ **6.** I thought you *said* we would be meeting your cousin.

_____ **7.** *This here* weather makes me lazy.

_____ **8.** Imena always acts *respectively* toward older people.

_____ **9.** What is the name of *that there* tree?

_____ **10.** Last evening the newscaster *says* we would have snow today.

_____ **11.** To *whom* do you think you're talking?

_____ **12.** I did better on today's test *then* on the one last week.

_____ **13.** Just before the sun *set*, the sky was streaked with purple.

_____ **14.** Keshia and Kosey are the president and vice president, *respectfully*, of the student council.

_____ **15.** When Calid *says* he is a computer freak, he means it.

Copyright © by Glencoe/McGraw-Hill

Usage

✓ Unit 10 Review

▶ **Exercise 1** **Underline the word in parentheses that best completes each sentence.**

Krista enjoys tennis more (<u>than</u>, then) softball.

1. The police did not (accept, except) the suspect's alibi.

2. The Millers hope to (adapt, adopt) a child next year.

3. Jourdan (respectfully, respectively) submitted his résumé to the company.

4. To get to the auditorium, go through (that there, that) door.

5. Ray Bradbury's science fiction was very popular (between, among) my classmates.

6. Even though several students were late, the teacher (preceded, proceeded) with the lesson.

7. Darla (hanged, hung) a wind chime on the front porch.

8. I thought you (all ready, already) did your report.

9. I can't help you (farther, further) without the computer instruction book.

10. Will the parade go (passed, past) this intersection?

11. We have to find a way to (raise, rise) money for the homeless shelter.

12. Hakeen swims every day, (irregardless, regardless) of the weather.

13. Don't forget to (take, bring) your new friend home for dinner.

14. I hope we don't (loose, lose) this important game.

15. Bring your friend (in, into, in to) meet us.

16. Walking is better for you (than, then) running if you have weak knees.

17. Whew, this hill is steep; I'll have to rest (a while, awhile).

18. Kwasi plays soccer (alot, a lot) so he knows the strategy.

19. Will you (lend, loan) me your notes from class?

20. We saw the sun (raise, rise) over the mountains.

21. I'll meet you in front of the Murphy Theater in (a, an) hour.

22. Ju-Yong thought for (a while, awhile) about her choices before making a decision.

23. Would you trust Harold's (advice, advise) on this matter?

24. I'm trying to discover the (affect, effect) decaffeinated coffee has on the nervous system.

Copyright © by Glencoe/McGraw-Hill

Usage

Cumulative Review: Units 1–10

▶ **Exercise 1 Underline the pronoun in parentheses that best completes each sentence.**

(<u>Who</u>, Whom) signed up for the camping trip?

1. (Who, Whom) did the director choose to play the king?

2. (Who, Whom) is that at the door?

3. To (who, whom) did Lally give the documents?

4. (Who, Whom) left some books on the bench?

5. (Whose, Who) voice is that on the recording?

6. To (whom, who) do these hubcaps belong?

7. (Whom, Whose) flag is that flying from the school?

8. (Who, Whom) did you know in the cast?

9. (Who, Whom) came to the house while we were gone?

10. (Whose, Who) speech was the most interesting?

11. Did you see (who, whom) was at the door?

12. To (whom, who) do you think you're talking?

13. Is this the student (whom, who) you mentioned?

14. The doctor (who, whom) came to treat Father is Pravat's uncle.

15. The comic (whose, who) impressions everyone applauded is my cousin.

16. Here is the gardener (who, whom) won the Best of Show.

17. Are those the lifeguards (who, whom) helped with the rescue?

18. (Who, Whom) did you beat in yesterday's match?

19. Aren't you the runner (who, whom) came in first?

20. I don't care (who, whose) car we take as long as we get there on time.

▶ **Exercise 2 Underline the verb in parentheses that best completes each sentence.**

Greg and Lois (expects, <u>expect</u>) to arrive by five o'clock.

1. One of my feet (is, are) asleep.

2. The paintings in the far gallery (was, were) painted by my brother.

3. Two of my science teachers (do, does) comet research on weekends.

Copyright © by Glencoe/McGraw-Hill

4. Neither Niran nor his brothers (speaks, speak) English.

5. The mayor, together with her aides, (is, are) coming to the rally.

6. The captain of the Falcons (say, says) the team is ready for the championship game.

7. Either a skunk or the cats (has, have) torn up the papers in the garage.

8. (Does, Do) the ferry and the fishing fleet tie up here?

9. The shoes on the floor (was, were) covered with mud.

10. Each of our relatives (brings, bring) a dish for Thanksgiving.

11. The signs along the highway (says, say) drive carefully.

12. The performance by the skaters (was, were) very colorful.

13. Both the Canadian and the magnolia warblers (has, have) black markings around their necks.

14. (Is, Are) the referee and the players arguing again?

15. The schedule, with all the new changes, (comes, come) out today.

16. The clerks at the counter (announces, announce) the incoming flights.

17. A call for help and supplies (was, were) answered.

18. Neither my clothing nor my sleeping bag (is, are) dry yet.

19. Bulldozers and jackhammers often (creates, create) a din outside.

20. The movies at the mall (looks, look) exciting.

▶ **Exercise 3** **Place a check (✔) before each compound sentence. Underline the subordinate clauses in each sentence.**

_____ The audience, who had arrived early, vigorously applauded the performers.

_____ 1. A park now graces the spot where the old Laurelville Bank and Trust once stood.

_____ 2. Tears sprang to her eyes, and she quickly turned away.

_____ 3. Cut along the fabric's fold, but do so very carefully.

_____ 4. Maria didn't arrive late; however, the ticket line moved slowly, and she missed the opening number.

_____ 5. I do not understand what you are saying.

_____ 6. The filling, only a temporary one, was made of inexpensive material, and it would have to be replaced.

_____ 7. When the days grow shorter, we know that winter is around the corner.

_____ 8. The popping and crackling sounds made me realize that the stereo was broken.

Copyright © by Glencoe/McGraw-Hill

_____ 9. Would you please start the coals burning and put the steaks into the marinade?

_____ 10. The woman who is standing by Mrs. Wolford is a talent scout.

_____ 11. Although the mail carrier is afraid of our Pomeranian, Musty is really quite gentle.

_____ 12. Gary is older than I had guessed.

_____ 13. You bring a movie, and I'll fix the snacks.

_____ 14. Kendra is glad that she passed that test.

_____ 15. Get well cards and letters poured in, and Cecil didn't rest until he had answered them all.

▶ **Exercise 4** **Write the correct word or words in the blank to replace each word or phrase in italics. If the word or phrase is correct, write *C* in the blank.**

___*respectively*___ The first two persons at the head table are the president and vice

president, *respectfully.*

_____ 1. Don't use the special paint *accept* for the outside work.

_____ 2. You have *an* unique way of perceiving the world.

_____ 3. I won't be back for *awhile,* so make yourself comfortable.

_____ 4. Is it *all right* for me to borrow your chess set?

_____ 5. We have had *all together* too much rain!

_____ 6. Who is that *besides* Ms. Taylor?

_____ 7. How can you tell the difference *between* all the puppies?

_____ 8. When you think you see water up ahead on a desert road, it is

probably an *allusion.*

_____ 9. *Being as* we are late, please go on without us.

_____ 10. I don't see that huge blackbird *anywheres.*

_____ 11. I hope you don't mind *borrowing* me your hockey stick.

_____ 12. The fire hurt the ecosystem *badly.*

_____ 13. I *can't hardly* get into your messy room!

_____ 14. Is there any way this epidemic *could of* been prevented?

_____ 15. Jake's house is no *farther* away than Malik's.

_____ 16. Ray and Pricha *doesn't* share the same taste in music.

_____ 17. There are *less* pieces in this game than in the one we played yesterday.

_____ 18. The school *don't* have a soccer team.

Copyright © by Glencoe/McGraw-Hill

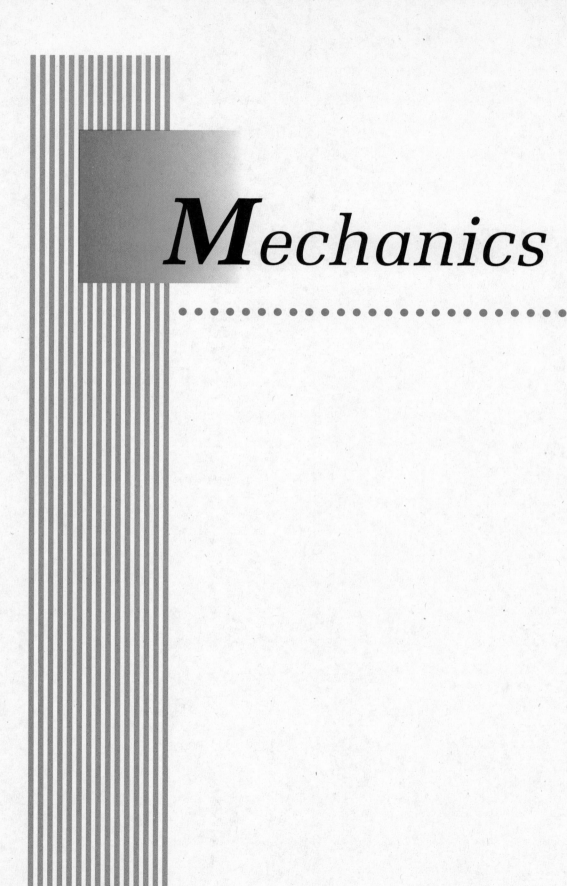

Mechanics

Unit 11: Capitalization

Lesson 72
Capitalization of Sentences and the Pronoun *I*

Capitalize the first word of every sentence. For sentences that appear in parentheses, capitalize the first word if the sentence stands by itself, but not if it is contained within another sentence.

We crossed the bridge yesterday. (**T**he bridge is 17 miles long.)
We crossed the bridge (**i**t is 17 miles long) yesterday.

Capitalize the first word of a direct quotation only if the quotation is a complete sentence.

A familiar adage states, "**T**oday is the first day of the rest of your life."
He called the adage "**i**nspirational and encouraging."

Do not capitalize an indirect quotation unless it is the first word in a sentence.

I heard the adage about **t**oday being the first day of the rest of your life.

Always capitalize the pronoun *I*.

Mary and **I** went to the play.

▶ **Exercise 1** **Draw three lines under each lowercase letter that should be capitalized. Draw a slash (/) through each capital letter that should be lowercase. If the sentence is correct, write *C* in the blank.**

_____ last week i got a letter from a friend who says He will visit me.

_____ **1.** the mechanic at the garage said my car is in excellent condition.

_____ **2.** Marla asked, "were you able to tour Europe last year?"

_____ **3.** she said that the king and queen will be crowned at the spring dance.

_____ **4.** my sister gave me a new tape. (it was my birthday present.)

_____ **5.** when i go to the store, i like to check the music section.

_____ **6.** the bookstore on the corner (it's the biggest in town) has a great selection of music.

_____ **7.** Theodore Roosevelt (he was our twenty-sixth president) led a far more interesting life than most history books describe.

_____ **8.** my older brother is a successful caterer in New Orleans. (he went to school to become a chef.)

_____ **9.** When I bought groceries for my mother, I asked the clerk if she would use paper bags.

Copyright © by Glencoe/McGraw-Hill

Mechanics

_____ **10.** my neighbors announced that they are starting a recycling program.

_____ **11.** Carlos began his speech by saying, "it is a pleasure to tell you of our recent successes."

_____ **12.** the dress in the museum (the white one just inside the door) is exactly like my

grandmother's wedding dress.

_____ **13.** My uncle is a realtor in Nashville. (he moved there from Chicago.)

_____ **14.** the reporter called the attack "Unexpected and devastating."

_____ **15.** In the future I will begin my homework by gathering everything I need.

_____ **16.** Kay asked if i would help rebuild her car. (she has to get a new transmission first.)

_____ **17.** it was Diane who said, "let's go to the concert."

_____ **18.** My mother said that she was glad she went to the concert.

_____ **19.** after everything was over (People stayed for hours after dinner), my sister and i had to

clean up the banquet hall.

_____ **20.** yesterday he said that Music is his greatest love.

_____ **21.** my best friend (We've been friends for years) works at Marshall Space Flight Center.

_____ **22.** Maria always says that Math homework is much more difficult than American history.

_____ **23.** on the other hand, Brian told me, "math is easier than English."

_____ **24.** mother says i will have to mend my shirt. (i ripped it when i was playing baseball.)

_____ **25.** Mrs. Smythe said she would give us our homework early in case the bell rings before

we finish the discussion.

_____ **26.** Barbara and I will work on the project together (it must be complete by March 1) so we

can finish by the deadline.

_____ **27.** last summer i had the opportunity to work for a landscape designer. (it's a field i would

like to enter myself someday.)

_____ **28.** my biology teacher says There are over 130 species of quail in the world.

_____ **29.** My sister (She is a college junior) is planning to work with my brother in the

catering business.

_____ **30.** this is still a new city to me, and i want to explore the downtown area. (it is a

fascinating place!)

Copyright © by Glencoe/McGraw-Hill

Mechanics

Lesson 73
Capitalization of Proper Nouns

Always capitalize proper nouns. If the noun is composed of several words, do not capitalize articles (*a, an, the*), coordinating conjunctions (*and, but, for, or, nor, yet*), or prepositions of fewer than five letters.

Center of **S**cience and **I**ndustry   **T**om and **R**on's **B**icycle **S**hop   **B**eauty and the **B**east

Capitalize titles before a proper name and titles used in direct address.

Do you know **S**ecretary **D**arleise **W**illiams?   **Y**es, **C**aptain, I will do that.

Capitalize a title showing family relationship when used with or in place of a proper noun. Do not capitalize it when preceded by an article or a possessive noun or pronoun.

Will my **grandma** go?   **W**ill **G**randma go?   **R**uth is a **grandma**.   **W**ill **G**randma **R**uth go?

Capitalize names of ethnic groups, religions, nationalities, and languages.

Native **A**mericans   **P**eruvian   **E**nglish   **H**induism

Capitalize names of clubs, organizations, institutions, and political parties.

Environmental **P**rotection **A**gency   **F**irst **N**ational **B**ank   **E**arlham **C**ollege   **D**emocrats

▶ **Exercise 1** Draw three lines under each lowercase letter that should be capitalized.

We enjoy traveling with uncle troy and our aunt in their motor home.

1. Yes, sir, I will complete my application to the university of michigan.

2. The democrats will hold a rally on the lawn of the smithsonian institution.

3. The boy scouts of america held a meeting at lincoln high school.

4. Does aunt gladys enjoy watching the chicago bulls?

5. Joshua's uncle is an orthodox jew.

6. The governor of our state is governor simon.

7. Yes, captain, I will send a telegram to admiral curtis.

8. I won't forget, mom, to say hello to aunt maren and uncle ben.

9. My sister told me that uncle Richard was a member of the peace corps.

10. The inuit are a people who live in and near the Arctic.

11. On our vacation dad got tickets to the washington national symphony.

12. I wanted to see the washington bullets.

Copyright © by Glencoe/McGraw-Hill

Mechanics

Capitalize names of monuments, bridges, buildings, ships, planes, and spacecraft.

Statue of **L**iberty   **B**rooklyn **B**ridge   **E**iffel **T**ower   *Concorde*

Capitalize trade names.

Microsoft   **P**rocter and **G**amble   **R**eebok   **P**entium

Capitalize geographical terms including cities, states, countries, bodies of water, roads, mountains, and specific sections of a country. Do not capitalize words that refer to direction.

Chicago   **R**ocky **M**ountains   the **S**outh   Go **s**outh one mile.

Capitalize holidays, historical events, eras, and calendar items.

Labor **D**ay   **A**merican **R**evolution   **R**oaring **T**wenties   **J**anuary

Capitalize titles of works including musical pieces, books, poems, plays, magazines, movies, television shows, and historical documents.

"**A**merican **P**ie"   the *New Yorker*   *The Lion King*   the **C**onstitution

▶ **Exercise 2** **Draw three lines under each lowercase letter that should be capitalized. Draw a slash (/) through each capital letter that should be lowercase.**

We visited new york city in the Spring and went to the top of the empire state building.

1. In june my family went digging for Rubies in the appalachian mountains of north carolina.

2. In virginia beach Moira went on a Dolphin Watch sponsored by the virginia marine science museum.

3. Yes, captain, I have learned a lot on board the ss *united states*.

4. On memorial day weekend the Rhoades family will drive west to the grand canyon.

5. When we were in tennessee in july, we drove to the top of lookout mountain.

6. Sutter's mill, where California Gold was first discovered, is on the sacramento river.

7. My brother goes to a college in the south that is right on the atlantic ocean.

8. A replica of the famous ship the *santa maria* sits in columbus, ohio.

9. Raul's grandparents tell him stories of the great depression.

10. We studied the renaissance in art class and analyzed the *mona lisa*, a famous painting in the louvre in paris, france.

11. In july of 1969, the spacecraft *columbia* was launched from cape canaveral in florida.

12. *How to be your own best friend* was a popular self-help book of the 1970s.

Copyright © by Glencoe/McGraw-Hill

Lesson 74
Capitalization of Proper Adjectives

Capitalize proper adjectives (adjectives formed from proper nouns).

Proper adjectives may be formed from names of people.

Marxist philosophy   **Jeffersonian thought**   **Orwellian foresight**
Jungian psychology   **Gregorian chant**   **Napoleonic delusions**

Proper adjectives may be formed from place names and names of national, ethnic, and religious groups.

Michigan waterways   **Egyptian hieroglyphs**   **Navajo blanket**   **Catholic ritual**

Proper adjectives may be formed from specific days, dates, or holidays.

February thaw   **Christmas tree**   **Friday night**   **Hanukkah candles**

▶ **Exercise 1** **Draw three lines under each lowercase letter that should be capitalized. Draw a slash (/) through each capital letter that should be lowercase.**

The july rains rusted the Metal fence.

1. I am reading a book of german Folktales.

2. Every saturday night Jonas goes hunting for june bugs.

3. Grandmother is planning to make a pot of irish stew for us.

4. My dad's favorite music is a beethoven symphony.

5. Aunt Marisa is an expert on norse Mythology.

6. No color quite matches alabama soil.

7. Grandfather taught me to play chinese checkers.

8. Miami is located on the atlantic side of florida.

9. Dr. Rudyard's english Degree required at least one course in victorian Literature.

10. Several steinbeck novels have been made into movies.

11. The speaker's reference to his brother was certainly a freudian slip.

12. Even the severe april shower couldn't keep us from our favorite mexican restaurant.

13. Yesterday's discussion topic was the rich variety of African Art.

14. Have you seen the rooms newly furnished in chippendale style?

15. My older sisters all enjoy italian Opera.

16. After lunch we drank Cinnamon tea.

Copyright © by Glencoe/McGraw-Hill

Mechanics

17. Eight U.S. presidents were ohioans.

18. Jordan visited Washington, D.C., and saw the lincoln memorial and The washington monument.

19. I prefer english muffins to bagels.

20. The american Red Cross is a great Volunteer Organization.

21. We have a small pembroke table in our front hallway.

22. For her november birthday, I gave my hungarian grandmother a large bowl of swedish ivy.

23. We are required to study jeffersonian philosophy in History class.

24. Many asian people arrived in the United States during the early part of the Twentieth Century.

25. George Voinovich was a republican governor from Ohio.

26. The hindu religion had a great impact on indian history.

27. Please play a gershwin tune on your Steinway Piano.

28. That hill was once the home of mississippian moundbuilders.

29. My russian friend took lessons in spanish dancing.

30. The Copper kettle is certainly the right thing for that Kitchen shelf.

31. An Insurance center in franklin county decided to use only microsoft products.

32. What a fine example of cherokee beadwork!

33. Most byzantine art of the Middle Ages came from the area that is now Turkey.

34. Sofia is the bulgarian capital.

35. Throughout the balkan peninsula, slavic languages are spoken.

36. Restoring the Ancient Castle proved to be a Monumental task.

37. The optimist sees the world through "Rose-colored glasses."

38. John Anthony West is an author and investigator of egyptian antiquities.

39. Jay asked, "how did the industrial Revolution change the labor Force?"

40. The punch was made by mixing syrup, Vanilla ice cream, and Carbonated water.

41. She said, "sharpen all the pencils in the drawer."

42. i agree with her about the time of the program. (she says 7:00 P.M. is too early.)

43. My grandmother attends northwestern university and is a member of alpha chi omega.

44. Ju-Yong wrote a report on mayor daley, the Mayor of Chicago.

45. While my Dad drove through the midwest, I was busy reading *A Tale Of Two Cities* by
charles dickens.

Copyright © by Glencoe/McGraw-Hill

✓ Unit 11 **Review**

▶ **Exercise 1** **Draw three lines under each lowercase letter that should be capitalized. Draw a slash (/) through each capital letter that should be lowercase. If the sentence is correct, write *C* in the blank.**

_____ Mia asked her Father, "may I go on a picnic in central park next sunday?"

_____ 1. mission san carlos borromeo was built near monterey, california, in 1770.

_____ 2. He asked us to drive with him to the top of henesy mountain to enjoy the fine Spring scenery.

_____ 3. The carmelite nuns have survived as a Religious order of the roman catholic church since the Thirteenth Century.

_____ 4. We will have a picnic high above the valley. (The valley is filled with flowers now.)

_____ 5. The columbus arts festival is an annual june event.

_____ 6. Dr. Hennig said, "diet is the most important element in maintaining Good Health."

_____ 7. Bruce studied Mechanics at indianapolis technical institute.

_____ 8. The Talk Show Host said The celebrity was late for the interview.

_____ 9. Some movies, like *Dances With Wolves*, make a lasting impression.

_____ 10. The poet John Donne wrote, "no man is an island entire of itself."

_____ 11. The northwest territory was created by congress under the Administration of president George Washington.

_____ 12. The redstone rocket was developed at the marshall space flight center in huntsville, alabama.

_____ 13. Mom said that Dad and my brother Jim will help me rebuild the lawn mower engine.

_____ 14. Jim's hobby is restoring Antique cars, particularly model t fords.

_____ 15. The voters will re-elect Senator Lopez because he is an excellent senator.

_____ 16. Contact nurse adams at the sleep disorder center, brady memorial hospital.

_____ 17. The next time we have lunch in the city (with its marvelous restaurants), let's eat at sylvan's steak place.

_____ 18. Dr. Kostyn, the new medical examiner for Northwestern Mutual Life Insurance Company, plays the coronet.

Copyright © by Glencoe/McGraw-Hill

Mechanics

Cumulative Review: Units 1–11

▶ **Exercise 1** Identify the type of pronoun in italics. Write *per.* (personal), *poss.* (possessive), *reflex.* (reflexive), *inter.* (interrogative), *rel.* (relative), or *indef.* (indefinite) in the blank.

_____poss._____   You many leave *your* coat hanging in the front closet.

_____   **1.** *Who* is in charge of tomorrow's program?

_____   **2.** Please tell *them* to give their work to Mrs. Massey.

_____   **3.** *He* is the only person who can make the copy machine work.

_____   **4.** The cat gave *itself* a bath.

_____   **5.** I can't wait to tell *everyone* the exciting news!

_____   **6.** Responsibility for a successful project is *ours* alone.

_____   **7.** Bring *me* the results of last night's contest.

_____   **8.** *His* glasses lay on the open book.

_____   **9.** To *whom* does this school jacket belong?

_____ **10.** Do you like the wallpaper *that* I chose?

_____ **11.** Carlos is the soccer player *who* won the MVP award.

_____ **12.** *Each* of the planets has its own unique atmosphere.

_____ **13.** *Which* is the best road to take to Phoenix?

_____ **14.** Let's ask *ourselves* if the risk is worth it.

_____ **15.** If you have a CD, bring *it* to the party.

▶ **Exercise 2** Draw three lines under each lower case letter that should be capitalized. For each italicized noun, write in the blank *con.* (concrete noun) or *abs.* (abstract noun).

_____con._____   Henry Ford founded the Ford motor *company*.

_____   **1.** A physician from edinburgh introduced *rhubarb* into scotland.

_____   **2.** The robert talbert armory is the largest building in our *town*.

_____   **3.** Our future teachers of america chapter sponsored a program on *ethics*.

_____   **4.** Atlanta's university hospital provides some of the best *care* in the south.

_____   **5.** Our high school holds class *elections* on the first thursday of october.

_____   **6.** Greg Hastings, the famous English *guitarist,* will give three concerts in the united states this year.

Copyright © by Glencoe/McGraw-Hill

_____ **7.** Terri's *hope* is to have her novel published.

_____ **8.** I have all the books in the *earthsea trilogy* by ursula k. le guin on audiotape.

_____ **9.** Mayfield *dormitory* is an old brick building.

_____ **10.** Just beyond that next *curve* is olentangy river park.

_____ **11.** Millions of people have died in search of *freedom*.

_____ **12.** Albrecht Dürer belonged to the german *tradition* of painters.

_____ **13.** The statue of liberty was a *gift* from the french people.

_____ **14.** We crossed the *bay* on the chesapeake bay bridge-tunnel.

_____ **15.** The *union* of the north and the south was tested by the civil war.

_____ **16.** We reveled in the *joy* of spending all day friday at the beach.

_____ **17.** The goethe *institute* is an international educational institution devoted to german language and literature.

_____ **18.** Gerbils are indigenous to the *wilds* of Africa and asia.

_____ **19.** Sir john hare, actor and manager of london's garrick *theatre* in the late nineteenth century, was recognized as the greatest character actor of his *day*.

_____ **20.** We need to make a *decision* concerning the upcoming memorial day events.

▶ **Exercise 3 Draw one line under each proper adjective. Draw a slash (/) through each capitalized letter that should be lowercase.**

I understood some of the Italian L̸yrics in that Ø̸pera.

1. The Hemingway book, *A Farewell to Arms,* became a Best-seller and a movie.

2. Joseph creates French Pastries that are Works of Art.

3. What important events took place during the Clinton Administration?

4. Isolationist Policies became popular between World War I and World War II.

5. "Mad Anthony Wayne" undertook a Canadian Expedition during the American Revolution.

6. I have three friends with Turkish heritage.

7. The official Brazilian Language is Portuguese.

8. Afghan carpets are handwoven, generally of wool or goat hair.

9. I often listen to Celtic melodies while I study.

10. Through the telescope we hoped to see Saturn's Rings.

11. American history is only a small portion of World history.

Copyright © by Glencoe/McGraw-Hill

Mechanics

12. Ingrid Bergman was a famous Swedish actress.

13. How many of the Germanic Languages have you studied?

14. Farmers in Angus County, Scotland, raise Angus cattle.

15. They are quite skilled at Chinese Cooking.

16. The Basque language is spoken by Basques living in the Spanish Pyrenees.

17. We seldom hear such excellent Irish Music.

18. He told us story after story from Mexican folklore.

19. Gothic Architecture has enjoyed several periods of popularity.

20. Let's end the day with a McDonald's hamburger.

▶ **Exercise 4 Underline the correct word or words in parentheses.**

My brother (<u>can</u>, may) do forty push-ups in a row.

1. (A, An) apple is always good with lunch.

2. We gathered (a lot, alot) of garbage from along the road.

3. I had to babysit my neighbor's children for (a while, awhile).

4. There was nothing to be done (accept, except) smile and keep going.

5. My sister and her husband were eager to (adapt, adopt) a child.

6. It's not always wise to depend totally on the (advice, advise) of others about which career to choose.

7. The (affect, effect) of changing the rule was to increase participation.

8. A crowd had (all ready, already) gathered when we arrived at the park.

9. "(All right, Alright)," the speaker said, "let's get started."

10. We were (all together, altogether) overwhelmed that over five hundred people attended the special event.

11. There was an (allusion, illusion) of friendliness among our class members.

12. Do you think the rain will (affect, effect) the new paint on the front porch?

13. Three people from here, (besides, beside) my mother, took the guided tour.

14. The five little boys bickered (between, among) themselves.

15. Mr. Rodham agreed to (advice, advise) the senior class on their graduation activities.

16. When you come to the picnic, please (bring, take) a dish of potato salad.

Copyright © by Glencoe/McGraw-Hill

Mechanics

Unit 12: Punctuation, Abbreviations, and Numbers

Lesson 75
End Punctuation: Period, Exclamation Point, and Question Mark

---

Use a **period** to end a declarative sentence and a polite command.

The photography exhibit is in Gallery F.
Show your membership pass to the guard at the door.

Use an **exclamation point** following strong feeling or a strong command.

Here comes the parade!   Look, one of the balloons is loose!   Catch it!

Use a **question mark** following a direct question. Do not use a question mark following a sentence with an indirect question.

Did you leave the door open?   I wonder who left the door open.

▶ **Exercise 1 Add periods, question marks, and exclamation points to complete the sentences.**

Think about the ways humans are like frogs.

1. Human beings belong to a group of animals called vertebrates

2. You might ask what this word means

3. It means simply that all these animals have a backbone

4. Did you think your backbone was that important

5. Invertebrates include amphibians, reptiles, birds, and three kinds of fish, in addition to mammals

6. Are you saying I'm in the same group with snakes

7. That's true, and we have many things in common with other vertebrates

8. For example, did you think your skull was just there to give shape to your head

9. Don't be silly

10. Your skull protects your brain, as in all vertebrates

11. Now, think of all the bones that make up your rib cage

12. They protect your heart and lungs

13. By now, I'm sure you know what your backbone protects

Copyright © by Glencoe/McGraw-Hill

Mechanics

14. You're right

15. The central nervous system is enclosed in your backbone

16. Think of some of the fossilized animals you have seen

17. What part of the animal do you think allows the fossil to be preserved

18. Well, you're certainly catching on fast

19. We have many brothers and sisters in the vertebrate family

20. This is the time to wonder what other characteristics vertebrates have in common

▶ **Exercise 2** **Revise the end punctuation to correctly complete each sentence. If the end punctuation is already correct, write _C_.**

_____ Can you imagine living 100 years, like the turtle.?

_____ **1.** Reptiles are one of the classes of vertebrates.

_____ **2.** There are three basic classes of reptiles!

_____ **3.** Remember that crocodiles and turtles make up two of the classes?

_____ **4.** The third class is, you guessed it, snakes!

_____ **5.** Wait a minute; what did you ask about alligators.

_____ **6.** Well, alligators join their crocodile cousins in that class?

_____ **7.** Don't you think you could have figured that out for yourself?

_____ **8.** Think of the kind of body covering that people and other mammals have!

_____ **9.** Skin and fur probably spring to mind?

_____ **10.** Reptiles have scales as body covering.

_____ **11.** On snakes and lizards, the scales are relatively thin!

_____ **12.** Turtles, however, grow thick protective plates on their bodies!

_____ **13.** What other purpose does this scaly skin serve?

_____ **14.** It keeps the animal's body from drying out!

_____ **15.** Since the scales keep moisture in, reptiles can go for long periods without water?

_____ **16.** Reptiles range in size from tiny to gargantuan.

_____ **17.** Small lizards measure no more than 2 inches in length!

_____ **18.** Pythons, on the other hand, can grow to 30 feet?

_____ **19.** Thirty feet is long. Wow.

_____ **20.** Hey, don't leave; I was just getting warmed up!

Copyright © by Glencoe/McGraw-Hill

Mechanics

Lesson 76
Colons

Use a colon to introduce lists, especially those that come after usages such as *these*, *the following*, or *as follows*.

The instruments in the string section are **these**: violin, viola, cello, and bass.
I have heard **the following** great violinists: Yehudi Menuhin, Itzhak Perlman, and Midori.
A famous violinist once gave **the following** humorous advice for success: (1) practice, (2) practice, (3) practice.

Do not use a colon to introduce lists that follow verbs or prepositions.

Three famous violin makers **were** Amati, Stradivari, and Guarneri.
I prefer violin composers **like** Vivaldi and Paganini.

Use a colon to introduce material that explains or restates material just stated.

My favorite courses are in the sciences: astronomy, botany, and geology are all on my current schedule.
The cause of the supernova was obvious: a star exploded.

Use a colon before long or formal quotations preceded by such words as *this*, *these*, *the following*, or *as follows*.

Chief Joseph of the Nez Percé people gave up his resistance to the U.S. government with **the following** words: "From where the sun stands now, I will fight no more forever."

Use a colon between the hour and minute of the time, between the chapter and verse of biblical references, and after the salutation of a business letter.

7:20 P.M.   John 3:16   Dear Dr. Randolph:

▶ **Exercise 1** Insert a colon where necessary in the following sentences. Write *C* in the blank if the sentence is correct.

_____   My toolbox holds the following: a hammer, wrench, plane, and screwdriver.

_____ **1.** I think the next feature begins at 830 P.M.

_____ **2.** Our orchard has the following fruit trees apple, plum, cherry.

_____ **3.** My favorite fresh fruits are bananas, oranges, and peaches.

_____ **4.** Who can resist these thrilling words of Nathan Hale "I regret that I have but one life to give for my country!"

_____ **5.** The counselor gave instructions as follows: (1) gather kindling, (2) dig a hole, (3) surround the hole with rocks, and (4) build a fire.

Copyright © by Glencoe/McGraw-Hill

Mechanics

_____ 6. That last inning ran from 840 to 935 P.M.

_____ 7. The teacher asked us to write a report on the following subject Famous Abolitionists in the South.

_____ 8. Any good children's library should contain the following: *Charlotte's Web, Sounder,* and *The Chronicles of Narnia.*

_____ 9. The reason for the crash was clear the fog made visibility zero.

_____ 10. The events to be held this afternoon are these the shot put, the javelin, the broad jump, and the high jump.

_____ 11. The first three runners to finish the race were Sergei, Ramón, and Sheila.

_____ 12. The following areas will be repainted next week Classroom A, Classroom C, the student lounge, and the meeting room.

_____ 13. What time is it in Philadelphia when it's 1000 A.M. in Denver?

_____ 14. As I dragged myself off the field, I remembered the following words "It's not whether you win or lose, it's how you play the game."

_____ 15. You'll need the following ingredients for the spaghetti sauce tomatoes, tomato sauce, mushrooms, onions, oil, and garlic.

_____ 16. Dear Ms. Larkin:

_____ 17. For the sleepover we'll need these things backpacks, sleeping bags, changes of clothing, food, and permission from our parents.

_____ 18. I love that line from Tennyson's poem "Ulysses": "To strive, to seek, to find, and not to yield."

_____ 19. The origin of the earthquake showed on the seismograph; it was below the town of Roland.

_____ 20. I wish I could swim like Colleen and Mariel.

_____ 21. The following crops were ruined by the cold blueberries, oranges, avocados.

_____ 22. The variety show consisted of these acts: a juggler, a magician, two comedians, and a mime.

_____ 23. If I leave this instant, I'll just make the 615 from the station!

_____ 24. Who was the famous cynic who said this "Winning isn't everything, it's the only thing"?

Copyright © by Glencoe/McGraw-Hill

Mechanics

Lesson 77
Semicolons

Use a semicolon to separate main clauses that are not joined by *and, but, or, nor, yet,* or *for.*

Randy finished first in the contest; he won a gold statue.

Use a semicolon to separate main clauses that are joined by adverbs such as *however, therefore, nevertheless, moreover, furthermore,* and *consequently* and expressions such as *for example* or *that is.*

Randy was overjoyed to win; however, he really had thought he would lose.
We did many fun things on our vacation; for example, we swam in the ocean, collected seashells, and went on a whale watch.

Use a semicolon to separate the items in a series when the items have commas.

I like foreign films such as *The Cars That Ate Paris,* from Australia; *Yojimbo,* from Japan; and *Z,* from France.

Use a semicolon to separate two main clauses joined by *and, but, or, nor, yet,* or *for* when the clauses contain several commas.

When we got home our dogs raced to meet us, leaped to lick our faces, and barked and barked; and when they had finished their greetings, they ran into the house to look for their meal.

▶ **Exercise 1 Insert a semicolon wherever necessary in each sentence. Write *C* in the blank if the sentence is correct.**

_____ I haven't been to the Antarctic; however, my uncle has.

_____ **1.** The Antarctic continent is the highest, driest, and coldest place on Earth nevertheless, scientists compete to do research there.

_____ **2.** The U.S. has three major research bases on Antarctica: McMurdo Station, on the Ross Sea Palmer Station, on the Antarctic Peninsula and Amundsen-Scott Station, at the South Pole.

_____ **3.** Dozens of other countries also maintain bases on the continent however, few are year-round.

_____ **4.** The winter climate is too cold during the winter months to allow much research moreover, air travel is also limited at this time.

_____ **5.** The Antarctic continent covers five and one-half million square miles this is an area larger than the United States and Central America combined.

Copyright © by Glencoe/McGraw-Hill

Mechanics

_____ 6. Ninety percent of the ice in the world is frozen into this region.

_____ 7. Astronauts orbiting Earth say the Antarctic ice sheet is the most distinctive feature of

our planet it shines like a giant light across the bottom of the world.

_____ 8. Many people think of the Arctic and Antarctic as the same kind of territory this is an error.

_____ 9. The Arctic is a large sea, while the Antarctic is a land mass.

_____ 10. The two climates are also very different many populations of people live comfortably in

the Arctic Circle, whereas there are no native human inhabitants of Antarctica.

_____ 11. There is no moisture on Antarctica all of its water is locked in ice.

_____ 12. The cold is bone-chilling; temperatures of −88° C have been recorded, more than 20°

colder than anywhere else on Earth.

_____ 13. Moreover, the wind rarely stops blowing one explorer recorded an average wind speed

for a month of about 65 miles per hour.

_____ 14. Photographers have taken amusing pictures of the effects of the Antarctic wind the

photographs show human beings leaning forward into the wind without falling to the

ground!

_____ 15. The absence of moisture makes fire a real danger on Antarctica.

_____ 16. Wooden buildings, zero humidity, and constant wind could all make a small fire into

an inferno and, in addition, all the firefighters on Antarctica are volunteers.

_____ 17. So what kinds of research can be done in such an inhospitable place, you might ask.

_____ 18. Researchers study climatology, the science of weather patterns plate tectonics, the

science of the movements of Earth's crust and astrophysics, the science of the origins of

the universe.

_____ 19. No one owns Antarctica consequently all countries are welcome to do research there.

_____ 20. Greenpeace has recently put pressure on the research stations to stop their polluting of

the continent however, there are decades of waste to clean up.

_____ 21. The U.S. base at the South Pole is 37 years old therefore, many people think it needs

an overhauling.

_____ 22. The National Science Foundation, which runs it, says the base may have to be closed

down if funds cannot be found to restore it.

Copyright © by Glencoe/McGraw-Hill

Mechanics

Lesson 78
Commas and Compound Sentences

Use a comma before the words *and, but, or, nor, yet,* or *for* when they join two main clauses.

I wanted to hike farther, but Kari was tired and wanted to rest.

Omit the comma if two very short main clauses are connected by *and, but, or, nor, yet,* or *for* unless you need to avoid confusion.

We can eat now or we can eat later. (clear)
We can eat now or maybe you'd like to wait until later. (unclear)
We can eat now, or maybe you'd like to wait until later. (clear)

▶ **Exercise 1 Add commas where necessary. Write *C* in the blank if the sentence is correct.**

_____ Sami slid into third base, but the umpire called her out.

_____ **1.** Don't walk on your sprained ankle or it will take longer to heal.

_____ **2.** I thought that old house would never sell but someone offered a high price for it yesterday.

_____ **3.** That movie is very sad and usually makes me cry.

_____ **4.** I've not met your brother before today yet there's something familiar about him.

_____ **5.** He is working on a project about whales and he'll need to use the research library at

the museum.

_____ **6.** I don't want to drive the old car, nor do I want to walk.

_____ **7.** Our cat eats the dog's food but the dog lets him get away with it.

_____ **8.** Ms. Trainor is very strict but very fair.

_____ **9.** I ran to third and Jordan advanced to second.

_____ **10.** I'll build the fire and the tents need to be put up.

_____ **11.** The alien leaped onto the screen and the entire audience screamed.

_____ **12.** I know you're tired but we really need to study some more.

_____ **13.** I hope you can come visit this summer for we really miss you.

_____ **14.** Will our photos be back tomorrow or do we have to wait through the weekend?

_____ **15.** This new dish is tasty yet low-fat.

_____ **16.** We ran and ran until we were out of breath yet we could not keep up.

_____ **17.** The dogs sniffed the ground and all took off in one direction.

Copyright © by Glencoe/McGraw-Hill

_____ **18.** Do you want to see the rock concert or the new movie?

_____ **19.** I think I have the flu but I hope I'm wrong.

_____ **20.** The tree came down in the storm and slammed into the attic.

_____ **21.** The soldiers raced for the pass, but the enemy had escaped.

_____ **22.** The floats came down the street first and the band followed them.

_____ **23.** Several kites headed for disaster but they all missed the electric wires.

_____ **24.** It's awfully cold yet I was really counting on our hike today.

_____ **25.** Ginger sings rock songs and tells jokes in her act.

_____ **26.** I don't see your skates but they may be under the couch.

_____ **27.** The climbers hoped to reach the peak by sunset but they were disappointed.

_____ **28.** The mail is late but I see the mail carrier down the street.

_____ **29.** We'll go with Mom, and you can come with Dad.

_____ **30.** The avalanche thundered down the slope but luckily it missed the chalet.

_____ **31.** I dared him to cross the river, and he took me up on it.

_____ **32.** Horace hopes to get an *A* in both history and geometry.

_____ **33.** That movie is so stupid yet it seems to be drawing crowds.

_____ **34.** The wind sprang up, and the air turned cold.

_____ **35.** The wolf howled over the hills and another answered him across the valley.

_____ **36.** Are the puppies blind or can they see already?

_____ **37.** I want neither sweets nor excess fats in my diet.

_____ **38.** I took several rolls of pictures and they'll be ready tomorrow.

_____ **39.** Can you operate your computer or do you want some help?

_____ **40.** The air is chilly yet it's a relief after the heat.

▶ **Writing Link** **Write two complete sentences about the weather in your community. Join the sentences with a comma and a conjunction.**

_____

_____

_____

_____

_____

Copyright © by Glencoe/McGraw-Hill

Lesson 79
Commas in a Series and between Coordinate Adjectives

Use commas to separate three or more words, phrases, or clauses in a series.

Alan's act was imaginative, funny, and entertaining.

Do not use commas when the items in a series are joined by conjunctions.

I don't want butter or sour cream or chives on my potato!

Do not use commas between words in a two-word pair. Do use commas to set off each pair in a series, however.

The menu offered bacon and eggs, ham and eggs, and pancakes and syrup.

Use a comma between coordinate adjectives that come before a noun. To see if adjectives are coordinate, try to change their order or insert the word *and* between them. If the sentence still sounds natural, the adjectives are coordinate. If it sounds stilted, the adjectives are not coordinate and a comma should not be used.

They served a spicy, appetizing meal. (use a comma)
They served an appetizing, spicy meal. (changed order sounds natural)
They served a spicy and appetizing meal. (*and* sounds natural)
We stood in front of the old brick building. (do not use a comma)
We stood in front of the brick old building. (changed order sounds unnatural)
We stood in front of the old and brick building. (*and* sounds unnatural)

▶ **Exercise 1** **Add commas where necessary. Write *C* in the blank if the sentence is correct.**

_____ The store will contribute tents, backpacks, and compasses to the trip.

_____ **1.** We collected bedding, clothing and canned food for the victims of the fire.

_____ **2.** Fresh fruits vegetables and bread are all at the back of the store.

_____ **3.** Phil likes biography best, but he prefers true adventure to horror films, science fiction, and fantasy.

_____ **4.** My cats' names are Huckleberry Jinx and Kneesox, and all three respond to their names.

_____ **5.** The villagers fled the erupting lava suffocating ash and deadly fumes of the volcano.

_____ **6.** Do the hammer, nails, and wrenches all go on the second shelf?

_____ **7.** Now where did I leave my books bookbag and skates?

_____ **8.** In the daylight we could see the mountain standing tall and strong and gleaming.

_____ **9.** Look that up in *The Chicago Manual of Style Words into Type*, or the dictionary.

Copyright © by Glencoe/McGraw-Hill

Mechanics

_____ 10. Is this product advertised as one of those new improved soaps?

_____ 11. Her eyes closed, her head dropped to her chest and she began to snore.

_____ 12. Does that small black kitten have a home?

_____ 13. The brothers came in first second and third in the marathon.

_____ 14. Would you like your eggs scrambled or fried or poached?

_____ 15. We are studying the history of radio and television.

_____ 16. The spy leapt from the roof ran through the alley, and disappeared into the crowd.

_____ 17. It was a long complicated rescue, but finally the boys were safe.

_____ 18. Who got mud on my expensive red boots?

_____ 19. Would you help me find the canned goods paper products and dairy foods?

_____ 20. Tim's favorite sports are baseball golf, and racketball.

▶ **Exercise 2** Delete (⸜) any commas that are unnecessary. Write *C* in the blank if the sentence is correct.

_____ Don't wear that old⸜stained shirt to dinner!

_____ 1. Stack the newspapers, in piles, tie them with twine, and put them out for recycling.

_____ 2. Are you going with Jamil, and Randy?

_____ 3. I can hear that old, broken-down car coming, down the street.

_____ 4. We left early, avoided rush hour traffic, and arrived at the motel by noon.

_____ 5. Should we go to the game, the movies, or the library, after school?

_____ 6. Do you want peanut butter, and jam on your sandwich?

_____ 7. The microbe exhibit showed us the paramecium, the euglena, and the volvox.

_____ 8. Will our guest use the couch, or the futon, or the sleeping bag?

_____ 9. I don't like to read about either Hitler, or Mussolini.

_____ 10. I showed Alana, Joanne, and Mabel my old, handmade quilt.

_____ 11. Should we have cereal, fruit, or eggs, for breakfast?

_____ 12. The dog turned around three times, curled itself into a furry ball, and fell immediately to sleep.

_____ 13. The snow loosened from the mountain, gained momentum, and rushed down, the mountain.

_____ 14. Should we rent a rock video, or a documentary, or a mystery?

_____ 15. Her posture, tone of voice, and mood all told me she wasn't feeling well.

Copyright © by Glencoe/McGraw-Hill

Mechanics

Lesson 80

Commas and Nonessential Elements with Interjections, Parenthetical Expressions, and Conjunctive Adverbs

Use commas to set off participles, infinitives, and their phrases if they are not essential to the sentence.

The dog ran from bush to bush, sniffing eagerly. (participle)
You should know, to satisfy your curiosity, that Beth is my cousin. (infinitive)

Use commas to set off a nonessential adjective clause.

The train from Omaha, which is usually late, comes in on that track.
(*Which is usually late* does not change the meaning of the sentence and, therefore, is nonessential.)

Do not use commas to set off an essential adjective clause. Such a clause gives information that is essential to the meaning of the sentence.

The people who work in that building are doctors.

Use commas to set off an appositive if it is not essential to the meaning of a sentence.

Janine, my mother's cousin, lives in Salt Lake City.

Use commas to set off interjections such as *oh* and *well*; parenthetical expressions such as *on the contrary, on the other hand, in fact, by the way, for example,* and *after all*; and adverbs and conjunctive adverbs such as *however, moreover,* and *consequently.*

Well, what are you doing here? In fact, I came to see you.
Oh, I'm busy; for example, I have to study.

▶ **Exercise 1 Add commas wherever necessary. Delete (⁊) commas used incorrectly.**

Oh, I see you've made the finals,⁊for the math competition.

1. The riders screaming plunged down the first major drop of the roller coaster.

2. Jean who laughs so hard she cries is a good audience.

3. John F. Kennedy a former U.S. president was born, in Massachusetts.

4. Well what do we have here?

5. The detective, that you met yesterday, will be in charge of the case.

6. Here's a suggestion to help you get started for something to do for your science project.

7. This paint which costs far too much will not add anything to the room.

Copyright © by Glencoe/McGraw-Hill

Mechanics

8. My mother to tell the truth does not care, about celebrities.

9. By the way where were you, when I came over?

10. Danielle worrying about her performance did not hear me call her.

11. Oh no what will I do if I miss the bus?

12. The character, that everyone mistrusted, turned out to be the hero.

13. The team made their triumphant way, off the field yelling wildly.

14. You could get to school another way; for example you could walk.

15. To prevent theft many homeowners have security systems.

16. Hank talks all the time; on the other hand he usually has something interesting to say.

17. The spy in the movie to give you a hint is someone you'd never suspect.

18. Someone who really cares about plants, should work in the school garden.

19. Okay I'll go if you insist.

20. The mother bear enraged charged the hunter threatening her cubs.

▶ **Exercise 2 Add commas wherever necessary. Delete (⸜) any unnecesary commas. Write _C_ in the blank if the sentence is correct.**

_____   Well, there is no longer any doubt; on the contrary, I am quite sure.

_____ **1.** Sonia went to the dentist, to get her teeth cleaned.

_____ **2.** The runners gasping for breath limped across the finish line.

_____ **3.** We met our parents at the restaurant for lunch.

_____ **4.** Warming up before exercise, is a way to prevent injury.

_____ **5.** Animals, that prey on other animals, are called predators.

_____ **6.** I have the strangest sense, that you're not telling the truth.

_____ **7.** Oh, is that, what you meant?

_____ **8.** His room, to give you an example, is covered with posters of explorers.

_____ **9.** I came too late for the award presentation unfortunately.

_____ **10.** By the way didn't I meet you at the film conference, last week?

_____ **11.** The ram made his way along the ledge stepping confidently.

_____ **12.** Arturo who loves animals takes in strays, all the time.

_____ **13.** My sister, who writes science fiction, wants to write for television.

_____ **14.** Yes I see that you have improved your backhand a lot.

Copyright © by Glencoe/McGraw-Hill

Mechanics

Lesson 81
Commas and Introductory Phrases

Use a comma after an introductory prepositional phrase to prevent misreading.

From the cliff above the lake looked like a mirror. (confusing)
From the cliff above, the lake looked like a mirror. (clear)

Don not use a comma if the prepositional phrase is followed immediately by a verb.

Over the mantelpiece hung a portrait of Aunt June.

Use a comma after a long prepositional phrase or after the final phrase in a series of phrases.

After a heartbreaking series of losses, the Lions finally won.
At the top of the hill on the ranch, we found the lost calf.

Use a comma to set off an introductory participle or a participial phrase.

Colliding, the two cars came to a crunching halt.
Hoping for the best, Rae Ellen checked the list of finalists.

▶ **Exercise 1** **Add a comma wherever necessary. Write *C* in the blank if the sentence is correct.**

_____ Around the honey, bees swarmed noisily.

_____ 1. For germination to work seeds must spread from place to place.

_____ 2. In a patch of bare soil outside your door new plants will spring up almost overnight.

_____ 3. Wondering at this process botanists have studied the migration of seeds.

_____ 4. To send their seeds out of the main plant and into the world, plants have evolved clever methods.

_____ 5. In certain plants seed pods explode.

_____ 6. In such an explosion seeds are flung into the air.

_____ 7. Traveling on the wind, some seeds fall on fertile ground.

_____ 8. Onto barren ground fall many more seeds that will not germinate.

_____ 9. Floating on the water some seeds are light enough to travel for many miles.

_____ 10. Developing inside berries many seeds are transported when animals eat the fruit.

_____ 11. Passing through the animal unharmed these seeds may come to rest on good soil.

_____ 12. Traveling inside an animal is only one way in which seeds make use of moving organisms.

Copyright © by Glencoe/McGraw-Hill

_____ **13.** Hitching a ride on the outside is yet another way.

_____ **14.** Walking through meadows or woodlands you have probably come home with many

plant parts stuck to your clothing.

_____ **15.** In their movement through the underbrush animals also pick up these seeds.

_____ **16.** Falling to the ground later on the seeds will often germinate.

_____ **17.** Some plants grow seeds that are very lightweight.

_____ **18.** Shaking in the wind such plants release their seeds.

_____ **19.** Into the air fly these lightweight seeds.

_____ **20.** Traveling much farther than heavy seeds, they spread the parent plant far and wide.

_____ **21.** Lacking locomotion plants cannot escape from their enemies.

_____ **22.** More than the ability to run away self-defense also comes in other forms.

_____ **23.** On some plants are thorns or stingers.

_____ **24.** Trying to eat such a plant animals soon become discouraged.

_____ **25.** On the edges and along the middle of other plants lie rows and rows of sharp barbs.

_____ **26.** Approaching the plant to eat it animals are stuck and quickly retreat.

_____ **27.** For some animals chewing a plant is a means of nourishment.

_____ **28.** Inside many plants are unpleasant tasting chemicals.

_____ **29.** Learning quickly, the chewers of such plants usually move on to other food sources.

_____ **30.** Making treaties with animals some plants trade a little food for a lot of safety.

_____ **31.** In the thorns of acacia trees is a substance that ants like to eat.

_____ **32.** In exchange for this food the ants attack animals that try to eat larger parts of the tree.

_____ **33.** On the teasel plant is a dangerous place for unwary animals.

_____ **34.** Meeting in the middle pairs of teasel leaves form a cup.

_____ **35.** During a rainstorm the cup fills with water.

_____ **36.** Climbing the plant to feed insects are faced with a small pool of water.

_____ **37.** Going on they risk getting trapped in the cup and drowning.

_____ **38.** Turning back they can avoid drowning and the plant is protected.

_____ **39.** With some plants it is not even necessary for an animal to try to eat it.

_____ **40.** On the rose vicious thorns stab an animal as it passes, which causes it to look for food

elsewhere.

Copyright © by Glencoe/McGraw-Hill

Mechanics

Lesson 82
Commas and Adverb Clauses and Antithetical Phrases

Use a comma to set off an introductory adverb clause and an internal adverb clause that interrupts the flow of the sentence.

Before you get angry, listen to my side of the story.
I hope, since we've always been friends, that you will understand.

In general, do not use a comma to set off an adverb clause at the end of a sentence.

I hope we get home before the storm breaks.

Use a comma to set off an antithetical phrase. An **antithetical phrase** uses words such as *not* or *unlike* to qualify what comes before it.

The auditorium, not the gym, has more space.
Basketball, unlike football, can be played year-round.

▶ **Exercise 1** **Add and delete commas to complete each sentence. Write *C* in the blank if the sentence is correct.**

_____ Fernando, not Enrique, enjoys hand-drawing and painting maps.

_____ 1. Before paper was invented maps were made of whatever materials were at hand.

_____ 2. The earliest known map, is made of mud not paper.

_____ 3. This map just so you know is believed to be Babylonian.

_____ 4. Mapmakers believe, that early maps were made to show people's possessions not to give directions.

_____ 5. A landowner would draw an outline, of his property, in order to protect it from theft.

_____ 6. Unlike the Babylonians, the Inuit of the Arctic made maps of animal skins.

_____ 7. The Egyptians to show the locations of precious ores engraved maps on gold, copper, and silver plates.

_____ 8. In order to identify their small islands the South Pacific islanders made maps using shells, and coral.

_____ 9. Many cultures, in fact seemed to evolve mapmaking, independently of one another.

_____ 10. The Chinese used silk, not cheap cloth, to make maps.

_____ 11. They used different symbols, to indicate towns and villages.

Copyright © by Glencoe/McGraw-Hill

Mechanics

_____ 12. The Chinese also distinguished between rivers and roads on their maps.

_____ 13. Early mapmakers used a lot of guesswork before people began to explore the world more fully.

_____ 14. Mapmaking was really a form of art not science.

_____ 15. When explorers returned, from trips new information was added to the mapmakers' store of knowledge.

_____ 16. Ptolemy unlike his predecessors began to put north at the top of maps.

_____ 17. He also in an attempt to add accuracy tried to show distances between landmasses on maps.

_____ 18. Until the printing press was invented maps had to be copied by hand.

_____ 19. This made them as you might guess very expensive.

_____ 20. When the printing press made maps widely available, interest in exploration flourished worldwide.

_____ 21. Maps basic tools for Earth scientists show a variety of things.

_____ 22. Topographical maps show the shape of the land just as road maps show the locations of streets and highways.

_____ 23. Although road maps show where roads lead they do not show the elevations of such roads.

_____ 24. A topographical map just so you know would be useful for you when you plan a day-long hike.

_____ 25. The map would show you before you got started how much climbing you would have to do.

_____ 26. In order to make plans for a highway engineers use topographical maps.

_____ 27. Such maps can tell them that the site they want to use for an underpass is one hundred feet high, not two hundred.

_____ 28. From the Greek word for "water," hydrology is the science of water distribution.

_____ 29. Hydrological maps as you might guess show the location of water sources on land.

_____ 30. Hydrological maps unlike some other kinds also show underground locations of water.

Copyright © by Glencoe/McGraw-Hill

Mechanics

Lesson 83
Commas with Titles, Addresses, and Numbers

Use commas to set off titles when they follow a person's name.

Frank Johns, professor of education, will speak tonight.
Rachel Cooney, mayor of Tisdale, will run for reelection.

Use commas to separate the parts of an address, a geographical location, or a date.

Salt Lake City, Utah, is the home of the Mormon Tabernacle Choir.
Chun-wei's new address is 12 Elm Street, Cleveland, Ohio 44113.
Friday, March 17, is St. Patrick's Day this year.

Do not use commas where only the month and the day or the month and the year are given.

On June 10 every year we celebrate the last day of school.
January 1991 was one of the coldest winters we ever had.

Use commas to set off the parts of a reference that direct a reader to an exact source.

The entry for *Computer* is found in *World Book*, Volume 4, pages 740–745.

▶ **Exercise 1** **Add and delete commas where necessary. Write *C* in the blank if the sentence is correct.**

_____ May I introduce Mabel Hawkins, the president of the board?

_____ **1.** The Grand Canyon is not far from Flagstaff Arizona.

_____ **2.** We plan to visit Yosemite in June 1996.

_____ **3.** An article in last week's edition of *The Free Times* page 6 says that Ted Hagan county commissioner will not be reappointed.

_____ **4.** Yesterday an unpopular bill was passed by the state senate in Columbus Georgia.

_____ **5.** When she told me her birthday was February 11 1978 I knew she was slightly older than I was.

_____ **6.** Next year we will visit London England and Madrid Spain.

_____ **7.** Jack Brown, the company CEO, was just fired.

_____ **8.** There are good satellite photos of Earth in the November 1994 issue of *Earth* pages 57–61.

_____ **9.** My new class will begin on March 29 1994.

_____ **10.** Harvey Webster my professor will teach us about the comeback of the peregrine falcon.

Copyright © by Glencoe/McGraw-Hill

Mechanics

_____ **11.** Is that new video store at 2240 Lee Road?

_____ **12.** The last day to sign up for camp is Monday June 5.

_____ **13.** My friend Marilyn and her daughters will spend the summer in Antigua, Guatemala.

_____ **14.** I think this blurred address reads 642 Shankland Ave., Metarie, Louisiana.

_____ **15.** Please have your reports to me no later than Monday May 6.

_____ **16.** Ho Chi Minh City, Vietnam, used to be called Saigon.

_____ **17.** Dr. Richards the veterinarian preformed delicate surgery on my cat.

_____ **18.** Our tour will visit Atlanta Georgia and Charleston South Carolina.

_____ **19.** Our championship game will be played in December 1996.

_____ **20.** School starts later next year, on September 10.

_____ **21.** I thought you said we had until July, 15 to apply.

_____ **22.** Fannie Lewis, is a city councilwoman.

_____ **23.** There is a good outdoor equipment shop in San Francisco California.

_____ **24.** Carl Sagan discusses the *Voyager* spacecraft discoveries in his book *Cosmos* pages 137–166.

_____ **25.** Linda Schele the Maya anthropologist will lecture here next week.

_____ **26.** My aunt's address is 126 Sapps Road, Danville, Ohio 43014.

_____ **27.** I will visit my friend Susan in Portland Maine in June, 1996.

_____ **28.** Elizabeth II queen of England has ruled since 1952.

_____ **29.** Please have your reports ready by April 5 1996.

_____ **30.** We hope to be completely moved by the end of October, 1996.

_____ **31.** I used to have a pen pal in Rio de Janiero, Brazil.

_____ **32.** Joseph Wood Krutch quotes from John Wesley Powell the explorer in his book *Grand Canyon* pages 97–98.

_____ **33.** Boston Massachusetts is the setting for many of Robert Parker's mysteries.

_____ **34.** K-Mart used to have two stores in Bloomington, Indiana but I think one has closed.

_____ **35.** Bruce Springsteen the "Boss" has been popular as a musician for many years.

_____ **36.** My doctor is Barry Brooks, M.D.

Copyright © by Glencoe/McGraw-Hill

Mechanics

Lesson 84

Commas with Direct Address and in Tag Questions and Letter Writing

Use commas to set off words or names in direct address.

Yuji, did you write this poem?   See, Jerry, you can do the backstroke.

Use commas to set off a tag question.

The store opens at 10 A.M., doesn't it?
You haven't been here before, have you?

Use a comma after the salutation of an informal letter and after the closing of all letters.

Dear Herb,   Dear Mr. Randall,   Sincerely,   As always,

Use commas in the heading of a letter as follows:

123 Elm Street
Springfield, Ohio 45313
June 6, 1997

▶ **Exercise 1** **Insert commas where necessary in the following letter. Write *C* in the blank if commas are used correctly or if no commas are needed.**

_____   Marcy, have you written to Satchi lately?

_____   **1.** Satchi Kwan

_____   **2.** 444 Randall Parkway

_____   **3.** Portland Maine 04101

_____   **4.** March 12 1995

_____   **5.** Dear Satchi

_____   **6.** Welcome to your new home my friend.

_____   **7.** We want to hear all about your move, but we really miss you you know?

_____   **8.** Satchi you'll be surprised to hear that Mona has moved, too.

_____   **9.** Her mother was transferred to the company branch in Dallas Texas.

_____   **10.** Pretty soon no one will be left of the old gang.

_____   **11.** Writing to you will improve my computer skills won't it?

_____   **12.** You after all have always kidded me about my distrust of computers.

_____   **13.** You were the first in our class to have an e-mail address weren't you?

Copyright © by Glencoe/McGraw-Hill

Mechanics

_____ **14.** Well, Satchi, you'll just have to wait until I get a modem.

_____ **15.** Oh, you should know that Sisay just got back from Salinas California.

_____ **16.** You visited there once didn't you?

_____ **17.** The news about the terrible floods was in your paper wasn't it?

_____ **18.** Well pal that's all the time I have for now.

_____ **19.** Your friend

_____ **20.** Marcy

▶ **Exercise 2** **Insert commas where necessary in the following letter. Write *C* in the blank if commas are used correctly or if no commas are needed.**

_____   May 16, 1995

_____ **1.** Mrs. Benito Salazar

_____ **2.** 749 Delgado St.

_____ **3.** Orlando, Florida 32821

_____ **4.** Dear Grandmama

_____ **5.** Your visit with us ended much too soon don't you think?

_____ **6.** I know you would have enjoyed a trip to the art museum.

_____ **7.** But the trip on the lake freighter was neat wasn't it?

_____ **8.** I really should become a tour guide shouldn't I?

_____ **9.** Mom wants me to take her to the botanical gardens.

_____ **10.** Mirna, she says, you know more about the city than I do.

_____ **11.** In the meantime Grandmama I am transcribing the tape you made.

_____ **12.** I love hearing about your early life with Grandpapa Diego.

_____ **13.** You and he have lived in many different places haven't you?

_____ **14.** When you talked about the church where you were married, I felt as if I were there.

_____ **15.** Florida was very different when you were young wasn't it?

_____ **16.** When I get the tape transcribed, I will send you a copy okay?

_____ **17.** Grandmama I wish we still lived in the same town.

_____ **18.** But until we see each other again, you will take care won't you?

_____ **19.** Your loving granddaughter

_____ **20.** Mirna

Copyright © by Glencoe/McGraw-Hill

Mechanics

Lesson 85
Misused Commas

Do not use a comma alone to join two main clauses. This forms a run-on sentence. Use a comma before a coordinating conjunction or use a semicolon.

Incorrect: The curtain rose slowly, the performance began.
Correct: The curtain rose slowly, and the performance began.
Correct: The curtain rose slowly; the performance began.

Do not use a comma before a conjunction that connects the parts of a compound predicate in a simple sentence.

Incorrect: That doctor never turns away anyone, but welcomes every patient.
Correct: That doctor never turns away anyone but welcomes every patient.

Do not use commas between a subject and its verb or between a verb and its complement.

Incorrect: Everything I like to snack on, is bound to have too much sugar.
Correct: Everything I like to snack on is bound to have too much sugar.
Incorrect: The recipe for chili contains, tomatoes, beans, and peppers.
Correct: The recipe for chili contains tomatoes, beans, and peppers.

▶ **Exercise 1** Delete (⌄) any commas used incorrectly, and correct the sentence. If the sentence is correct, write *C* in the blank.

                                              ; *or* , and
_____   I had not seen Yosemite before, it took my breath away.

_____ **1.** I hope the Andrewses can come, I've invited the whole family.

_____ **2.** Every sport you like, is one that I don't play.

_____ **3.** I called the company for help, their ad gave a toll-free number.

_____ **4.** We don't watch television news but read the newspapers.

_____ **5.** My favorite courses include, geology, algebra, and art.

_____ **6.** The dog refused to chase the cat, but instead ate its food.

_____ **7.** The art you call avant-garde, is art I call silly.

_____ **8.** I came to pick you up for the party, you were gone.

_____ **9.** The senator spoke at our graduation, his speech was very inspiring.

_____ **10.** These vegetables contain, Vitamin A, Vitamin C, and several minerals.

Copyright © by Glencoe/McGraw-Hill

Mechanics

_____ 11. The things you consider old-fashioned are dear to me.

_____ 12. The audience cheered the recipient of the award, and called for a speech.

_____ 13. Sarah was exhausted by noon, she kept going.

_____ 14. Each bibliography entry should include author, title, and publisher.

_____ 15. Sheila had never come in first before, but usually won a second prize.

_____ 16. The starter fired the gun, the runners were off.

_____ 17. Whatever you're thinking about my grade is wrong.

_____ 18. The supernova was quite distant, it shined brighter than everything else in the sky.

_____ 19. I tried to beat the storm home, I lost.

_____ 20. My backpack includes an army knife, cooking utensils, and waterproof matches.

_____ 21. Socrates achieved fame as a philosopher, people still study his teachings today.

_____ 22. Whoever crosses the finish line first, gets the trophy.

_____ 23. The squirrel isn't satisfied with its sunflower seeds, but tries to get into the bird feeder.

_____ 24. The audience burst into applause, they kept applauding for ten curtain calls.

_____ 25. The spy hoped to exit through the kitchen, the door was locked.

_____ 26. Which grocery sack contains, the potatoes, rice, and beans?

_____ 27. We tried to clean up the river, it was too severely polluted.

_____ 28. I hope we're including, Ralph, Manny, and Paul on the list.

_____ 29. He will never forget that performance, it made him laugh till he cried.

_____ 30. Suellen finished first in the race and also broke the record.

_____ 31. I never would have believed it, had I not seen it.

_____ 32. We heard about the tragic accident, an eyewitness told us the tale.

_____ 33. I love homework more than watching TV, well, there are some good shows on.

_____ 34. The king assembled his dukes, barons, and earls in a parliament.

Copyright © by Glencoe/McGraw-Hill

Mechanics

Lesson 86
Commas in Review

▶ **Exercise 1** Add commas where necessary and delete (⌣) any that are not needed. If the sentence is correct, write *C* in the blank.

_____ If you want to study deserts, you should move to the Southwest, don't you think?

_____ **1.** Hari and Kirti are both good singers but Kirti is a better guitar player.

_____ **2.** I talked, and June listened.

_____ **3.** Alice Walker writes poetry essays and short stories about African American women's experience.

_____ **4.** I don't think Jason that the two cases are at all alike.

_____ **5.** The villain really should be more terrifying, don't you think?

_____ **6.** The man who heads up the legal department, is a Harvard graduate.

_____ **7.** In the room over the garage Celeste worked on her painting.

_____ **8.** James Earl Jones was in John Sayles's film *Matewan.*

_____ **9.** Josh is a better dancer than Sergei, and I much prefer Josh's acting.

_____ **10.** Toward the horizon, sped the jet plane.

_____ **11.** That chair is lovely, and expensive, and chic but I don't want to sit in it.

_____ **12.** Your old, torn pants indicate that this is not a formal visit.

_____ **13.** It's not a good idea to use your computer during a storm you know?

_____ **14.** After the long game we went out for hot chocolate.

_____ **15.** I'll tell you since you ask that I think the film lacks merit.

_____ **16.** The person who gave you that information is mistaken.

_____ **17.** We need to leave soon don't we?

_____ **18.** Giggling the children watched the antics of the clown.

_____ **19.** You can either accept the judges' decision or you can contest it.

_____ **20.** I didn't read his best-seller; moreover I haven't read any of his books.

_____ **21.** Aunt Emma, who runs the sales department, said she would hire me for the summer.

_____ **22.** Are you a ham, and eggs kind of person, or a rice, and beans kind?

_____ **23.** Prescott Arizona unlike Tucson is not excessively hot.

Copyright © by Glencoe/McGraw-Hill

_____ 24. During the semester, we hosted speakers from several political parties.

_____ 25. Starting out in the mail room she soon became the head buyer for our company.

_____ 26. For your salad dressing you can choose one of the following: oil and vinegar garlic and oil or yogurt and spices.

_____ 27. On March 17, 1995, my father had open heart surgery in Mercy Hospital.

_____ 28. Jamil ran triumphantly under the high, wide goalposts to score the winning touchdown.

_____ 29. I think in fact that you would be very good as the hero of the play.

_____ 30. To make such a splendid bowl takes extraordinary pottery skills.

_____ 31. Albany not New York City is the capital of New York state.

_____ 32. Christa before going to college scored very high on her SATs.

_____ 33. The rescuers racing against the clock lowered the stretcher into the mouth of the cave.

_____ 34. She used to live at 4030 Lander Road Chagrin Falls Ohio 44022.

_____ 35. We hope to visit London England and several cities in Yorkshire.

_____ 36. Toshiro Mifune who has acted in so many wonderful Japanese films was actually born in China.

_____ 37. Sprinting the last few yards, Ayita ran for the ball.

_____ 38. Our school picnic last year was better than the one in June, 1994.

_____ 39. Jake what took you so long?

_____ 40. The best-loved book, written by E.B. White, is probably *Charlotte's Web.*

_____ 41. The puppy is a growling, chewing, eating terror.

_____ 42. I should try to do my homework, shouldn't I?

_____ 43. She didn't finish the portrait, but put the paints aside for later.

_____ 44. Well I never thought I'd hear you say that Gene.

_____ 45. The player everyone else thought was so good, seemed ordinary to me.

_____ 46. When I have something to say no one ever listens.

_____ 47. For dinner tonight we plan to eat, hamburgers, french fries, and pecan pie.

_____ 48. My grandfather and I used to go fishing, but that was some time ago.

_____ 49. You didn't look did you when I asked you to?

_____ 50. I thought she was, beautiful wise and intelligent.

Copyright © by Glencoe/McGraw-Hill

Mechanics

Lesson 87
Dashes to Signal Change and to Emphasize

Use a dash to indicate an abrupt break or change in thought within a sentence.

Have a seat in the dining—well, look who's coming up the walk!

Use a dash to emphasize appositives, or to set off a series of them.

We'll meet the new coach—James Greer—after lunch.
We'll meet the replacements—Harkins, Snell, and Kirk—tomorrow.

Use a dash to emphasize a parenthetical clause.

Her new book—I think it's called *Life in Space*—is on order.

Use a dash to show hesitation.

You—you mean you didn't get my letter? But—but that's impossible!

▶ **Exercise 1** **Insert a dash where necessary.**

The Spanish word for mustang *mestengo* means "wild."

1. I'll be studying with Corrine did you see her goal in the game today?

2. The cats we call them the herd will come running for dinner now.

3. I I I can't remember what I was doing last Tuesday.

4. The basic tools hammer, wrench, and screwdriver are all in your kit.

5. Her book you must have read it has been on the best seller list for weeks.

6. I think your scarf is in the oh, I don't know where it is!

7. A neutron star a small, very dense star weighs an incredible amount.

8. She she's the one I saw driving away from the crash scene!

9. The signs of spring robins, daffodils, and spring peepers are in evidence.

10. The two finalists Amy and Namid will compete for first prize.

11. Two of the brothers Lash and Karl are pianists for our town's orchestra.

12. Please make yourself at home do you smell something burning?

13. My favorite character the one who really solves the mystery is Rob MacCracken.

14. The mezzanine from the Latin for "middle" is the seating area between the main floor and the balcony.

15. What what what have you done?

Copyright © by Glencoe/McGraw-Hill

Mechanics

16. Halle, this is oh, I didn't know you two had met.

17. Jim's grandfather he's our mayor, as you know will speak at commencement.

18. The heroine of the book is a war photographer, and she sorry, I have to get the phone.

19. You you shouldn't have jumped out at me like that!

20. Names of animals many of them from Native American languages are usually very colorful.

21. We held dinner for you oh my, what did you do to your arm?

22. Mrs. Carter she's Adam's grandmother, you know is our science teacher this year.

23. He he he almost ran into the garage wall!

24. Many animal names *burro, bronco,* and *pinto* are three come from the Spanish language.

25. Do you want to eat what's the score, by the way? while you watch the rest of the game?

26. You you mean you knew it was Jack all the time?

27. Now, when you divide fractions, you is that the baby crying?

28. Jean's brother you met him at the game is going to Cornell University in Ithaca, New York.

29. Shanna exercises every day an hour each morning to prepare for the track meet.

30. The movie was directed by Steven Spielberg but you know that.

31. There there there must be some mistake!

32. The Dutch have given us words that name pastries *cookie, cruller,* and *waffle,* for example.

33. The rainy season in India it's called the *monsoon* season is about to begin.

34. Our mail comes every day but Saturday, that is just after noon.

35. What what do you mean by that?

36. Early outlaws Billy the Kid and Jesse James, for example are very popular subjects for movies.

37. A planet's orbit that is, its path around the sun is elliptical, not circular.

38. I I I'm sorry I hurt your feelings, Caroline; can you forgive me?

39. Some words *laundromat* and *smog* are examples are compounds made from two other words while dropping some letters.

40. The strings I mean the violins, violas, and cellos are my favorite instruments.

41. That huge wave Asford, what are you doing? is going to hit us!

42. The horse oh, look how swiftly he runs is coming this way.

43. The movie started why couldn't you be here on time? so you missed the opening scenes.

44. We saw the iceberg how enormous it looked float past us.

Copyright © by Glencoe/McGraw-Hill

Lesson 88
Parentheses, Brackets, and Ellipsis Points

Use parentheses to set off supplemental material, that is, material not closely related to the rest of the sentence.

Anna Pavlova (1881–1931) was a famous Russian ballerina.

If material within parentheses is a complete sentence, but is part of a larger sentence, do not add end punctuation. If a sentence in parentheses stands by itself, use both a capital letter and end punctuation.

Anna Pavlova (she was known as the "Dying Swan") was born in St. Petersburg.
Anna Pavlova was born in St. Petersburg. (St. Petersburg was renamed Leningrad during the period of the Soviet Union.)

Place a period, question mark, or exclamation point inside the parentheses if it is part of the parenthetical expression. Place a period, question mark, or an exclamation point outside the parentheses if the parenthetical expression is part of the whole sentence.

Anna Pavlova was prima ballerina of the Imperial Ballet Company in Russia. (Later, after leaving Russia, she formed her own company.)
Pavlova was known for her graceful movements (which contributed to her nickname).

▶ **Exercise 1 Insert parentheses where necessary.**

Flannery O'Connor (1925–1964) wrote many excellent short stories.

1. Ms. Star my teacher wants us to enter our themes in the contest.

2. I can't imagine and I've tried! Jeremy in that role.

3. The President will speak at 10:00 A.M. Eastern 9:00 A.M. Central.

4. Rollerblading is very popular now even though I get dizzy just watching someone do it.

5. Will you return these videos they're due today on your way to work?

6. Rachel told me not that it's any secret that she's thinking of changing her major.

7. If you like nuts and I know you do, you'll love this selection.

8. Today is the birthday of composer Wolfgang Amadeus Mozart 1756–1791.

9. Theodore Roosevelt known as T.R. was an avid conservationist.

10. Jo put the props dishes, water glasses, tray on the backstage table before the performance.

11. We will visit Great Britain England, Wales, and Scotland next year.

12. The thermometer read −30° yes, 30° below zero.

Copyright © by Glencoe/McGraw-Hill

Mechanics

Use **brackets** to enclose information that you, the writer, insert to clarify a quotation from someone else's work.

"We want full manhood suffrage [voting rights], and we want it now, henceforth and forever." Booker T. Washington

Use brackets to enclose a parenthetical phrase that appears within parentheses.

The word *bacteria* comes from the Greek *baktron* (meaning "rod" [from its shape]).

Use **ellipsis points**, or **ellipses**, a series of three spaced points, to indicate that material from a quotation has been left out. Use three ellipsis points if the omitted material occurs at the beginning of a sentence. If the material is omitted in the middle or at the end of a sentence, use any necessary punctuation plus the ellipsis points.

". . . In short, our school needs a new gymnasium," Emily said.
Bill began his poem, "A light shone in the window. . . ."

▶ **Exercise 2** **Insert parentheses, brackets, and ellipsis points where necessary. Use the marks of punctuation named at the end of each sentence.**

My grandpa (people called him "Doc") was a veterinarian. (parentheses)

1. What comes next after "Roses are red, violets are blue"? (ellipses)

2. James Earl Jones the voice of Darth Vader is in a new television drama. (parentheses)

3. The campaigner ended his speech with " and if elected, I promise to lower taxes." (ellipses)

4. George S. Patton "Old Blood and Guts" was one of our most famous generals. (parentheses)

5. The teacher said, "This pointing to Japan on the map is our biggest challenge in business for the next decade." (brackets)

6. The mayor, a Republican, was quoted as saying, "We will fight the opposition Democrats on this important issue." (brackets)

7. He stated, "We know the enemy, here referring to passivity, and we will fight it." (brackets)

8. My sister is a well-known biologist. She writes for *Discovery* magazine. (parentheses)

9. We studied mushrooms members of the fungus family last week. (parentheses)

10. Our star, the sun, is about 150 million kilometers 93 million miles from Earth. (parentheses)

11. The review stated, "The sisters, played by Joy and Alice Hollis who are sisters themselves, were strong and believable." (parentheses)

12. Help me finish this Shakespearean sonnet, "When in disgrace with fortune and men's eyes," (ellipses)

Copyright © by Glencoe/McGraw-Hill

Lesson 89
Quotation Marks for Direct Quotations

Use quotation marks to enclose a direct quotation. When a quotation is interrupted by explanatory words such as *he said* or *she wrote,* use two sets of quotation marks. Use two punctuation marks, such as two commas or a comma and a period, to separate each part of the quotation from the intervening phrase. If the second part of the quotation is a complete sentence, begin it with a capital letter.

"I'm not sure," replied Mark, "that I want to go to the game tonight."
"We can leave early," said his sister. "I know you have to get up at five o'clock."

Do not use quotation marks if you do not repeat a person's exact words.

Thoreau said that truth requires two people, one to say it and the other to hear it.

Use single quotation marks around a quotation within a quotation.

The speaker said, "I know you've all heard James Thurber's cartoon caption, 'Well, if I called the wrong number, why did you answer the phone?'"

When you write dialogue, begin a new paragraph and use a new set of quotation marks each time the speaker changes.

"Why are you skipping those rocks across the river?" I asked, idly watching the clouds.
"My father used to do it," he replied. "I'm trying to beat his record."

▶ Exercise 1 **Insert quotation marks where necessary.**

John Muir, renowned American explorer and conservationist, said of his school days, "We

were simply driven pointblank against our books like soldiers against the enemy. . . . "

1. Born in Scotland, Muir loved the natural world, where, as he says, Wildness was ever sounding

   in our ears, . . .

2. Muir remembers his journey to America in 1849 with his brothers and father as the first grand

   adventure of my life.

3. John was creative, crafting dozens of clocks—There's nothing else like them in the world,

   exclaimed a neighbor—and other devices.

4. Muir began to travel and study and to continue inventing, saying, Living is more important than

   getting a living.

5. When he invented new machines for a broom- and rake-making factory, his employer said, It

   was a delight to see those machines at work.

Copyright © by Glencoe/McGraw-Hill

Mechanics

6. Flowers are born every hour, Muir wrote to a friend; living sunlight is poured over all, and every thing and creature is glad.

7. Muir soon began walking over the natural paths of America; I might have become a millionaire, he later said, but I chose to become a tramp!

8. I'll acquaint myself with the glaciers and wild gardens, he wrote, and get as near the heart of the world as I can.

▶ **Exercise 2 Insert quotation marks where necessary. Write *C* in the blank if the sentence is correct.**

_____   When she was a child, Rachel Carson said, "I spent long days out of doors . . . happiest with the wild birds and creatures as companions."

_____ 1. Carson's mother taught her daughter that intelligence and personal worth were more valuable than money or success.

_____ 2. Her biographer, Philip Sterling, said that Rachel Carson did not make friends readily or carelessly.

_____ 3. The young Carson wrote poems and stories, and when a story was accepted by a magazine, she wrote, The pay, I believe, was a cent a word.

_____ 4. Once in college, she was drawn to science, but her friends told her to stick to writing because there was no future for a woman in science.

_____ 5. I thought I had to be one or the other, she wrote. It never occurred to me . . . that I could combine the two careers.

_____ 6. When her studies in biology and zoology led her to write scripts for a radio program, she said, It dawned on me that by becoming a biologist I had given myself something to write about.

_____ 7. Learning to scuba dive, Carson wrote about the colors and animals she observed under the waters off the Florida Keys.

_____ 8. Miss Carson's science cannot be questioned, said oceanographer William Beebe.

_____ 9. But when Carson wrote her classic *Silent Spring, Time* magazine labeled the book, an emotional and inaccurate outburst.

_____ 10. It was a spring without voices, she said in the introduction to the book that described how the pesticide DDT damaged current and future generations of both animals and humans.

Copyright © by Glencoe/McGraw-Hill

Lesson 90

Quotation Marks with Titles of Short Works, Unusual Expressions, Definitions, and with Other Marks of Punctuation

Use quotation marks to enclose titles of short works, such as short stories, short poems, essays, newspaper and magazine articles, book chapters, songs, and single episodes of television series.

"Raymond's Run" (short story)   "Annabel Lee" (poem)
"Nature" (essay)   "Instant Theater" (newspaper article)
"Brothers and Sisters" (chapter)   "Bridge Over Troubled Water" (song)

Use quotation marks to enclose unfamiliar slang and unusual or original expressions.

A slang phrase for *died* is "bought the farm."

Use quotation marks to enclose a definition that is stated directly.

Merganser comes from two Latin words meaning "diving goose."

Place a comma or period inside closing quotation marks.

"It's dishonest," said Mack, "and I want no part of it."

Place a semicolon or a colon outside closing quotation marks.

Alice Walker wrote the poem "In Love and Trouble"; it was also the title of one of her books of poetry.

Place a question mark or exclamation point inside the closing quotation marks when it is part of the quotation.

I'd like to memorize Shakespeare's sonnet "Shall I Compare Thee to a Summer's Day?"

Place a question mark or exclamation point outside the closing quotation marks when it is part of the entire sentence.

Do you understand Henry James's story "The Beast in the Jungle"?

▶ **Exercise 1** **Insert quotation marks wherever necessary. Write *C* in the blank if the sentence is correct.**

_____   Our class is doing reports on various aspects of American culture, from Emerson's

essay "Nature" to contemporary music.

_____ 1. Angel is researching the original sound films, known as talkies.

_____ 2. Many silent stars could not make the transition, he says, because they did not have good

speaking voices.

Copyright © by Glencoe/McGraw-Hill

_____ 3. *The Jazz Singer*, about Al Jolson, was the first sound film.

_____ 4. Doraline is reading the work of Ernest Hemingway, one of the group of writers in Paris whom writer Gertrude Stein named the lost generation.

_____ 5. When Hemingway wrote for the *Kansas City Star*, the newspaper's style sheet instructed him to . . . write short sentences, . . . short first paragraphs, . . .and vigorous English.

_____ 6. Hemingway said, These were the best rules I ever learned. . . .

_____ 7. Three students will research and report on the life of Walt Whitman, who was nicknamed Good Gray Poet by one of his disciples.

_____ 8. The three—Jackie, Myron, and Shanna—will read Whitman's poem Song of Myself from his most famous work, *Leaves of Grass*.

_____ 9. Whitman loved America and said, "The proof of a poet is that his country absorbs him as affectionately as he has absorbed it."

_____ 10. Binte is looking into the history of jazz, starting with New Orleans, which is often called the cradle of jazz.

_____ 11. W. C. Handy composed the first blues numbers, Memphis Blues and St. Louis Blues.

_____ 12. Other big names were Thomas Waller, known as Fats, and Jelly Roll Morton.

_____ 13. Duke Ellington recorded a song called It Don't Mean a Thing If It Ain't Got That Swing, which ushered in the era known as swing.

_____ 14. Did you know Benny Goodman became known as the King of Swing?

_____ 15. Amiri will be talking about Langston Hughes, an African American writer who contributed to the Harlem Renaissance, which began in the 1920s.

_____ 16. Ninety percent of his poetry was written, in Hughes's own words, "to explain and illuminate the Negro condition in America."

_____ 17. Amiri's favorite of Hughes's poems is The Negro Speaks of Rivers.

_____ 18. I myself like Mother to Son, in which a mother tells her son, Life for me ain't been no crystal stair.

_____ 19. James Baldwin wrote the long essay, The Fire Next Time, according to our teacher.

_____ 20. Baldwin helped create what is now called the protest novel.

Copyright © by Glencoe/McGraw-Hill

Lesson 91
Italics

Italics is a form of type. *It looks like this.* When you type, you indicate italics type by underlining, <u>like this</u>.

Use italics for the titles of books, lengthy poems, plays, films, television series, paintings, sculpture, and long musical compositions. Also italicize the names of court cases (but not the "v."), newspapers, magazines, ships, trains, airplanes, and spacecraft.

Emma (book)   *Gilgamesh* (long poem)   *Nova* (television series)
Mona Lisa (painting)   *The Thinker* (sculpture)   *Marbury* v. *Madison* (court case)
Chicago Zephyr (train)   *Lusitania* (ship)   *Washington Post* (newspaper)
Concorde (airplane)   *Discovery* (spacecraft)   *E.T.* (film)

Italicize foreign words and expressions that are not used frequently in English, but not those that are in common usage.

The scientific name for the red maple is *acer rubrum.*
That restaurant has particularly good chop suey.

Italicize words, letters, and numerals used as themselves.

I use the word *very* too much.
My small *a*'s always look like *e*'s.
There are three *4*'s in my address.

▶ **Exercise 1 Underline each word or phrase that should be italicized.**

I think <u>Don Quixote</u> is far better than any modern novel.

1. The National Geographic Special airing tonight is a documentary about elephants.

2. Which of the three Alien movies did you like best?

3. My sister's name is Helene, with an e.

4. Agnes de Mille's ballet Rodeo was a smashing success.

5. Can we get the Wall Street Journal newspaper here?

6. I prefer the Guardian, from London, for international and European news.

7. Smithsonian is a great magazine for articles in all fields of endeavor.

8. They've made a film about the Apollo 13 near disaster on the way to the moon.

9. I loved the Star Trek: The Next Generation episode called "I, Borg," about a lost alien.

10. My grandmother was born in 1912, the same year the Titanic sank in the North Atlantic.

11. Tom Stoppard's play Hapgood, about quantum mechanics, must be fascinating!

Copyright © by Glencoe/McGraw-Hill

12. Do you have the latest copy of Cultural Survival, the magazine about indigenous cultures?

13. That restaurant has such an air of gemütlichkeit, or "coziness," as the Germans would say.

14. She uses like and you know too often in her speech.

15. I hate subtracting 9's!

16. My favorite Thomas Hardy novel is Jude the Obscure.

17. Verdi wrote the opera Falstaff when he was eighty years old.

18. Our school is doing a production of the play Arsenic and Old Lace.

19. There is no k in the word accelerate, is there?

20. The documentary is about the battle between the warships Monitor and Merrimack.

21. My new copy of Astronomy magazine came today.

22. Few television shows have become popular more quickly than E.R.

23. We read several chapters of Sherwood Anderson's novel Winesburg, Ohio.

24. The play we saw last night is based on Edward Lee Masters's Spoon River Anthology, a collection of poetry.

25. Wasn't Thomas Hardy's novel Far From the Madding Crowd made into a movie?

26. An arrested person's rights were strengthened under the Supreme Court's case Miranda v. Arizona.

27. The word decorations is misspelled on this list of tasks.

28. Mozart's opera The Magic Flute has some astonishing characters in it.

29. The crew aboard the Endeavor space shuttle repaired the Hubble Space Telescope.

30. Our local ballet company performed Leo Delibes's work Coppelia.

▶ **Writing Link Write a paragraph about your favorite book, film, or television program. Use underlining to indicate which parts of your sentences should be italicized.**

_____

_____

_____

_____

_____

_____

Copyright © by Glencoe/McGraw-Hill

Mechanics

Lesson 92
The Apostrophe

Use an apostrophe and *-s* to form the possessive of singular nouns, singular indefinite pronouns, and plural nouns that do not end in *-s*. Use an apostrophe alone to form the possessive of a plural noun that ends in *-s*.

the bus**'s** horn   each one**'s** alibi   the books**'** covers   the children**'s** room

Put only the last word of a compound noun in the possessive form. If two or more persons possess something jointly, use the possessive form for the last person named. If two or more persons possess an item individually, put each one's name in the possessive form. Also use the possessive form to express amounts of money or time that modify a noun.

my sister-in-law**'s** recipe   Lewis and Clark**'s** journeys
Rita**'s** and Mark**'s** reports   six hours**'** difference

Use an apostrophe in place of the letters omitted in contractions:

I will = I**'**ll   She is = She**'s**   They would = They**'d**

Use an apostrophe in place of numerals omitted from a year, but not with the plural of full dates.

the **'**93 Midwest floods   the Depression of the 1930s

Use an apostrophe and *-s* to form the plural of letters and words used as themselves. Italicize only the letter or word, not the apostrophe or *-s*.

The *o***'s** in *Ohio* look very much alike in that script.

▶ **Exercise 1 Write in the blank any word that requires an apostrophe or an apostrophe and -s.**

_____crusader's_____   Marjory Stoneman Douglas was born with a crusaders spirit.

_____   1. Marjorys birth took place over a century ago, in 1890.

_____   2. She grew up in Massachusetts, where, she says, "You couldnt drag me away from books. . . ."

_____   3. Soon Marjory and her mother went to live at her grandparents house.

_____   4. During her college years, Marjory became an advocate of womens suffrage.

_____   5. After college, Marjory worked for one of St. Louis well-known department stores.

Copyright © by Glencoe/McGraw-Hill

_____ 6. After her marriage to Kenneth Douglas ended, Marjory moved to Miami, Florida, to live with her father Frank and Franks new wife, Lilla.

_____ 7. Frank Stoneman, the publisher of Miamis morning newspaper, crusaded against developers plans for the Everglades.

_____ 8. His editorials didnt stop the governor from a first assault on the Everglades, however.

_____ 9. Marjory responded to her familys and many friends affection.

_____ 10. During World War I, Marjory joined the American Red Cross, Clara Bartons organization.

_____ 11. The Red Cross mission focused on helping wounded soldiers and other war victims, regardless of which side they were on.

_____ 12. The volunteers duties were hard.

_____ 13. Everywhere she went, Marjory saw the despair in refugees faces.

_____ 14. She visited childrens hospitals and clinics throughout France.

_____ 15. Since she had begun to write for her fathers newspaper, Marjory filed several stories from France.

_____ 16. Stationed in Paris at the end of the war, she wrote of the Parisians joy at the armistice.

_____ 17. Returning to Miami, Marjory became the *Miami Heralds* assistant editor.

_____ 18. She and all the writers earned twenty dollars per week because there was no difference between mens and womens wages at the paper.

_____ 19. Marjory wanted her writing to open peoples eyes to social problems, such as labor camps or children in poverty.

_____ 20. Eventually she met Ernest Coe, who wanted to protect the Everglades unique characteristics.

_____ 21. Marjory was impressed by Ernest because a panthers scream in a thicket never bothered him.

_____ 22. Soon the campaign became Marjorys crusade and Ernest's passion.

_____ 23. Marjory and her friends would visit the Everglades to observe herons nests, spoonbills flights, and egrets at rest.

_____ 24. Exhausted by the battle, Marjory took her doctors advice and resigned from the paper.

_____ 25. She wrote short stories, and soon the *Saturday Evening Posts* editor began publishing her writings.

Mechanics

Copyright © by Glencoe/McGraw-Hill

_____ **4.** You just ate one third of the pie!

_____ **5.** There's a lot of antiintellectual feeling in our culture, it seems to me.

_____ **6.** We need three fourths of the vote to win.

_____ **7.** We counted sixty three houses with flags on the Fourth of July.

_____ **8.** The thief made off with his ill gotten gains.

_____ **9.** There are only fifty one cards in this short deck.

_____ **10.** Our new oven, which was delivered yesterday afternoon, is self cleaning.

_____ **11.** From 1861 to 1865, the United States fought a terrible civil war.

_____ **12.** These colorful, amazing paintings are certainly post Dadaist!

_____ **13.** "Seventy Six Trombones" is the name of a famous song from the musical *The Music Man.*

_____ **14.** This is a richly deserved award for you to receive, Asford.

_____ **15.** You'll find the information about Mars on pages 760 792.

_____ **16.** Do we say former President Carter or exPresident Carter?

_____ **17.** Persons who see the good in everything are said to look at the world through rose

colored glasses.

_____ **18.** Many people consider Ludwig van Beethoven (1770 1827) the greatest composer in

Western musical history.

_____ **19.** My new pants are red striped.

_____ **20.** We will surely win the all Scholastic tournament this season!

▶ **Exercise 2** **Rewrite each word with a hyphen to indicate where it would be divided.**

wobble ___wob-ble_____

1. lassos	_____		**10.** carton	_____
2. cookies	_____		**11.** baffle	_____
3. circus	_____		**12.** guesses	_____
4. curtain	_____		**13.** tender	_____
5. annexes	_____		**14.** pictured	_____
6. boxes	_____		**15.** fiddle	_____
7. tarnish	_____		**16.** priceless	_____
8. insect	_____		**17.** engines	_____
9. yellow	_____		**18.** office	_____

Copyright © by Glencoe/McGraw-Hill

Mechanics

Lesson 93
The Hyphen

Use a hyphen to join a prefix to a proper noun or adjective, after the prefixes *all-, ex-, self-, anti-* (when it joins a word beginning with *i-*), and *vice-* (except for *vice president*).

post-Vietnam years	all-seeing	ex-astronaut
anti-inflationary	vice-mayor	self-confident

Use a hyphen in a compound adjective that precedes a noun, but not one that follows the noun. Also use a hyphen in compound adjectives beginning with *well, ill,* and *little,* except if the compound adjective is modified by an adverb.

a well-known musician (The musician is well known.)
a little-understood theory (That is a very little understood theory.)

Do not hyphenate an expression that includes an adverb ending in *-ly* and an adjective.

a poorly made car   a wretchedly unhappy person

Use a hyphen in cardinal or ordinal numbers that are spelled out, up to ninety-nine, in fractions used as adjectives, and to separate two numerals in a span.

sixty-six   a one-fifth increase   1941-1945   pages 7-24

Do not use a hyphen if numeral spans are separated by the word pairs *from/to* and *between/and.*

from 1941 to 1945   between 1776 and 1789

Use a hyphen to divide words at the end of a line of type. If a word contains two consonants between two vowels, or a double consonant, divide the word between the two consonants.

Though it was late, the child's mother couldn't bear to interrupt his mer-
riment by insisting he go to bed.

If a suffix has been added to a complete word that ends in two consonants, divide the word after the two consonants.

Sally could not believe the race car driver's rash-
ness in taking the turn at such a great speed.

▶ **Exercise 1** **Insert a hyphen where necessary. Write *C* in the blank if the sentence is correct.**

_____   We visited the post-impressionist show at the Art Museum.

_____   **1.** Mona came in twenty seventh in her Graduate Record Exams.

_____   **2.** My brother thinks he is all knowing and often tries to prove it.

_____   **3.** Mr. Cobb is a well intentioned person.

Copyright © by Glencoe/McGraw-Hill

Mechanics

Lesson 94
Abbreviations

Capitalize the abbreviations of proper nouns, including titles.

Wed.   Oct.   Jr.   Ph.D.   Ms.   Mr.   Dr.

Use all capital letters and no periods for abbreviations that are pronounced letter by letter or as words. Exceptions are U.S. and Washington, D.C., which do use periods.

IRS   PIN   NCAA   SAT   YWCA   NASA

Abbreviations for a person's first and middle names require periods and spaces after each initial. Three initials used together require no periods and no spaces between initials.

Ulysses S. Grant   F. Scott Fitzgerald   T.S. Elliot   JFK   FDR

Use the abbreviations A.M. (*ante meridiem*, "before noon") and P.M. (*post meridiem*, "after noon") for exact times. For dates use B.C. (before Christ) and, sometimes, A.D. (*anno Domini*, "in the year of the Lord," after Christ).

The bus leaves at 2:20 P.M.
The novel was set in A.D. 250.

Abbreviations for units of measure are generally used only in scientific writing, not in ordinary prose. Note that the metric abbreviations use no periods. Each abbreviation stands for both the singular and plural forms.

ENGLISH SYSTEM		METRIC SYSTEM	
ft.	foot	cg	centigram
gal.	gallon	cl	centiliter
in.	inch	cm	centimeter
lb.	pound	g	gram
mi.	mile	kg	kilogram
oz.	ounce	km	kilometer
pt.	pint	l	liter
qt.	quart	m	meter
tbsp.	tablespoon	mg	milligram
tsp.	teaspoon	ml	milliliter
yd.	yard	mm	millimeter

▶ **Exercise 1** **Write the correct abbreviation for each of the following.**

1. February   _____

2. *anno Domini*   _____

3. Saturday   _____

4. North Atlantic Treaty Organization   _____

5. Public Broadcasting System   _____

Copyright © by Glencoe/McGraw-Hill

Mechanics

6. Medical Doctor _____

7. *ante meridiem* _____

8. National Aeronautics and Space Administration _____

9. kilometer _____

10. Junior _____

11. American Automobile Association _____

12. teaspoon _____

13. National Collegiate Athletic Association _____

14. kilogram _____

15. *post meridiem* _____

16. John Fitzgerald Kennedy _____

17. Internal Revenue Service _____

18. Zoning Improvement Plan _____

19. Thursday _____

20. Franklin Delano Roosevelt _____

21. Scholastic Aptitude Test _____

22. intelligence quotient _____

23. Doctor of Veterinary Medicine _____

24. Occupational Safety and Health Administration _____

25. December _____

▶ **Exercise 2** **Using the abbreviation for each word in parentheses, complete the following chart.**

Measurement Equivalents

1 _____ (yard) = 3 _____ (feet)	= 36 _____ (inches)	
1 _____ (gallon) = 4 _____ (quarts)	= 8 _____ (pints)	
1 ton = 2000 _____ (pounds)	= 32,000 _____ (ounces)	
1 _____ (meter) = 100 _____ (centimeters)	= 1,000 _____ (millimeters)	
1 _____ (liter) = 100 _____ (centiliters)	= 1,000 _____ (milliliters)	
1 _____ (gram) = 100 _____ (centigrams)	= 1,000 _____ (milligrams)	

Copyright © by Glencoe/McGraw-Hill

Mechanics

Lesson 95
Numbers and Numerals

Some **numbers** are spelled out and others are expressed in figures. Those expressed in figures are called **numerals**.

In general, spell out cardinal and ordinal numbers that can be written as one or two words. Spell out any number that occurs at the beginning of a sentence, even if it is longer than two words.

one   twelve   twenty-six   ninety-nine   fifty-first   thirty-second
Four hundred seventeen runners entered the marathon.

Write large numbers as numerals followed by a noun of amount, such as *million* or *billion*.

The planet Neptune is about **2.8** million miles from the sun.

In a sentence, if one number is in numerals, related numbers must be in numerals.

We had only collected **69** signatures by Friday, but over the weekend, we reached **529**.

Use numerals to express decimals, percentages, and amounts of money involving both dollars and cents; write out amounts of money that can be written in one or two words.

We'll need about **3.5** gallons of paint.   The total is **fifty-five** dollars.
Of the voting population, **30** percent went to the polls.
The shirt cost **$9.95**.

Use numerals to express the year and day in dates and to express the exact time, and with the abbreviations A.M. and P.M. Spell out expressions of time that do not use A.M. or P.M.

My birthday is April **17, 1981**.   The court session opens at **9:15** A.M.
I thought we were supposed to meet at around **nine** o'clock.

To express a century with the word *century,* spell out the number. To express a decade when the century is clear, spell out the number.

The twentieth century experienced a decade known as the "roaring twenties."

When a century and a decade are expressed as a single unit, use numerals followed by *-s.*

The Great Depression reached its peak in the **1930s**.

Use numerals for streets and avenues above ten and for house, apartment, and room numbers. Spell out numbered streets and avenues with numbers of ten or under.

The parade will proceed down **Fourth** Avenue.   Room **2173** at **1200** East **26th** Street

Copyright © by Glencoe/McGraw-Hill

Mechanics

▶ **Exercise 1** Write in the blank any numbers or numerals that are incorrectly. Write *C* if the sentence is correct.

_____Three hundred_____ 300 people attended the meeting.

_____ 1. There are three hundred and fifty fruit trees in the orchard.

_____ 2. The sun is about ninety-three million miles distant.

_____ 3. The shorter buildings are only about fifty feet high and are overshadowed by the taller ones, some as high as 450 feet.

_____ 4. I thought that book cost seventeen dollars and ninety-five cents.

_____ 5. One mile equals 1.6 kilometers.

_____ 6. Only 26 percent of the students have cable.

_____ 7. 762 transactions took place in the first hour.

_____ 8. The weekly tests averaged about seventy-five multiple-choice questions, but the final had over 150!

_____ 9. Australia has about two point nine million square miles in land area.

_____ 10. Did your great aunt really live to the age of 102?

_____ 11. This package weighs twelve and a half ounces.

_____ 12. You owe me three dollars and twenty-six cents change, right?

_____ 13. You won 5,000 dollars in the lottery?

_____ 14. A light-year is the distance light travels in a year, about 6,000,000,000,000 miles.

_____ 15. I bought my house when the interest rate was twelve percent!

_____ 16. I need another twenty-seven cents to pay for this notebook.

_____ 17. Mark's birthday is April twenty-eighth, nineteen seventy-four.

_____ 18. We drove two hundred seventy-five miles on the first day of our vacation.

_____ 19. People call the nineteen seventies the "Me" decade.

_____ 20. Our new office is on 7th Avenue.

_____ 21. The Civil War was fought in the eighteen sixties.

_____ 22. The afternoon movies are cheaper—only three dollars and seventy-five cents.

Copyright © by Glencoe/McGraw-Hill

Mechanics

Unit 12 **Review**

▶ **Exercise 1** **Add all necessary punctuation marks, including end punctuation. Draw a line under words or phrases that should be in italics.**

Robert Frost, who wrote the poem "The Road Not Taken"—have you read it ?—is one of my favorite poets.

1. In musical notation the word vivace from the Italian means played in a lively manner or with great speed

2. George Gershwin s musical Of Thee I Sing (1931) written over sixty years ago is still popular our local playhouse performed it just last year.

3. Poet Robert Frost who read a poem at JFK s inauguration said of poetry We play the words as we find them

4. Adrienne Rich s name is not as well known as that of other American poets which is a shame because her collection Diving into the Wreck is splendid

5. Nikos Kazantzakis who wrote the novel Zorba the Greek declared I am a mariner of Odysseus (wasn't he the Greek hero?) with heart of fire but with mind ruthless and clear

6. Shakespeare s Much Ado About Nothing has been made into a film like many of his comedies is a tale of love conspiracy mistaken identity and oh see it for yourself

7. Percy Bysshe Shelley wrote the poem Ode to the West Wind (1820) from which comes that wonderful line If winter comes, can spring be far behind

8. The magazine we know as Harpers Magazine has had two other names Harper's New Monthly Magazine between 1850 and 1900 and Harper's Monthly Magazine (between 1900 and 1925)

9. The famous refrain A boy s will is the wind s will, And the thoughts of youth are long long thoughts comes from Longfellow s poem My Lost Youth (1855)

10. Musicals that deal with the lives of ordinary persons—Hair Grease and Chorus Line are three have become more popular in recent decades

11. At Gettysburg Pennsylvania the Union troops of Gen George Meade beat back Gen Robert E Lee and the Army of Northern Virginia during three days of battle July 1–3 1863

12. Have you read Shirley Jackson s hair raising short story The Lottery

Copyright © by Glencoe/McGraw-Hill

Mechanics

Cumulative Review: Units 1–12

▶ **Exercise 1** Underline the word in parentheses that best completes each sentence.

The speaker started out (bad, <u>badly</u>).

1. I finished my homework (already, all ready).

2. This dessert tastes (all together, altogether) too sweet for my teeth!

3. I (can't hardly, can hardly) stand it when people scratch a blackboard with their fingernails.

4. When was this warning (hanged, hung) on the wall?

5. Don't (loose, lose) your hall pass, or the guard will stop you.

6. We won't be there for (a while, awhile), so go ahead and eat without us.

7. Alice (doesn't, don't) live here anymore.

8. Well, the refrigerator is practically empty, so I guess someone (must of, must have) been

   really hungry!

9. Meet me for basketball practice (in, into) the gym.

10. Standing up here so high, I can hardly believe a major river (lays, lies) far below.

11. (Besides, Beside) your cello lessons, what else do you do after school?

12. I don't know if I (can, may) make it up that cliff.

13. Well, this is certainly (a, an) inconvenience, Stanley!

14. The sporting event will take place (irregardless, regardless) of the weather.

15. Your twin sister Anastasia acts very (different than, different from) you, Alice.

16. Even from the air, we could see that the damage from the earthquake looked (bad, badly).

17. I don't like (these kinds, this kind) of pencils because they smear.

18. The grand jury will look into the matter (farther, further).

19. (Take, Bring) this video back when you go to the store.

20. I don't know what else to do (accept, except) to admit I was wrong.

▶ **Exercise 2** Underline the verb form in parentheses that best completes each sentence.

Billy and Sheila always (mislays, <u>mislay</u>) their toys.

1. The mayor, together with his staff, (has, have) left for the day.

2. The highest wave during the storm (was, were) ten feet!

3. The long-term effects of pollution (remains, remain) unknown.

4. In a case at the back of the antique store (sits, sit) several priceless vases.

5. Ashford (has, have) the mumps!

6. The students painted the mural that (covers, cover) those three walls of the cafeteria.

7. I think she (gives, give) too much money for her clothes.

8. Every article, advertisement, and graphic (was, were) checked for accuracy.

9. Each of the violinists (plays, play) at least one other instrument in the youth orchestra.

10. My hat, in addition to my gloves and pants, (is, are) caked with mud from the horseback ride in the rain.

11. A group of several hundred protesters (gathers, gather) in front of the courthouse.

12. Neither the driver nor the passenger (seems, seem) hurt in the crash.

13. None of the boys on the team (likes, like) their last defeat at the hand of their archrivals.

14. Can you believe that some of these clothes (has, have) already faded?

15. Several members of our carpool (wants, want) to start biking.

16. Either an opossum or some raccoons (strews, strew) the garbage all over the porch.

17. Where (does, do) these shoes go?

18. Either the radio or the newspapers (covers, cover) all our championship games.

19. Neither of those talk shows that you insist on listening to all the time (interests, interest) me at all!

20. (Is, Are) either of the office telephones in the conference room free just now?

▶ **Exercise 3** **Add all necessary punctuation marks, including end punctuation. Draw a line under words or phrases that should be in italics.**

If you want to read a weird novel, and I know you do, try Thomas Pynchon's <u>V</u>.

1. The blues a specifically American form of music was popularized by three giants Bessie Smith Ma Rainey and Louis Armstrong

2. Scott Joplin composer of the song Maple Leaf Rag 1899, is the best known composer of the music known as ragtime surely you remember his music from the movie The Sting

3. Onomatopoeia is the forming of words that imitate sounds buzz hiss and twitter are good examples

4. J M Barrie wrote Peter Pan or the Boy Who Wouldnt Grow Up yes its a long title which is why everyone just calls it Peter Pan

Copyright © by Glencoe/McGraw-Hill

Mechanics

5. Mary Renault pen name of Mary Challans 1905 1983 wrote wonderful historical novels about Athens and Sparta including The King Must Die

6. William Kennedy wrote a novel Ironweed that became a film and also wrote the script for Francis Ford Coppolas film The Cotton Club 1984

7. Big jazz festivals are held in Newport R I. and Monterey California

8. Jack Kerouac wrote the novel On the Road which has become synonymous with the period of American writing known as the beat movement

9. Can there be a movie called Alien 4 if the heroine you know Sigourney Weavers Ripley died in Alien 3

10. Arent you confusing Francis Scott Key 1779 1843 who wrote The Star-Spangled Banner with Francis Parkinson Keyes 1885 1970 the novelist who wrote Dinner at Antoines (1948)

11. When the writer Thoreau was arrested for refusing to pay taxes to support the Mexican War his friend Emerson visited and said Henry what are you doing in here

12. Supposedly they are making Star Wars movies that predate the current ones for example I guess well get to know the ancestors of Luke Skywalker and Han Solo

13. American humorist James Thurber cartoonist for the New Yorker for years is often identified with one of his short stories The Secret Life of Walter Mitty

14. Bill Haley and His Comets were the first famous rock band and their recording of Rock Around the Clock from the film Blackboard Jungle 1955 was a major hit

15. A A Milnes characters Pooh Tigger Roo and Piglet are some of the most beloved in all of fantasy literature

16. Georgia OKeeffe 1887 1986 painted haunting pictures of the Southwest and hey youre not listening to a thing I say are you

17. Do you know if its Jim or Tim the one with the beard who published a story in The Antioch Review

18. Nina a member of the seraph society is the headstrong heroine in a Teresa Vitale book.

Mechanics

Copyright © by Glencoe/McGraw-Hill

Vocabulary and Spelling

Unit 13: Vocabulary and Spelling

Lesson 96
Building Vocabulary: Learning from Context

Many times you can determine the meanings of new words by clues from the context. Specific clue words often provide contextual help as follows:

Restatement—An unfamiliar word explained by a more familiar expression. Clue words include *or*, *in other words*, *also known as*, and *also called*.

During our tour of the palace, we saw the king's **diadem,** *or* crown.

Contrast—Unfamiliar words shown as opposites of familiar words. Clue words include *whereas, but, although, on the contrary, however, on the other hand,* and *in contrast to*.

Katya was very **lethargic** *in contrast to* her usual bubbly manner.

Comparison—Gives clue by likening unfamiliar words to familiar ones. Clue words include *like, also, likewise, similarly, in the same way, similar to, resembling,* and *as*.

The **repugnant** scamp tried to hide among his *likewise* disgusting friends.

Cause and effect—Unfamiliar cause explained by familiar effect. Clue words include *because, as a result, therefore, when,* and *consequently*.

The man was **indigent** and *therefore* could not afford food, clothing, or shelter.

Definition—Unfamiliar word is actually defined after a clue word. Clue words include *which is, which means,* and *that is*.

Hope is a **numismatist,** *which means* that she collects coins.

Example—Illustrates unfamiliar words. Clue words include *like, such as, for example, for instance, these, including,* and *especially*.

Mr. Maxwell raised several **ovine** species *such as* Caracul sheep.

▶ **Exercise 1** **Draw a line under the clue words. Write a definition for the italicized word.**

Most of the soldiers were eager volunteers, <u>but</u> some of the regiment were *conscripts.*

soldiers that were forced into service _____

1. The alarm system was very *sophisticated,* in other words, complicated. _____

_____

2. Cheryl *truncated* her speech because she ran out of time. _____

3. Whereas the courts have *abrogated* the helmet laws, the seat belt laws are strictly enforced.

_____

Copyright © by Glencoe/McGraw-Hill

Vocabulary and Spelling

4. Terrence's injury was *euplastic;* on the other hand, Mickey's twisted knee took three weeks

longer to heal. _____

5. The parks were *replete* with deer, which means that the deer population was extremely high.

_____

6. Stella was blessed with a *pacific* nature including the ability to stay calm under pressure.

_____

7. *Remnants* of ancient cultures, like mounds, tell us much of their way of life. _____

_____

8. Her good reputation was *sullied* as a result of the vicious rumors. _____

9. During the war, Mr. Orton was a *liaison* officer, which is a person who is in charge of

cooperation and communication. _____

10. Emilio had made several *overtures* of friendship, in contrast to Frieda, who ignored the

newcomer. _____

_____

11. Jason *gorged* himself on the snacks and, similarly, Yoshika overate until she felt

uncomfortable. _____

12. The agency kept a *dossier,* or a personal file, on each employee. _____

_____

13. Winona was in the *vanguard* of the reform movement, while Marta held back till she saw that

things were going well. _____

14. The *introverted* Mr. Keung, however, appeared on television to make his case for the bond

issue._____

15. The suspect had no record of *felonious* activity, even though he had been seen leaving the

scene of the crime. _____

16. Eileen seemed very *culpable* because of her suspicious actions. _____

_____

17. Because Lonnie would not *eschew* gossip, his loose tongue got him into trouble.

_____

18. Ms. Alvarez was *ambiguous* in her instructions, which means that her directions were not

clear. _____

Vocabulary and Spelling

Copyright © by Glencoe/McGraw-Hill

Lesson 97
Building Vocabulary: Word Roots

The main part of a word is called its **root**. When the root is a complete word, it is called a **base root**. The root supplies the basic meaning of a word. Roots are often combined with a *prefix* (a syllable preceding the root), a *suffix* (a syllable following a root), or another root. These syllables change the direction of a word's meaning. Here is a list of some common roots.

ROOTS	MEANINGS	ROOTS	MEANINGS
aqua, aqui	water	*junct*	join
astr, astro	star	*jur, jus*	law
biblio	book	*log, logy*	word, thought, speech
bio	life	*meter, metr*	measure
chron	time	*nym*	name
clin	bend, lean	*op, oper*	work
cogn	know	*path, patho*	suffering
crypt	hidden, secret	*ped*	foot, child
culp	fault, blame	*psych*	soul, mind
fin	end, limit	*reg, rig*	rule, straight
fix	fasten	*scop*	examine, instrument
gen	birth, kind	*spect*	sight
graph, gram	write, writing	*terr*	earth
jac, ject	throw, cast, hurl	*verb*	word
jud	judge	*vid, vis*	see

▶ **Exercise 1 Draw a line under the root of each word. Define each word, using a dictionary when needed. When there is more than one definition, use one that emphasizes the meaning of the root.**

incandescent _emitting a visible white glow as a result of being heated_____

1. nurture _____

2. incline _____

3. abject _____

4. intercede _____

5. visage _____

6. anhydrous _____

7. epigram _____

8. autonomy _____

9. chronograph _____

10. verbose _____

Copyright © by Glencoe/McGraw-Hill

Vocabulary and Spelling

11. aquamarine _____

12. terrestrial _____

13. retrospection _____

14. regimen _____

15. psychosis _____

16. peddler _____

17. aster _____

18. conjunct _____

19. empathy _____

20. aquarelle _____

21. cognizant _____

22. congenital _____

23. transfix _____

24. crypto grapher _____

25. bibliophile _____

26. injudicious _____

27. anonymity _____

28. culpable _____

29. psychotherapy _____

30. introspection _____

31. trilogy _____

32. verbiage _____

33. seismograph _____

34. pseudonym _____

35. psychopath _____

36. dialogue _____

37. conjecture _____

38. chronometer _____

39. pedometer _____

40. cryptogram _____

Vocabulary and Spelling

Copyright © by Glencoe/McGraw-Hill

Lesson 98
Building Vocabulary: Prefixes and Suffixes

Prefixes are attached to words to change their meaning. They may show quantity, size, time, direction, or position. Some prefixes have more than one meaning.

PREFIX	MEANING	PREFIX	MEANING
post-	after	pre-, pro-	before
re-	again	syn-	together
a-, an-	not, without	ant-, anti-	against
de-, dis-	do the opposite	non-, un-	not
semi-, hemi-	half	bi-, di-	two
uni-, mono-	one	cent-	hundred
circum-	around	in-, im-	into
sub-	below, outside of	trans-	across, over

Suffixes each have their own meaning. They are added to the end of a root word to create a new word with a new meaning. Suffixes may change the part of speech of a word.

SUFFIX	MEANING	SUFFIX	MEANING
-ee	receiver of action	-ance, -ence	state, quality
-ant, -eer	agent, doer	-ist	one who
-ness	action, state	-tion, -ion	the act of
-ate	become, form	-en	make, cause to be
-ify	cause, make	-ize	make, cause to be
-ic	characteristic of	-ous, -ful	full of, having
-ial	relating to	-al	characterized by
-ly	akin to	-less	lacking

▶ **Exercise 1** Draw a line under the prefix in items 1 through 10 and under the suffix in items 11 through 18. Write the meaning of the prefix or suffix and the meaning of the word in the blank. Use a dictionary if necessary.

defrost ___do the opposite; to remove from being frosted or frozen_____

1. circumnavigate _____

_____

2. bistate _____

_____

3. amoral _____

_____

4. synergistic _____

_____

Copyright © by Glencoe/McGraw-Hill

Vocabulary and Spelling

5. trilateral _____

_____

6. intercede _____

_____

7. antebellum _____

_____

8. prologue _____

_____

9. peristyle _____

_____

10. monocle _____

_____

11. culpable _____

_____

12. somnambulist _____

_____

13. nullify _____

_____

14. scurrilous _____

_____

15. ablution _____

_____

16. proliferate _____

_____

17. spastic _____

_____

18. reverence _____

_____

Copyright © by Glencoe/McGraw-Hill

Vocabulary and Spelling

Lesson 99
Basic Spelling Rules: I

Adding a prefix does not change the spelling of the original word. Use a hyphen only when the original word is capitalized or with the prefix *ex-* meaning *previous* or *former.*

anti- + social = antisocial   *un-* + stable = unstable
non- + Celtic = non-Celtic   *ex-* + director = ex-director

Most words do not change spelling when a suffix is added. When adding *-ly* to a word that ends in a single *l,* keep the *l.* If the word ends in a double *l,* drop one *l.* If the word ends in a consonant + *le,* drop the *le.*

partial + *-ly* = partially   dull + *-ly* = dully   dangle + *-ly* = dangly

Drop a final silent *e* before a suffix that begins with a vowel.

line + *-er* = liner   value + *-able* = valuable

Keep the silent *e* before a suffix beginning with a consonant.

infinite + *-ly* = infinitely   trite + *-ness* = triteness
Exceptions: silent *e* after *u* or *w:* argue + *-ment* = argument   due + *-ly* = duly

Keep the final *e* when the word ends in *-ee* or *-oe,* before the suffix *-ing,* and with words ending in *-ce* or *-ge* that have suffixes beginning with *a* or *o.*

see + *-ing* = seeing   woe + *-ful* = woeful   trace + *-able* = traceable

Double the final consonant if:

• the original word is a one-syllable word   (stop, stopping)

• the accent remains on the last syllable of the original word after the suffix is added (defer, deferred)

• the original word is a prefixed one-syllable word   (regret, regretting)

Do not double the final consonant if:

• the accent is not on the last syllable or the accent shifts when the suffix is added (confer, conference)

• the final consonant is *x* or *w*   (row, rowing)

• the original word ends in a consonant and the suffix begins with a consonant (ship, shipment)

▶ **Exercise 1 Write the word that results when the given prefix or suffix is added to the root word. Check your dictionary for variations in spelling.**

define + *-ing* _____defining_____

1. final + *-ly* _____   **2.** probable + *-ly* _____

Copyright © by Glencoe/McGraw-Hill

3. hoe + -ing   _____

4. repel + -ent   _____

5. sew + -ing   _____

6. home + -ly   _____

7. swift + -ly   _____

8. un- + American   _____

9. grace + -ful   _____

10. shrill + -ly   _____

11. sit + -ing   _____

12. defer + -ence   _____

13. annul + -ment   _____

14. precut + -ing   _____

15. free + -ing   _____

16. advise + -er   _____

17. awe + -ful   _____

18. hope + -ful   _____

19. terrible + -ly   _____

20. ex- + president   _____

21. tax + -ing   _____

22. rebel + -ion   _____

23. confine + -ment   _____

24. contend + -ing   _____

25. befit + -ing   _____

26. cage + -y   _____

27. shoe + -ing   _____

28. full + -ly   _____

29. refer + -ence   _____

30. ex- + claim   _____

31. change+ -able   _____

32. fatal + -ly   _____

33. pop + -er   _____

34. make + -er   _____

35. singe + -ing   _____

36. neat + -ness   _____

37. common + -ness   _____

38. argue + -ment   _____

39. dis- + like   _____

40. accuse + -er   _____

▶ **Writing Link** **Write several sentences about opposite things, such as matter and antimatter or aliens and nonaliens.**

_____

_____

_____

_____

_____

_____

_____

_____

Copyright © by Glencoe/McGraw-Hill

Spelling

Lesson 100
Basic Spelling Rules: II

Plurals Add -*s* to most nouns (including proper nouns) to form the plural. Add -*es* to nouns ending in -*ch*, -*s*, -*sh*, -*x*, or -*z*. When a noun ends in a consonant + *y*, change the *y* to *i* and add -*es*. Some nouns ending in -*f* (especially -*lf*) become plural by changing the *f* to *v* and adding -*es*.

atom + -*s* = atoms   box + -*es* = boxes   bush + -*es* = bushes   candy + -*es* = candies
chief + -*s* = chiefs   cliff + -*s* = cliffs   loaf + -*es* = loaves   half + -*es* = halves

Some nouns have irregular formations for the plural and some have the same form for both singular and plural.

child = children   woman = women   physics = physics   sheep = sheep

Words with *ie* and *ei* The *i* comes before the *e* except when both follow a *c* or when they are sounded together as an $\bar{a}$ sound. However, there are many exceptions.

believe (*i* before *e*)   deceive (*e* before *i*)   neighbor ($\bar{a}$ sound)   seize (exception)

Words with -*ceed* and -*cede* Most words that end in a -*sede* sound use the suffix -*cede*. *Supersede* is the one word with the -*sede* suffix. *Proceed* is a spelling exception.

con**cede**   re**cede**   inter**cede**

An **unstressed vowel** is a vowel that is not emphasized in pronunciation. To determine correct spelling, think of a related word where the vowel or syllable is stressed.

mag*net* - mag*netic*   med*icine* - med*icinal*

Compound words usually do not change spelling when they are formed; however, some form one word, some use a hyphen, and some remain as two words.

bare + foot = barefoot   know + how = know-how   cross + section = cross section

Many spelling challenges exist with words that are homonyms or near homonyms. Other words contain unusual combinations of letters. The dictionary is the source to end the confusion. Be aware that computer spell checkers do not find wrong word choices or errors that result in a correct word that is wrong for the context. Proofreading is still necessary.

Copyright © by Glencoe/McGraw-Hill

Vocabulary and Spelling

▶ **Exercise 1 Write the new word in the blank. Use a dictionary to check your answers.**

plural of beach _____beaches_____   shoe + maker _____shoemaker_____

1. plural of calf _____   5. plural of clock _____

2. plural of parody _____   6. plural of matrix _____

3. sun + set _____   7. soft + drink _____

4. plural of rich _____   8. plural of legacy _____

9. high + chair _____

10. plural of chief _____

11. plural of doe _____

12. vice + president _____

13. thunder + head _____

14. plural of dispatch _____

15. plural of mathematics _____

16. book + keeper _____

17. plural of goose _____

18. plural of clef _____

19. wind + shield _____

20. plural of peach _____

21. cheer + leader _____

22. plural of stress _____

23. plural of sheaf _____

24. plural of fox _____

25. jewelry + box _____

26. plural of deer _____

27. plural of grass _____

28. plural of buzz _____

29. mother + in + law _____

30. plural of rash _____

31. after + math _____

32. plural of ravine _____

▶ **Exercise 2** **Write the missing letter or letters in each word.**

rec__ei__ve   re__cede____   com__a__tose

1. pun____tive

2. h____ght

3. antece____

4. l____ (garland)

5. succe____

6. pr____st

7. magn____tize

8. interce____

9. perc____ve

10. fr____ght

11. fall____cy

12. pre____de

13. s____ve

14. gr____f

15. col____ny

16. ex_____

17. conc____ve

18. h____r

19. sed____tive

20. proce____

21. ach____ve

22. v____n

23. dram____tize

24. super_____

25. w____gh

26. dec____ver

27. com____dy

28. ac_____

29. retr____ve

30. rec____pt

31. comb____nation

32. con_____

33. f____gn

34. ch____f

35. dec____t

36. ____ght

37. effic____nt

38. rec_____

39. bel____f

40. crit____cism

41. n____ce

42. fant____sy

Copyright © by Glencoe/McGraw-Hill

Vocabulary and Spelling

Unit 13 **Review**: Building Vocabulary

▶ **Exercise 1** **Write the definition of the word in italics. Draw a line under any clue words.**

The audience rose in *unison*; <u>that is</u>, they stood up at the same time.

altogether; as one _____

1. Building a racer is *unfathomable* to me because I know nothing about engines.

   _____

2. Mario enjoyed his work as a *typographer,* especially when the owner of the print shop assigned

   him to design advertising brochures. _____

3. The country was ruled by a *triumvirate* consisting of a general, a politician, and an economist.

   _____

4. Because of her outstanding work, Eileen's supervisor wrote a glowing *testimonial* for her

   portfolio when she moved to California. _____

   _____

5. Pablo showed a *tendency* toward kindness while An-Li was usually glum. _____

   _____

6. The Johnsons found the movie *tedious* in contrast to the thrills experienced by the Sanchez

   family. _____

7. The judge *sustained* the defense objections; consequently, the prosecution could not introduce

   the new evidence. _____

8. Jaleel's voice was rich and *resonant* like that of a professional announcer. _____

   _____

9. The driveway became a *quagmire* because of the heavy rains during the month. _____

   _____

10. Mr. Bearclaw *prunes* his rosebushes every fall while Ms. Ramirez allows hers to grow at will.

    _____

11. The speaker's *opulence* was evident; for example, she arrived in a chauffeur-driven limousine.

    _____

Copyright © by Glencoe/McGraw-Hill

Vocabulary and Spelling

12. The choir so completely *mesmerized* the audience that, when the concert was over, no one

rose to leave. _____

13. All of the woman's knowledge was *notional* rather than based strictly on facts. _____

_____

14. My subscription to that newsletter *lapsed* because I forgot to renew it. _____

15. All our *kindred*, or relatives, attended the reunion. _____

16. Soon after completing his apprenticeship, the young man became a respected *journeyman* for

the Wurlitzer Company. _____

17. Andrea attempted to fix the washer in spite of her mother's opinion that it was *irreparable*.

_____

18. Sally abandoned her *humanitarian* concerns after she became preoccupied with becoming

famous. _____

19. While the rest of the group fell asleep, Kendra maintained her *vigilance* throughout the night.

_____

20. Because of the lack of closet space in the old house, the Chins put a *wardrobe* in each bedroom.

_____

21. Despite his extensive world travel, Mr. Mitchell remained a *xenophobe*. _____

_____

22. Although her husband was content with the old sedan, Mrs. Smith had a *yen* to buy a

conversion van. _____

23. Each of the council members provided *zonal* representation except for Kim and Teresa, who

were elected as members at large. _____

24. Mary's thoughts were so *confounded* by the conflicting stories, so that consequently she could

make no decision. _____

25. Mr. Franco enjoyed the chance to revisit his childhood *haunt*, which means his favorite hang-out.

_____

26. Merry spent the entire evening trying to impress the conductor, while Joan was less *gushy*.

_____

Copyright © by Glencoe/McGraw-Hill

Vocabulary and Spelling

Unit 13 **Review**: Basic Spelling Rules

▶ **Exercise 1** **Draw a line under the correct spelling of the word in parentheses. Use a dictionary if necessary.**

How many (correcttions, corrections) were necessary?

1. President Lincoln was (fatally, fataly) wounded in Ford's Theater.

2. The letter expressed his congratulations and best (wish's, wishes).

3. Harley conducted himself with an impeccable (mein, mien).

4. When did King Edward VIII (abdicate, abdacate) his throne?

5. Because of a lack of cash flow, the future of our company is (un-stable, unstable).

6. Juan detests (hoing, hoeing) the garden.

7. Grandad designed the kitchen with plenty of cabinets and (shelfs, shelves).

8. The seminar dealt with handling (grief, greif) and sorrow.

9. This light bulb has a tungsten (filiment, filament).

10. Is Ms. Giles (arrangeing, arranging) a meeting for Tuesday?

11. Miette viewed the entire ridiculous situation as (humerous, humorous).

12. Kang (percieved, perceived) a faint cry coming from the cellar.

13. The scholarship was sponsored by the faculty (wifes, wives).

14. Are carry-out food orders (taxxable, taxable)?

15. Keep a copy of your sales slip to (verafy, verify) your purchase if you decide to return it.

16. The radical group espoused several (unAmerican, un-American) principles.

17. There is no room for (deciet, deceit) in a friendship.

18. The menu was the result of recipes collected from three famous (cheffs, chefs).

19. Wise use of cosmetics enhanced Kara's already (comly, comely) appearance.

20. Teresa's presence gave Mikhail a (tingley, tingly) sensation.

21. Have you ever ridden in a horse-drawn (sliegh, sleigh)?

22. Ms. Hughes's bid for the Senate was supported by several (exmembers, ex-members).

23. Four stone (quarrys, quarries) are located in Greenfield County.

24. The (play ground, playground) is only a block from our house.

25. Diana doesn't like going down the (basment, basement) steps.

Copyright © by Glencoe/McGraw-Hill

Vocabulary and Spelling

26. Yolanda has the (knowhow, know-how) to plan a successful campaign.

27. Ali could not fix the tire because he was out of (patches, patchs).

28. This emerald (wieghs, weighs) over three carats.

29. (Anti-social, Antisocial) behavior will not be tolerated.

30. In her speech, Willa made several (referrences, references) to Kathy's expertise.

31. High mountain (pass's, passes) in the Rockies are open only a few months each year.

32. Carlos spent most of his time on the fairway (replaceing, replacing) his divots.

33. The War of 1812 (preceeded, preceded) the Civil War.

34. Larry and Gary are going (skiing, sking) this weekend.

35. Who is your (adviseor, adviser) for your science project?

36. Are any of your (greatgrandparents, great-grandparents) living?

37. By 7:00 A.M., Martin was shaved and (fuly, fully) dressed.

38. The royal party included two (princeses, princesses).

39. Ms. Chung will not (consede, concede) any possibility of defeat.

40. My time is (arrangable, arrangeable) to suit your schedule.

41. We will have no job openings in the (foreseable, foreseeable) future.

42. Is the (steeringwheel, steering wheel) on this model adjustable?

43. Wu's Cafe is the best (dinner, diner) in town.

44. My doctor (refered, referred) me to a skin specialist.

45. This new song has an (unforgetable, unforgettable) melody.

46. Each (contestant, contestent) had to answer ten questions.

47. Cameron's essay explains his (beliefs, believes) quite thoroughly.

48. The sky turned a (strangely, strangly) beautiful shade of blue.

49. The Drama Club is (planing, planning) a reception for the first-night audience.

50. Troy and Julio will monitor the debate (fairly, farely).

Vocabulary and Spelling

Copyright © by Glencoe/McGraw-Hill

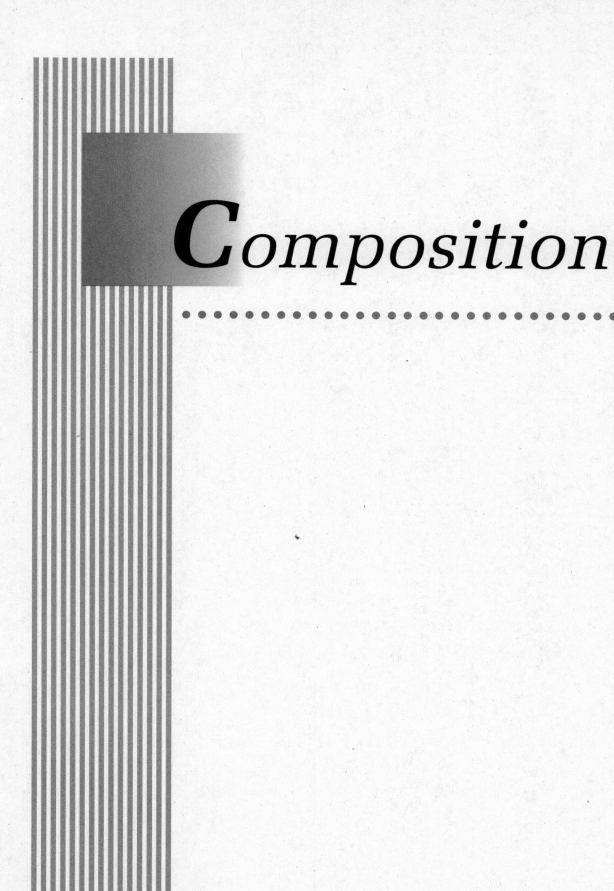

Composition

Unit 14: Composition

Lesson 101
The Writing Process: Prewriting

In the prewriting stage you decide *what* you want to say (topic), *how* to say it (purpose), and *to whom* you want to say it (audience). First you need to decide on your topic, the subject of your piece of writing. You can decide on a topic using any of the following techniques.

Freewrite Begin writing about anything that comes into your mind. You can think of freewriting as having a conversation with yourself or thinking on paper.

Collect Gather facts and information from various sources. Ponder the information, compare facts, and see what interesting topics emerge.

List Make a list of events, experiences, people, ideas, or even words that interest you. Use this list as a starting point.

Ask Think of questions that you would like to explore. Ask *What if...? How...? Is it possible that...?*

▶ **Exercise 1** **Spend 10 minutes prewriting, using any of the techniques described above.**

_____

_____

_____

_____

_____

_____

_____

_____

_____

_____

_____

_____

Copyright © by Glencoe/McGraw-Hill

Composition

▶ **Exercise 2** Identify five possible topics you could write about based on the prewriting in Exercise 1. Be specific.

_____

_____

_____

_____

_____

Make sure your topic is **narrow**, or specific, enough to cover thoroughly. If you are writing a three-page essay about the history of basketball, "Great Teams of the 1990s," while still far too broad, would be a more manageable topic than "50 Years of NBA Champions." Further narrow the topic to an essay about a championship game of the 1990s, and you'll have a solid topic that fits the available space.

Next, decide on a **purpose** for your writing. What do you want to do with your topic? Do you want to inform? amuse? describe? persuade? A single piece of writing may have more than one purpose. Think of the purpose as a way of narrowing the topic.

Finally, decide on your **audience**. Who do you want to read your piece? Knowing who your intended audience is before you begin writing will help you decide what style, tone, and vocabulary to use.

▶ **Exercise 3** Rewrite each sentence to match the indicated audience.

How do you do? (your sister) _How's it going?_____

1. Thanks a million for giving me a hand. (person to whom you have written a letter of complaint)

_____

2. I think if you believe that you must be out of your mind! (grandparent) _____

_____

3. The player hyperextended the anterior cruciate ligament in his left knee. (a friend) _____

_____

4. Mozart wrote symphonies, rondos, sonatas, concertos, oratorios, and comic operas. (person who knows very little about classical music) _____

_____

5. My grades are OK, pretty decent, actually. (potential employer) _____

_____

Copyright © by Glencoe/McGraw-Hill

Composition

6. The enemy tank is over there somewhere and going pretty fast toward the east or whatever.
   (a fighter pilot to whom you are reporting critical information) _____

   _____

7. The flat thing that you push on with your foot to make the car go is sticking. (a car mechanic)

   _____

   _____

8. Put some of that stuff in the test tube. (your lab partner for a chemistry experiment)

   _____

   _____

9. That poor section of town is a real dump; nobody goes there. (a descriptive brochure for

   visitors to your city) _____

   _____

10. The quarterback threw three interceptions! (a foreign student in your high school who has

    never seen a football game) _____

    _____

▶ **Exercise 4 Write a sentence that conveys the topic and purpose and is appropriate for the audience listed.**

   Topic: the advantages of being computer-literate; Purpose: describe; Audience: a grandparent
   Computers are everywhere these days, Grandma, and if I want to get a good job, I need to know how to use
   them.

1. **Topic:** roller blading; Purpose: persuade; Audience: high school students _____

   _____

2. **Topic:** new movies; Purpose: inform; Audience: city newspaper readers _____

   _____

3. **Topic:** an embarrassing incident; Purpose: amuse; Audience: group of friends _____

   _____

4. **Topic:** great fictional detectives; Purpose: describe; Audience: a mystery readers book club

   _____

   _____

Copyright © by Glencoe/McGraw-Hill

Composition

5. Topic: need for building a new middle school; **Purpose:** persuade; **Audience:** members of the

school board _____

_____

6. Topic: the most exciting basketball game of the season; **Purpose:** narrate; **Audience:** a friend

who missed the game _____

_____

7. Topic: traffic safety; **Purpose:** persuade; **Audience:** third-graders _____

_____

8. Topic: the most fantastic car you've ever seen; **Purpose:** describe; **Audience:** high school

students _____

_____

9. Topic: practical jokes you have played; **Purpose:** amuse; **Audience:** a stranger _____

_____

10. Topic: why you need a larger allowance; **Purpose:** inform; **Audience:** a parent _____

_____

_____

▶ **Exercise 5 Choose one of the audiences below, and write a paragraph that reflects the purpose listed.**

your family doctor (to describe a typical exercise workout)
a group of your friends (to entertain with an amusing story)
readers of the community newspaper (to inform about the need to build a jogging track in a park)
adults who do not get enough exercise (to persuade them about the need to exercise)

_____

_____

_____

_____

_____

_____

_____

_____

_____

Copyright © by Glencoe/McGraw-Hill

Composition

Lesson 102
The Writing Process: Drafting

The next step after prewriting is **drafting**, or writing the piece in paragraph form. Based on the topic and the purpose, develop a theme, the main point you want to make in the piece. State this theme in a thesis statement in the first paragraph. Each paragraph is made of a topic sentence, which states a main idea related to the theme, and sentences that support the main idea with details. You may adopt a different style or voice, depending on your theme, audience, and purpose. The writing style or tone gives the piece its "feel."

▶ **Exercise 1** **Write a thesis statement that is appropriate for the topic and purpose indicated.**

Topic: violence on television; **Purpose:** to persuade. <u>Programs containing violence should carry a</u> <u>warning to viewers.</u>

1. **Topic:** getting a driver's license; **Purpose:** to entertain and to inform. _____

   _____

2. **Topic:** preparing a meal at our house; **Purpose:** to entertain. _____

   _____

3. **Topic:** sports; **Purpose:** to persuade. _____

   _____

4. **Topic:** frying an egg; **Purpose:** to narrate. _____

   _____

5. **Topic:** hair styles; **Purpose:** to describe. _____

   _____

6. **Topic:** pets; **Purpose:** to entertain. _____

   _____

7. **Topic:** money; **Purpose:** to persuade. _____

   _____

8. **Topic:** the most influential person in my life; **Purpose:** to describe. _____

   _____

Copyright © by Glencoe/McGraw-Hill

Composition

9. Topic: my most embarrassing moment; **Purpose:** to entertain. _____

_____

10. Topic: recycling; **Purpose:** to persuade. _____

_____

▶ **Exercise 2 Draft a brief paragraph that begins with the thesis statement provided. Choose an appropriate writing style and tone.**

1. The Art Club is looking for anyone interested in painting, drawing, printmaking, or any other

fine art to become a member of the best club at Rodgers High! _____

_____

_____

_____

_____

_____

2. I am responding to your ad in the Daily News for a lawn care worker. _____

_____

_____

_____

_____

_____

3. I am writing in regards to a defective compact disc player that I recently purchased at your store.

_____

_____

_____

_____

_____

4. Thanks a million, Aunt Patricia, for the new baseball cap. _____

_____

_____

_____

_____

Copyright © by Glencoe/McGraw-Hill

Composition

5. You would think that opening a can of cat food would not be beyond the capabilities of a

relatively intelligent, reasonably coordinated eleventh-grader. _____

_____

_____

_____

_____

_____

▶ **Exercise 3 Write a paragraph containing four related sentences that provide details to support
the topic sentence below.**

Studying history can help people avoid the mistakes of the past. _____

_____

_____

_____

_____

_____

▶ **Exercise 4 Draft a brief paragraph on each theme. State the main idea in a topic statement.
Include several sentences that provide details to support the main idea.**

1. **Theme:** to request information about vacation cruises. _____

_____

_____

_____

_____

_____

2. **Theme:** to urge a network not to cancel your favorite television program. _____

_____

_____

_____

_____

_____

_____

Copyright © by Glencoe/McGraw-Hill

Composition

3. Theme: to describe what you like about your neighborhood. _____

_____

_____

_____

_____

_____

4. Theme: to express an opinion on a community or national issue. _____

_____

_____

_____

_____

_____

5. Theme: to thank a good friend for doing you a big favor. _____

_____

_____

_____

_____

_____

6. Theme: to give an account of an exciting or humorous experience. _____

_____

_____

_____

_____

_____

Copyright © by Glencoe/McGraw-Hill

Composition

Lesson 103
The Writing Process: Revising

After you have completed your draft, the next step is to revise, or improve, your writing. First, check for meaning. Does your thesis statement communicate the point you wanted to make? Have you included all the important details needed to support your thesis? Next, check for unity. Is the organization logical? Do the details clearly support your thesis? Last, check for coherence. Is each sentence clear? Does the writing flow smoothly from one part to the next? Have you provided transitions?

▶ **Exercise 1** **Revise and rewrite each paragraph below for meaning, unity, and coherence.**

Doing this will solve the burnt toast problem in most cases. My mom likes her toast pretty dark, but I definitely don't. The thermostat is usually a screw or knob on the bottom of the toaster. Readjusting a toaster thermostat is not difficult. It is often responsible for charred toast. It is very important to follow a few safety rules. Always unplug the toaster before working on it, and never stick any metal object like a fork or knife into a toaster. Turn the thermostat adjustment knob so that its tip is about a quarter-inch from the keeper release switch contact. You'll probably have to turn the toaster upside down and open the crumb tray.

_____

_____

_____

_____

_____

_____

_____

_____

_____

_____

_____

_____

_____

Copyright © by Glencoe/McGraw-Hill

Composition

Name _____ Class _____ Date _____

Mark Isambard Brunel was an industrialist and inventor. He became Chief Engineer of New York and started a cannon factory. He is one of the most fascinating figures of the early nineteenth century. His production line became the marvel of its time. It was one of the most popular tourist attractions of the day, too. Mark Isambard Brunel is also a father of modern industrial development. Born in France in 1769, Brunel received a technical education. After that, he moved to the young United States. Because he grew up speaking French, he had to learn English, which is quite different from his native language. One of his friends was Alexander Hamilton. One day he was eating dinner with Hamilton in 1798. They talked and he learned that the British Royal Navy had a severe problem. They couldn't obtain enough wooden blocks. They needed 100,000 blocks a year to rig sailing ships each year. Brunel moved to Portsmouth, England. He set up the world's first automated production line. Using specially designed machines to cut, shape, polish, and finish the wooden blocks. It was so well designed and built that one of Brunel's machines was still manufacturing blocks almost two hundred years later! It was operated by 10 workers. It replaced 110 expert artisans.

_____
_____
_____
_____
_____
_____
_____
_____
_____
_____
_____
_____
_____
_____
_____
_____
_____

Copyright © by Glencoe/McGraw-Hill

Composition

Lesson 104
The Writing Process: Editing

After you have revised your work, the next step is to **edit** what you have written. As you edit, look for correct word usage, subject-verb agreement, correct verb tenses, clear pronoun references, run-on sentences, and sentence fragments. You can cross out weak or inappropriate words and write better ones in the margins or spaces between the lines. Next, **proofread** your writing to correct spelling, punctuation, and capitalization errors. Use the following proofreading marks:

insert ∧	disater
delete	electrical
insert space #	mostoutlandish
close up space	over protective
capitalize ≡	Empire state building
make lowercase /	Director
check spelling	Plymoth
switch order	yellow little
new paragraph ¶	. . . in three places. Next on the list. . . .

▶ **Exercise 1** **Edit each sentence for clarity and correct grammar.**

I suggest ordering the freid chicken, the fish, or the roast beef.

1. Your gumchewing bother almost every one here.

2. What time you do think ashley and I should arriv?

3. If you were to visit Holmes county, Ohio, youd see many Amish people.

4. It's quite important to get a good nights sleep before takeing a test.

5. The very first hollywood movie was filmmed in 1911.

6. Two important civil war battles were fought at bull run, also known as Manassas.

7. If you never see a person ride a unacycle, you in for a real treet.

8. Darnell was suprised to learn that hawaii is the only place in the United States where Coffee is grow.

Copyright © by Glencoe/McGraw-Hill

Composition

9. The humble fruit fly has made some important contributons to ourunderstanding of genetics.

10. We took my Sister Janelle to the air port, where she caught her plain to Miami.

▶ **Exercise 2** **Edit the following paragraph, then rewrite the paragraph based on your editing marks.**

My grandmother is avid gardener. Eachwinter she pores over gardening boooks trying to decide what to plan in the spring. She al ways chooses plats that will blend witht he perennials already in her garden. every year adds she more flowers—hyacinths, pansies, tulips, and snapdragons each have their specail place. This year is adding purple petunias and more white Snapdragons. grandmother's garden is all ways a peace ful retreat from bustling the city.

_____
_____
_____
_____
_____
_____
_____
_____
_____
_____
_____
_____
_____
_____
_____
_____

Copyright © by Glencoe/McGraw-Hill

Composition

Lesson 105
The Writing Process: Presenting

After completing a piece of writing, you may want to present, or share your work with others. You can begin thinking about presentation as early as the prewriting stage when you define your audience. The nature of your piece also affects how and where you might present your writing.

An outlet for presenting your writing to a specific audience is called a market. As an eleventh-grade student, several markets are available to you. Some of these markets are school forums, such as school newspapers and classroom presentations; community forums, such as local organizations and community newspapers; contests, often sponsored by magazines; and open-market forums, such as special-interest magazines and newsletters. The *Market Guide for Young Writers*, available in many libraries, will provide many ideas for marketing your work.

To decide how to present your writing, first analyze the piece and pinpoint the audience. Then search for an outlet that serves that audience. Some outlets, such as classroom presentations, radio programs, community productions, or speech contests, offer a chance for oral presentation. In these cases, visual aids can add to your presentation.

▶ **Exercise 1** **Suggest an outlet or market for each piece of writing described below.**

a short story ___a school literary magazine or national student literary publication___

1. a review of a current movie or video release _____

2. a how-to article on preparing a farm animal for the state fair livestock show _____

_____

3. an essay on what you have learned from your grandparents _____

_____

4. an adventure story with sound effects _____

5. a speech about the value of recycling programs _____

6. a description of a typical day at your school _____

7. an editorial on an important community issue _____

8. a review of new computer software _____

9. a listener's guide to new music CDs _____

10. a poem about the seasons _____

Copyright © by Glencoe/McGraw-Hill

Composition

Name _____ Class _____ Date _____

▶ **Exercise 2** **Suggest a visual aid to increase the effectiveness of each presentation below.**

an oral reading of a poem written in dialogue ___costumes or props for the readers___

1. a classroom presentation about sports-card collecting _____

2. a cable-television commercial to raise money for a new animal shelter _____

_____

3. a presentation about Appalachian folk music _____

4. a speech to the student body about your qualifications for student office _____

_____

5. a report on various devices used by people who are physically challenged _____

_____

6. the steps of the publishing process _____

_____

7. a discussion of different painting techniques _____

8. a presentation about foods from different parts of Asia _____

_____

9. a report on the population growth of your state or city _____

10. a research paper on the Great Pyramid _____

▶ **Exercise 3** **Draft a topic, purpose, and theme for a piece of writing intended for a specific audience or market. Then describe how and to whom you might present the piece.**

Topic: _____

_____

Purpose: _____

_____

Theme: _____

_____

Intended audience: _____

Form of presentation: _____

Reasons for choice of presentation: _____

_____

_____

Copyright © by Glencoe/McGraw-Hill

Composition

Lesson 106
Outlining

Outlining is a method for organizing the information in a piece of writing. It is often helpful to begin an outline after the prewriting phase, before you start drafting your piece. One handy way to make an outline is to transfer information from your prewriting material to index cards. You can then arrange the cards by main topic and supporting details. In your outline, use Roman numerals to indicate main topics. Use capital letters for subtopics. Under each topic, you can list details (called subdivisions) using regular numbers. (If you use subtopics or subdivisions, always give at least two.) Part of an outline for an informational piece on in-line skating might look like this:

I. Important Techniques
  A. Stopping
    1. First bend knees
    2. Move left foot backward
    3. Move right foot forward
  B. Maintaining balance
    1. Keep knees slightly bent
    2. Put pressure on balls of feet
    3. Look straight ahead
  C. Skating with safety
    1. Wear protective pads
    2. Don't skate at night or in traffic
    3. Watch your speed
II. Safety Equipment

▶ **Exercise 1 Evaluate the outline below.**

  I. String instruments
    A. Made of wood, use strings of nylon or sheep gut
    B. Played with bows of horsehair
    C. Members
      1. Violin
      2. Viola
      3. Cello, contrabass
    D. Most numerous section in orchestra
      1. Most orchestras have about 100 musicians
  II. Brass family
    A. Includes trumpet, trombone, French horn, tuba
      1. Tuba is lowest
    B. Trombone is loudest
    C. Made of metal tubes of different lengths
      1. The longer the tube, the lower the instrument
    D. Tuba can be 35 feet long

Copyright © by Glencoe/McGraw-Hill

Composition

_____

_____

_____

▶ **Exercise 2** **Organize the following topics and details into an outline for a piece about the Andean countries of South America.**

Venezuela is one of the wealthiest countries in South America, while Bolivia is poor and landlocked. Colombia and Bolivia are two of the world's most important coffee producers. Mineral exports from this region include tin from Bolivia; oil from Venezuela (one of the world's largest oil exporters), Ecuador, Peru, and Colombia; zinc from Peru; bauxite from Venezuela; and coal from Colombia and Venezuela. Ecuador produces bananas, while Peru and Ecuador are important sources of fish. Bauxite is used to make aluminum. Capital cities of the countries are La Paz, Bolivia; Caracas, Venezuela; Bogotá, Colombia; Quito, Ecuador; and Lima, Peru.

_____

_____

_____

_____

_____

_____

_____

_____

_____

_____

_____

_____

_____

_____

_____

_____

_____

Copyright © by Glencoe/McGraw-Hill

Composition

Lesson 107
Writing Effective Sentences

Effective sentences are one of the most powerful tools a writer can use. You can vary the tone and style of a piece by changing the patterns of your sentences. When writing, consider these strategies for making your sentences as effective as possible. Vary the length of your sentences. Don't use all long sentences or all short sentences. Also vary the structure of the sentences. Following a rigid sentence pattern quickly becomes repetitive and boring. Parallelism is deliberate repetition of certain words, phrases, or sentence structures to achieve certain effects. Another strategy is to use interruption for emphasis. A sudden break in thought calls attention to itself. Use this device to emphasize an important point or detail. One more way to add emphasis is to use an unusual sentence pattern that stands out from all the other sentences.

A **topic sentence** states the main idea of the paragraph. Be sure it is specific and interesting enough to arouse the reader's interest.

Use the **active voice** as often as possible. In a sentence in the active voice, the subject performs the action (*It eats*). In a **passive-voice** sentence, the subject is acted on (*It is eaten*). Active verbs are stronger than passive verbs. As a general rule, only use passive when the "doer" of an action is not known, is unimportant, if you do not wish the doer to be known, or when you want to emphasize something other than the subject.

▶ **Exercise 1 Reword the sentences below into an effective topic sentence of a paragraph.**

Silk has been cultivated from silkworms for thousands of years. It is one of nature's marvels.
Cultivated from silkworms for thousands of years, silk is one of nature's marvels.
_____

1. Knowledge of color is important. Interior decorators have to know all about it. They use it in

their work. Their work is designing rooms. _____

_____

2. Santa Fe is fascinating. It is the capital of New Mexico. It has been strongly influenced by three

cultures. They are Native American, Hispanic, and Anglo-American. _____

_____

3. Being a lifeguard is not one big party. Many people think this. Lifeguards have important

responsibilities. They may be called on to save a life at any time. _____

_____

Copyright © by Glencoe/McGraw-Hill

Composition

4. Charles Babbage was a great inventor. He is little known today. He developed a "Difference Engine." It was one of the world's first computers. _____

_____

_____

5. My mom and I visited colleges. We visited several. I liked Piedmont College best. Mom preferred Southern Tech. _____

_____

_____

6. Chariot races were popular in Ancient Rome. People cheered for one of the four teams. The four teams were the Blues, Greens, Reds, and Whites. They were all owned by the emperor.

_____

_____

_____

7. The door of the house creaked open. It was extremely dark. I couldn't see anything. I began to feel more than a little frightened. _____

_____

_____

8. Kangaroos are marsupials. They are the largest members of this order. They have become a symbol of Australia. Australia is the only country where they are found. _____

_____

_____

9. Jeanine stood at the free throw line. Her team was down by one point. She had two foul shots. There was no time left on the clock. _____

_____

_____

10. More and more people are working at home. It is more convenient. It cuts down on commuting time. Computers have made much of this possible. _____

_____

_____

Copyright © by Glencoe/McGraw-Hill

Composition

▶ **Exercise 2** **Write an effective sentence or group of sentences using the strategy indicated.**

(repetition of words)   "No," said the man at the video store. "No," said the woman at the bakery; I was
beginning to think they were trying to tell me something!

1. (unusual pattern) _____

_____

2. (varied sentence length) _____

_____

_____

3. (interruption for emphasis) _____

_____

_____

4. (varied sentence length) _____

_____

_____

5. (varied sentence structure) _____

_____

_____

6. (appropriate use of passive voice) _____

_____

7. (unusual sentence for emphasis) _____

_____

_____

8. (interruption for emphasis) _____

_____

_____

9. (repetition of phrases) _____

_____

_____

10. (parallelism) _____

_____

Copyright © by Glencoe/McGraw-Hill

Composition

Name _____ Class _____ Date _____

▶ **Exercise 3 Rewrite the paragraph using effective sentences.**

   Louis Armstrong was a pioneer of jazz. His nickname was Satchmo. Louis Armstrong was one of

the most respected of all jazz trumpeters. He joined the New Orleans band of King Oliver when he

was quite young. He formed his own jazz band in 1927. Then he went on to worldwide fame.

Armstrong's trademark was his raspy, but expressive voice. Everyone recognizes it immediately as

the voice of Satchmo the Great!

_____

_____

_____

_____

_____

_____

_____

_____

_____

_____

_____

_____

_____

_____

_____

_____

_____

_____

_____

_____

Copyright © by Glencoe/McGraw-Hill

Lesson 108
Building Paragraphs

You can arrange the supporting details in a paragraph in **chronological order**, which places events in the order in which they happened; in **spatial order**, the way in which objects appear to an observer; or in **compare/contrast order**, which shows similarities and differences between the items you are writing about.

The following example uses spatial order in the first paragraph, chronological order in the second paragraph, and compare-and-contrast order in the third paragraph.

My brother and I paid our admission and entered the park. Turning left past the concession stand, we headed straight toward the Shrieker, the new roller coaster we'd heard so much about. There, looming ahead of us, towering above the ferris wheel on the right and the log ride on the left, was the biggest coaster I'd ever seen!

The first thing was to get our tickets. After waiting in line about ten minutes, we reached the booth and plunked down our money. An attendant directed us to the loading ramp. Then, as the screams of riders grew louder, the Shrieker appeared at the end of the track and zoomed up next to us.

The Shrieker was incredible! It's not quite as fast as the Banshee, but it twists and turns more often. We went upside down four times, which is one more than on the Blue Beast. In all, my brother and I gave the Shrieker an A plus, a grade matched only by the legendary Sea Dragon.

▶ **Exercise 1** **Use compare/contrast order to write a paragraph about one of the following topics.**

two of your favorite sports
writing with a pencil and paper versus writing on a computer
paintings and photographs
what you enjoy in a movie
the ideal pet

_____
_____
_____
_____
_____
_____
_____
_____
_____

Copyright © by Glencoe/McGraw-Hill

Composition

▶ **Exercise 2** **Write the following paragraph in chronological order.**

The sheep have to be dry when they're sheared; otherwise the wool goes into the bag wet and never dries out. If it looks like rain, we have to gather the sheep inside the barn. After arranging a time for the shearer to come, we have to watch the skies. When the shearer arrives, my father and I help him set up his equipment and make sure the sheep are gathered. He takes about three minutes on each animal, then we push them out into a new pasture. And no, it doesn't hurt them at all to be sheared! After they're sheared they look a little funny, but believe me, they feel light and easy. Once he starts shearing, it's our job to ensure a smooth flow of sheep. Getting our flock of sheep ready for the shearer is a big job.

_____

_____

_____

_____

_____

_____

_____

_____

_____

_____

_____

_____

_____

_____

_____

_____

_____

_____

_____

_____

Composition

Copyright © by Glencoe/McGraw-Hill

▶ **Exercise 3 Write the following paragraph in spatial order.**

The first floor windows to either side of the door reached almost to the ground. Up on the second floor, the curtains in the windows had always been closed tightly, sealing in whatever secrets they held. As long as he could remember, Anthony had been fascinated by the old house at the end of the street. "I intend to remain a mystery," the tower seemed to whisper. "Leave me my secrets." Maybe it was the color, a dirty gray that reminded him of old newspapers. Finally, the tower that jutted up into the sky always seemed to be warning him away. It was difficult to imagine dance music and happy laughter streaming out of them on a summer's evening. There was something about its appearance that, somehow, just didn't seem right. The front door, too, looked like it had seen grander days, when guests would have been proud to walk through it.

_____

_____

_____

_____

_____

_____

_____

_____

_____

_____

_____

_____

_____

_____

_____

_____

_____

_____

Copyright © by Glencoe/McGraw-Hill

Composition

▶ **Exercise 4** **Write a two-paragraph essay about a subject that interests you. Choose an appropriate method of ordering paragraphs in your essay, and explain your choice.**

_____

_____

_____

_____

_____

_____

_____

_____

_____

_____

_____

_____

_____

_____

_____

_____

_____

_____

_____

_____

_____

_____

_____

_____

_____

_____

_____

_____

_____

_____

_____

Copyright © by Glencoe/McGraw-Hill

Composition

Lesson 109
Paragraph Ordering

When you revise a first draft, check the unity and coherence of paragraphs. Each paragraph should include a topic sentence, which states the main idea of the paragraph, as well as supporting details related to the topic sentence. Be sure the comparisons are understandable. Check chronological details for proper order and make sure that spatial details are clear. (See Lesson 108.) Finally, link the ideas together properly by using effective transitions.

▶ **Exercise 1   Revise the following paragraphs for unity and coherence. Rewrite the paragraphs based on your revisions.**

The armadillo's armor covers the creature from head to toe to the tip of its tail, which is protected by bony rings. The animal's most distinctive feature is the hard, bony shield that protects its soft body from a host of predators. Most mammals are covered with fur, hair, or wool. The shield is formed of bony plates connected by skin. Without a doubt, one of the oddest animals of the Western Hemisphere is the armadillo, found in North, Central, and South America, primarily in dry climates.

While different species of armadillos have different plate placement, many are able to fit head and tail armor tightly together. To render it even more difficult for a predator to make a meal of it, the armadillo can roll its body into a tight ball. It is an almost impregnable barrier to an attacker. Perhaps the most unusual member of the family is the little fairy armadillo. It sports a pink shell, attached only at the ridge of its back. Under the shell is long, soft white fur. The animal uses this broad tail to block the entrance to its underground burrow in case of danger. The fairy armadillo's tail is large and flat—so heavy, in fact, that it cannot be lifted. Particular species of armadillos have some odd habits and capabilities, in keeping with their unusual appearance. For example, the female nine-banded armadillo always gives birth to a litter of identical quadruplets.

The creatures are extremely good diggers, often able to bury themselves so firmly that people need shovels or picks to break through the dirt. By covering themselves with dirt, armadillos add another layer of defense. Perhaps the only attacker that armadillos need fear is the automobile; the highways of the American Southwest often witness the truth of this statement. Armadillos spend most of the daylight hours in underground burrows, emerging at night to feed on insects and plants.

Copyright © by Glencoe/McGraw-Hill

Composition

Composition

Copyright © by Glencoe/McGraw-Hill

Lesson 110
Personal Letters

A **personal letter** is frequently a letter to a friend or a relative. Personal letters describe recent events in your life, as well as your opinions, thoughts, and feelings about various topics. They also ask the person to whom you are writing questions about his or her life. Personal letters can maintain friendships and deepen understanding. Invitations and thank-you notes are other kinds of personal letters.

Personal letters are usually written in indented form. Each paragraph is indented, as well as each line in the heading and the signature line.

▶ **Exercise 1** **Read the following personal letter. Answer each question.**

450 Browning Boulevard
Dubuque, IA 52001
March 6, 1996

Dear Dan,
    Are you still working as hard as ever? I know I am. With school, studying, choir, and working at the grocery store, I don't have a lot of free time left—about five minutes a day, I think!
    The reason I'm writing is to get your opinion on something. I have the chance to buy a second-hand car. It's a good car, and I know the owner has taken good care of it. Do you think it's a good idea? It would be great to have a car, but I'm hesitating because I'm afraid having a car would take up too much time and money. You know I'm saving for college. You had a car when you were in high school. Did you run into (ha-ha, pun intended) any of these problems with your car? Please let me know what you think as soon as you can.

                                    Your buddy,
                                    Kwame

1. What do you think is the relationship between Kwame and Dan? _____

_____

2. What is Kwame's attitude about having a car? Why is he asking Dan's opinion? _____

_____

_____

3. How is this a good example of a personal letter? _____

_____

_____

Copyright © by Glencoe/McGraw-Hill

Composition

4. What might Dan include in a response to Kwame's letter? _____

_____

▶ **Exercise 2 Write a personal letter to a friend.**

_____

_____

_____

_____

_____

_____

_____

_____

_____

_____

_____

_____

_____

_____

_____

_____

_____

_____

_____

_____

_____

_____

_____

_____

_____

Copyright © by Glencoe/McGraw-Hill

Composition

Different situations call for different kinds of personal letters. You would probably use a different tone and style in writing to an adult relative than you would in writing to your best friend. In writing to your relative, your tone would probably be more formal, while you might use slang or secret code words when writing to your best friend. You would also write differently to a favorite author, performer, or sports figure.

▶ Exercise 3 **Write a letter to an adult relative describing the ups and downs of your school year so far. Explain what successes you have enjoyed, as well as what you would like to improve.**

_____

_____

_____

_____

_____

_____

_____

_____

_____

_____

_____

_____

_____

_____

_____

_____

_____

_____

_____

_____

Copyright © by Glencoe/McGraw-Hill

Composition

▶ **Exercise 4** **Write a letter to a class of seventh-graders persuading them to stay in school. Include appropriate information on the advantages of graduating from high school and the disadvantages of dropping out. Use a tone and style that match your intended audience.**

_____

_____

_____

_____

_____

_____

_____

_____

_____

_____

_____

_____

_____

_____

_____

_____

_____

_____

_____

_____

_____

_____

_____

_____

_____

_____

_____

_____

_____

_____

_____

Copyright © by Glencoe/McGraw-Hill

Composition

Lesson 111
Business Letters: Letters of Request or Complaint

A **letter of request** asks for information or services. It is important to be both clear and courteous when writing a letter of request. Make sure to explain what information you need and why you need it. Be sure to include any information the receiver may need to answer your request.

Business letters are usually written in block form or semiblock form. In block form, everything is lined up with the left margin. In semiblock form, the heading, complimentary close, and the signature are indented.

▶ **Exercise 1** Examine the following letter. Is it a good example of a letter of request? Why or why not? Write your critique below.

Dear Sonic Solutions:
I need to be able to plug my CD player into the car radio. Get into my tunes on long trips. The guy at the music store said I could write to you for the part I need. Can you send it to me right away at the adress on the outside of this envelope?

Sincerly,
Kyle Lorenzo

_____

_____

_____

_____

▶ **Exercise 2** Write a short letter of request for one of the following topics. Be sure to use proper business letter format.

requesting information from a military recruiter on how to join the service after graduation

requesting information from a computer manufacturer on accessories it offers for your computer

requesting information from a local college on how to buy tickets to an upcoming play

requesting information on an after-school volunteer tutoring program you want to join

_____

_____

_____

_____

Copyright © by Glencoe/McGraw-Hill

Composition

A **letter of complaint** describes a problem or concern and sometimes requests a specific action. It should be clear, concise, and reasonable. Never let your anger get the best of you when you are writing a letter of complaint. Begin by stating the problem and telling briefly how it happened. Provide supporting details as evidence of your problem. Explain what you would like done about the matter. Always avoid insults and threats.

▶ **Exercise 3** **Read the following letter of complaint. Describe any problems and suggest how to correct them.**

Dear rip-off artist:

Thanks for making me miss the concert of the year. When I ordered tickets for it, you sent me ones with the wrong date when me and my friends got to the concert they had the write ones. But I didn't. I had to wait outside cause the jerk at the door wouldn't let me in. Thanks to your mistake. I'll never buy tickets from you lousy company again. I hope your happy.

A disatisfied customer

_____

_____

_____

_____

▶ **Exercise 4** **Revise and rewrite the above letter of complaint.**

_____

_____

_____

_____

_____

_____

_____

_____

_____

_____

_____

_____

Copyright © by Glencoe/McGraw-Hill

Composition

Lesson 112
Business Letters: Résumés and Cover Letters

A résumé is a summary of your work experience, school experience, talents, and interests. You use your résumé when applying for a job or for admittance into a school or an academic program. A résumé should be clear, concise, expressive, and informative. Use expressive language to describe your accomplishments and abilities (*supervised* four people, *computer-literate*). Because a résumé is a summary, it is not necessary to use complete sentences. However, use a consistent format, as in the following example.

William Ramirez
2225 Martin Street
Austin, TX 78746
(512) 784-0985

Objective:	Full-time summer employment as a lifeguard
Training:	Junior and Senior Lifesaving Course, Austin YMCA, 1995, 1996
Education:	Austin East High School, August 1995 to present, 3.1 grade point average
	Decatur Middle School, August 1992-June 1995, 3.2 grade point average
Awards:	Most Improved Sophomore Swimmer, Austin East High School swim team
References:	Elizabeth Hollings, teacher, Austin East High School, (512) 555-489-2911
	Robert Steinberg, water safety instructor, Austin YMCA, (512) 555-4862

▶ **Exercise 1 Answer each question.**

1. How might the headings (Objective, Training, Education, and so on) be ordered if William were applying for an academic program? Why? What else might he include if he were applying for a school program? _____

_____

_____

_____

2. The headings William used are not the only ones you can use on a résumé. What are some others? _____

_____

_____

_____

_____

Copyright © by Glencoe/McGraw-Hill

Composition

3. If you were the manager of a swimming pool considering hiring William, would you be

impressed by his résumé? Why or why not? _____

_____

_____

_____

4. Who are some other people William might have used as references? Why is it a good idea to get

permission before you use someone as a reference? _____

_____

_____

_____

_____

_____

_____

_____

_____

_____

_____

_____

▶ **Exercise 2 You are applying for one of the following:**

    a position on an important school committee
    an internship with a local television station
    a summer job as a recreation program assistant for physically challenged children
    a special advanced study program in a field that interests you
    a part-time job at a fast-food restaurant

**Freewrite for ten minutes about the information you would want to include in your
résumé.**

_____

_____

_____

_____

_____

Copyright © by Glencoe/McGraw-Hill

Composition

▶ **Exercise 3 Write your résumé.**

_____

_____

_____

_____

_____

_____

A **cover letter** is a letter of introduction that often accompanies a résumé. In your cover letter, say what you are applying for and where you can be contacted. You may also want to refer the reader to specific sections of your résumé that you feel are especially appropriate for the job or program you are applying for. By using your cover letter to call attention to, or highlight, certain abilities, interests, and experiences, you can create a "customized" presentation, one that is tailored to the specific job or program you are interested in.

The following is an example of a well-formatted, concise cover letter. Note that the letter follows business letter style rules and that it is directed to a specific person. Note also how William highlights his swimming award and lifesaving classes to tailor his application to the specific job. Finally, notice that he is beginning his summer job search several months before he wants to begin working.

2225 Martin Street
Austin, TX 78746
April 19, 1996

Ms. Natalie O'Shaughnessy
Personnel Director, Oak Hills Swim Center
7906 Wright Boulevard
Austin, TX 78746

Dear Ms. O'Shaughnessy:

    I am a student and swimming team member at East High School. I am interested in full-time summer employment as a lifeguard. I feel my extensive training in water safety, as well as my abilities as a swimmer, makes me a strong candidate for employment at Oak Hills. When I received the swimming award last winter, Coach Halsey praised my work ethic and willingness to do whatever it takes to get the job done. I would like to put these qualities to work to help make this the safest summer yet at Oak Hills.

    Enclosed is a copy of my résumé. I hope you agree that I am well qualified to become a member of your staff. Please feel free to contact me if you have any questions. I hope to hear from you soon.

Sincerely,
William Ramirez

Copyright © by Glencoe/McGraw-Hill

Composition

▶ **Exercise 4** Write a cover letter to send with your résumé for the position you chose in Exercises 2 and 3.

_____

_____

_____

_____

_____

_____

_____

_____

_____

_____

_____

_____

_____

_____

_____

_____

_____

_____

_____

_____

_____

_____

_____

_____

_____

_____

_____

_____

_____

_____

Copyright © by Glencoe/McGraw-Hill

Composition

*I*ndex

Index

Copyright © by Glencoe/McGraw-Hill

and compound sentences, 15, 249

and conjunctive adverbs, 253

between coordinate adjectives, 15, 251

in direct address, 15, 261

in direct quotations, 15–16, 271

and interjections, 43, 253

and introductory phrases, 42, 255

with nonessential elements, 15, 42–43, 253

with numbers, 259

for parenthetical elements, 15, 43, 253

in references, 15, 259

after salutations and closings in letters, 15, 261

in series, 15, 44, 251

in tag questions, 15, 261

with titles of persons, 259

Common nouns, defined, 2, 47

Comparative degree (form), modifiers, 9–10, 195, 197

Compare/contrast order, 18, 327

Comparison

of adjectives, 9–10, 61, 195, 197

of adverbs, 9–10, 195, 197

double and incomplete, 10, 199

irregular, 10, 197

Complements, 6, 79, 81–82

diagraming, 119

direct objects, 6, 79

indirect objects, 6, 79

object, 6, 81

subject, 6, 82

Complete predicates, defined, 6, 74

Complete subjects, defined, 6, 74

Complex sentences, defined, 7, 101

Compound elements

numbers, hyphens in, 16, 279

predicates, 6, 75

prepositions, 5, 65

sentences, 7, 99, 249

subjects, 5, 75, 163

Compound-complex sentences, 7, 101

Concrete nouns, defined, 2, 47

Conjunctions, defined, 5, 67

conjunctive adverbs, 5, 69, 257

coordinating, 5, 67

correlative, 5, 67

list, 67

subordinating, 5, 67, 97

list, 67, 97

Conjunctive adverbs, 5, 69, 257

Context clues, 17, 291

Continual, continuous, 12, 220

Conversations, punctuating, 15–16, 271

Coordinate adjectives, 15, 251

Coordinating conjunctions, 5, 67

Correlative conjunctions, 5, 67

Could of, might of, must of, should of, would of, avoiding, 12, 220

D

Dangling modifiers, avoiding, 10, 38–39, 207

Dashes, 15, 267

Dates, punctuating, 15, 283

Declarative sentences, defined, 8, 109

Definite article, 61

Degrees of form (comparison), 9–10, 61, 195, 197

Demonstrative pronouns 2, 54

Dependent (subordinate) clauses, 7, 97, 101, 103–105, 107, 257

punctuating, 257

Diagraming

sentences with clauses, 123–126

simple sentences, 119–120

simple sentences with phrases, 121–122

Different from, not *different than,* 12, 221

Direct address, 15, 235

Direct objects, defined, 6, 79

Doesn't, don't, 12, 221

Double comparisons, avoiding, 10, 199

Double negatives, avoiding, 10, 203

Drafting, 18, 311

chronological order, 18, 327

compare/contrast order, 18, 327

spatial order, 18, 327

style, voice, 311

theme, 311

thesis statement, 311

topic sentence and related sentences, 311

E

Each, agreement with, 8, 29, 31 ,167

Editing, 18, 317

proofreading marks, 317

Effect, affect, 11, 218

Either, agreement with, 167

Ellipses (ellipsis points), 15, 270

Emigrate, immigrate, 12, 221

Emphatic verbs, defined, 4, 142

Everywheres, anywheres, avoiding, 11, 219

Except, accept, 11, 217

Exclamation points, 14, 109, 243

and quotation marks, 16, 273

Exclamatory sentences, defined, 8, 109

F

Farther, further, 12, 221

Fewer, less, 12, 221

Fragments, sentence, defined, 22–23, 111

Freewriting, 18, 307

Further, farther, 12, 221

Future perfect tense, 3, 137, 139

Future tense, 3, 135, 139

G

Gerund phrases, 7, 89, 93

Gerunds, defined, 7, 89

Good, well, 12, 201, 222

H

Had of, avoiding, 12, 222

Hanged, hung, 12, 222

Hardly, in double negatives, 220

Helping (auxiliary) verbs, 3, 59

Hung, hanged, 12, 222

Hyphens, rules, 16, 279

I

Illusion, allusion, 11, 219

Immigrate, emigrate, 12, 221

Imperative mood, verbs, 4, 147

Imperative sentences, defined, 8, 109

In, into, in to, 12, 222

Incomplete comparisons, avoiding, 10, 199

Indefinite articles, 61

Indefinite pronouns, defined, 2, 54, 167

agreement with verb, 8, 29, 167

as antecedents 31, 187

list, 54, 167

Independent (main) clauses, 7, 97, 99, 101

Indicative mood, verbs, 4, 147

Indirect objects, defined, 6, 79

Indirect quotations, 233, 271

Infinitive phrases, 7, 91, 93

Infinitives, defined, 7, 91

as adjectives, 7, 91

as adverbs, 7, 91

as nouns, 7, 91

Copyright © by Glencoe/McGraw-Hill

Copyright © by Glencoe/McGraw-Hill

Subject-verb agreement, 8, 26–29, 153, 155, 157, 159, 161, 163, 165, 167, 169
  in adjective clauses, 8, 169
  and collective nouns, 2, 27, 49, 161
  and compound subjects, 8, 28, 163
  and indefinite pronouns, 8, 29, 167
  and intervening expressions, 8, 29, 165
  in inverted sentences, 8, 26, 77, 159
  and linking verbs, 12, 26, 157
  and predicate nominatives, 8, 26, 157
  and prepositional phrases, 8, 26, 155
  and special subjects, 8, 161
  with titles, 8
Subjects
  agreement of verb with, 8, 26–29, 153, 155, 157, 159, 161, 163, 165, 167, 169
  complete, 6, 74
  compound, 5, 75, 163
  gerunds and infinitives as, 7, 89, 91
  noun clauses as, 7, 107
  simple, 5, 73
Subjunctive mood, verbs, 4, 147
Subordinate (dependent) clauses, 7, 97, 101, 103–105, 107, 257
Subordinating conjunctions, 5, 67, 97
  list, 67, 97
Suffixes, 17, 18, 295, 297, 299
Superlative degree (form), 9–10, 61, 195, 197

T

Take, bring, 11, 220
Teach, learn, 12, 223

Tenses, defined, 3, 35–37, 135, 137, 139
  compatibility, 143
  future, 3, 135, 139
  future perfect, 3, 137, 139
  past, 3, 135, 139
  past perfect, 3, 137, 139
  present, 3, 135, 139
  present perfect, 3, 137, 139
  shifts in, avoiding, 35, 143
Than, then, 13, 225
That there, this here, avoiding, 13, 225
Theme, writing, 18, 311
Then, than, 13, 225
Thesis statement, writing, 18, 311
This here, that there, avoiding, 13, 225
This kind, these kinds, 12, 223
Topic outlines, 19, 321
Topic, prewriting, 18, 307–308
Topic sentences, 311, 323, 331
Transitive verbs, defined, 3, 55

U

Underlining, 16, 275
Understood subject, 77, 109
Unity, in writing, 18, 315, 331

V

Verb phrases, defined, 3, 6, 59
Verbal phrases, 7, 87, 89, 91, 93
Verbals, defined, 7, 93
  See also Gerunds, Infinitives, Participles
Verbs, defined, 3, 55
  action verbs, 3, 55
    intransitive, 3, 55
    transitive, 3, 55
  agreement with subjects, rules, 8, 26–29, 153, 155, 157, 159, 161, 163, 165, 167, 169
  auxiliary (helping), 3, 59

  emphatic, 4, 142
  intransitive, 3, 55
  irregular, regular, 3–4, 131, 133
  linking, 3, 57, 157
  list, 3–4, 57, 133
  moods of, 4, 147
  principal parts of irregular, 3–4, 133
  principal parts of regular, 3, 131
  progressive, 4, 141
  tenses of, 3, 35–37, 135, 137, 139
  See Tenses
    compatibility, 143
    shifts in, avoiding, 35, 143
  transitive, 3, 55
  voice of, active and passive, 4, 145, 323
Vocabulary building, 17–18, 291, 293, 295
  from context, 17, 291
  prefixes and suffixes, 17–18, 295
  word roots, base words, 17, 293
Voice of verbs, defined, 4, 145, 323
  active, 4, 145, 323
  effective use of, 145, 323
  passive, 4, 145, 323
Voice or style, 311, 323

W

Well, good, 12, 201, 222
Who, whom, 9, 13, 181, 225
Writing letters, 19–20, 333, 335, 337–339
Writing paragraphs, 18, 327, 331
Writing process. *See specific steps.*
Writing sentences, 323

Y

You, as understood subject, 77, 109

Copyright © by Glencoe/McGraw-Hill